Ethics and the Profession of Anthropology

Ethics
and the Profession of
Anthropology

Dialogue for a New Era

edited by
Carolyn Fluehr-Lobban

uℏℏ

University of Pennsylvania Press
Philadelphia

Library of Congress Cataloging-in-Publication Data

Ethics and the profession of anthropology: dialogue for a new era /
   edited by Carolyn Fluehr-Lobban.
        p.   cm.
   Includes bibliographical references and index.
   ISBN 0-8122-8157-8
   I. Anthropological ethics.   I. Fluehr-Lobban, Carolyn.
GN33.6.E84   1991
174'.9309—dc20   90-13043
                                                       CIP

for Richard,
and the rich life we share

Contents

Acknowledgments

MANY SINGLE-AUTHOR BOOKS are made possible by the collaboration and support of others, and, certainly, edited volumes can only come into existence through the efforts of multiple contributors. And so my first debt of gratitude is to the group of concerned colleagues who responded to the crisis in anthropology over ethics, and who worked in a professional and constructive fashion to foster a dialogue within the discipline. Many of these colleagues are contributors to this volume, but several deserve special mention.

To my colleague, David Hakken, the founder and driving force behind the Action Network for Responsible Anthropological Professionalism (ANRAP), I owe the greatest debt of gratitude. By inviting me to cochair this group, he served to draw me into this specific set of issues, and in doing so, provided a meaningful framework for my reinvolvement with the discipline. His organization of the 1985 American Anthropological Association (AAA) symposium, "Ethics, Professionalism and the Future of Anthropology," set the agenda for the ensuing dialogue. Three papers in this volume are drawn from this session, including those of David Hakken, Gerald Berreman, and Erve Chambers.

Arnold Pilling responded to the emotionally charged debate over ethics, and we worked together, both on a 1986 AAA panel entitled "Appropriate and Inappropriate Secrecy in Research: Dialog for a New Era" and on an early, proposed version of this book. It is to Arnold Pilling that credit is due for his coining the apt phrase that has become the subtitle of this volume, "dialogue for a new era."

A third invited session at the American Anthropological Association in 1987 was co-organized with my colleague and friend, Barbara Frankel, and was entitled "Ethics and Professionalism in the 1980s: Academic and Practicing Anthropologists Confront the Issues." To her, I am also grateful for her energy, sense of balance, and concern for these issues; with her involvement in both academic and applied branches of the discipline, she provided important linkages between the two. Our session on ethics produced three chapters for this book, those of Barbara Frankel and M. G.

Trend; Jean Gilbert, Nathaniel Tashima, and Claudia Fishman; and my own.

The chapter offered by William Graves and Mark Shields grew out of their own experience with ethical decision-making in conducting research for clients. I am grateful to them for the care they took in examining the issues, and for providing a framework for their resolution.

I want to express my sincere gratitude to the Institute for the Study of Applied and Professional Ethics at Dartmouth College, and to its Director, Deni Elliott, for extending to me the opportunity to work on this project while holding a Rockefeller postdoctoral fellowship during 1990. The seminars with Bernard Gert, Stone Professor of Intellectual and Moral Philosophy at Dartmouth, and the Center's Fellows and Associates helped me clarify the particular relationship of issues of ethics in anthropology to other fields of knowledge. The collegial and supportive working environment afforded me during my residence at Dartmouth, where I was affiliated with both the Ethics Institute and the Department of Anthropology, will always be appreciated.

I am grateful to Rhode Island College and its Summer Research Stipend Program, which provided funds in 1987 to work on a project related to ethics and professionalism in anthropology that has, ultimately, become part of this volume. Specifically, I am grateful to Willard F. Enteman, Provost of the College until 1990, who was an initiator of this program, and who also is a specialist in philosophy and ethics. Through discussion with him, I came to appreciate some of the larger issues in the professions and in the social sciences which impact upon the discipline of anthropology. I am also grateful to Rhode Island College's Faculty Research Committee for a grant which funded the production of the index, and to Robert Tidwell, who compiled the index for this volume.

Further, I would like to recognize that segment of the community of scholars who have earned their doctorates during the past difficult fifteen years, or more, when traditional, academic employment opportunities were nearly nonexistent. The creative approach to job-hunting that they mustered, the dedication to their field that seemed not to waver, and the sheer force of will that kept many in the discipline despite this bleak employment picture is a part of the history of the field that is very much to be admired, and should be examined more closely. This may say something about the power of anthropology, and the resourcefulness of those who are attracted to it. You all have my admiration and respect, and to the degree that this volume speaks to your needs, I welcome that personal service to you.

I leave my last acknowledgment to my husband, Richard Lobban, Jr., to whom this book is dedicated. Over twenty-two years of marriage, we have shared many joint projects, including several extended field trips, the parenting of two beautiful daughters, employment at the same institution, the coauthorship of numerous works, and, mostly, the richness and the complexity of a relationship that combines so much. The challenges we have faced as an academic couple have created a dialectic that has enriched every day and every year together.

*Ethics and the Profession
of Anthropology*

Carolyn Fluehr-Lobban

Introduction

Ethics in Anthropology, the Past and the Present

HISTORICALLY, discussions of ethics in anthropology have reflected the issues and events of the day. The 1980s have demonstrated that there is a crisis in ethics in basic U.S. institutions such as business, government, law, medicine, and religion. Indeed, a confusion over ethical principles and practices is pervasive in American society today, with very few clear standards for which there is general consensus. This crisis has developed along with rapid changes in society that have emphasized individualism and uprooted traditional values. Decisions regarding right and wrong have become a matter of personal judgment without much reference to societal needs and the commonweal.

Current discussion on anthropological ethics has been prompted somewhat by these broader developments, but is also a consequence of an internal evolution that is peculiar to the field itself. In anthropology, the old order is no longer operative. Throughout this century until the 1970s, anthropologists were trained to conduct field research among Native Americans ("American Indians" then) or in other small-scale, non-Western cultures with the understanding that they would return to spend their lives as scholars and teachers in secure academic positions. However, in the post–Vietnam War period, the number of available jobs in the social sciences and humanities dropped off markedly, affecting the discipline of anthropology severely. By the end of the 1970s, anthropology and philosophy were tied for last place in their ability to place new Ph.D.'s in academic positions. For the next decade, academic openings in anthropology were nearly frozen at all levels, but were especially critical in the entry-level instructor and assistant professor categories.

The discipline struggled to come to terms with this new reality. A number of new initiatives were undertaken in an effort to find employment for a generation of professionally trained anthropologists with few or no prospects for academic work. A crisis developed and deepened as the field found itself torn between the old, established academic traditions of anthropology and the need to assist in the construction of a new reality, one that would embrace the concept of nonacademic employment as legitimate for anthropologists. New organizations appeared, such as the Washington Area Practicing Anthropologists (WAPA) and the National Association of Practicing Anthropologists (NAPA). Applied anthropology, which had an established semiautonomous organization, the Society for Applied Anthropology (SfAA), since 1941, changed in the 1980s from its tributary status to join the mainstream, conceptually, if not organizationally.

By the mid-1980s, the demographic composition of anthropology had been transformed. More professionally trained anthropologists were employed in nonacademic jobs than in the academy. Through its major professional organization, the American Anthropological Association (AAA), the discipline hoped to find a solution to its crisis through reorganization and "reprofessionalization," to use Hakken's term from this volume.

The reorganization of the AAA began in 1981 and was justified as addressing the growing specialized needs of the professional in anthropology. This process was finalized with the formal reorganization of the AAA in 1984, when nine affiliated societies signed a merger agreement with the AAA. Five new AAA units were created: General Anthropology, Archaeology, Biological Anthropology, Linguistics, and the Practice of Anthropology. These, together with the newer Societies for Psychological Anthropology, for Humanistic Anthropology, for Medical Anthropology, and for Latin American Anthropology, joined the venerable American Ethnological Society (est. 1842) to form a new, and presumably stronger, AAA.

The reorganized association was to be more democratic and more accessible to the scholarly and professional needs of the membership. As of this writing (1990) fourteen affiliated societies or units are now included in the organizational structure of the AAA, and doubts have been raised as to the ability of the organization to bind all of these diverse affiliates together into a coherent whole called "anthropology." Certain large and long-lived organizations, such as the Society for Applied Anthropology and the Society of American Archaeology, however, declined to join the AAA as affiliated organizations, thus a very considerable number of professional and practicing anthropologists would not claim, after reorganization, membership in the American Anthropological Association.

For generations, anthropologists have been trained in the importance of holism, a unified view of humanity embracing physical and cultural anthropology as well as archaeology and linguistics. The unifying concept has been *culture,* that uniquely human attribute, that could be studied throughout time and space from diverse research perspectives. Despite the hopeful words that holism would be maintained in the restructuring, it may be that the discipline was fostering its own dismemberment. Articles began to appear in the *Anthropology Newsletter* regarding the crisis in the General Anthropology Division and the future of the association (e.g., Forman et al. 1987). The problem of the progressive fragmentation of the field as a whole was raised openly for the first time, while a plea was made to investigate the long-term, unintended consequences of the restructuring process.

The Employment Crunch

The overriding context within which the ethics crisis has occurred has been the drastic reduction in available academic positions for anthropologists since the mid-1970s. The decline that began in the 1970s was reflected in unemployment figures in the 1980s: 11 percent in 1981–82 and 19 percent in 1985–86 of the visible, actively searching anthropological professionals were unable to find any employment. Many of the younger professionals who obtained their Ph.D.'s in the decade between 1975 and 1985 entered a marginal academic job market where they were forced to move from one temporary or part-time teaching position to another, and the term "Gypsy scholar" was coined to describe this new phenomenon.

A further group of "invisibles," estimated in 1986 at between two thousand and five thousand, were unemployed professionals no longer seeking jobs in anthropology or maintaining membership in the American Anthropological Association (Helm, 1987).

In 1986, for the first time since the founding of the AAA in 1902, more anthropologists (51 percent) were employed *outside* academia than inside. Given the significant numbers of unemployed and "invisible" anthropologists, academic employment had even less importance in the field.

In the 1985–86 survey conducted by the AAA (*Anthropology Newsletter,* 1987), the average anthropologist was described as thirty-eight years old, female, white, married, childless, with average earnings of twenty-four thousand dollars. She funded her own field research in cultural anthropology, most commonly in North America. (The relatively higher age average apparently reflects a large number of older women who have pursued advanced degrees later in life.) The 52 percent majority of females in the profession is consistent with the discipline's historical openness to women. However, the low salary average of this majority demonstrates both the competitive weakness of the field as well as the overall lower earning power of women in the United States.

These figures offer a more general context for the discussion of the deepening crisis in anthropology. During the same time period in most major American cities, the average salary for public school teachers exceeded the twenty-four-thousand-dollar average for the employed anthropologist. While the appropriate terminal degree for a teacher is the bachelor's degree, for the anthropologist it is the Ph.D. Not only does the crisis affect younger anthropologists, whether newly employed, underemployed, or unemployed, but a malaise has spread to more established academically employed professionals whose earning power after ten or fifteen years in the field may be worse than, or certainly no better than, public school teachers.

As a result, many academic anthropologists have sought to supplement their incomes with consulting work, while others have left the field entirely to assume more lucrative jobs. In the 1985–86 survey, the majority of respondents indicated that, given the opportunity, they *would* do it all again and become anthropologists despite the difficulties. However, 32 percent responded that they would not become anthropologists, given a second chance. Still, the discipline continues to produce about four hundred new Ph.D.'s each year, a figure that has remained constant since 1974; despite the apparent bad news about academic jobs, professors continue to encourage students, and they continue to respond to the call to become anthropologists. One disturbing response indicated in the 1985–86 survey is that 71 percent of professionals reported "poor" or only "fair" job counseling from their Ph.D.-granting institutions and professors. This clearly violates one of the ethical principles enunciated in the AAA's Principles of Professional Responsibility (PPR), that anthropologists should realistically counsel their students regarding career opportunities.

Coming to terms with the depth of the economic crisis and the poor career opportunities in the field has been extremely painful and, for the most part, ex post facto. Once the crisis was apparent, the AAA responded by holding job fairs and seminars at the annual meetings on "nontraditional" employment in anthropology, on how to market oneself as a generic social scientist. Indeed, the average anthropologist in the 1985–86 survey employed outside of academia most frequently held a job with the title "Program Director," a position where research and writing are typically combined with administration and program evaluation.

Overall, nonacademic anthropologists earned more in salary than academic anthropologists, and men earned more than women in both arenas, although the discrepancy was less in the nonacademic positions. The mean academic salary for a new male Ph.D. was $21,768 in 1985–86, while the new female Ph.D. in academia earned a mean salary of $16,960. For nonacademic work, salaries are better. The mean salary for a male Ph.D. was $25,879 in 1985–86, while it was $23,879 for the woman Ph.D. The message is clear. While nonacademic employment may be viewed as less prestigious in terms of traditional values in anthropology, it clearly pays better and is more equitable. By 1986, the old order in anthropology was profoundly disturbed.

Tensions in the Arena of Ethics and the Discipline's Response

Thus contemporary issues of ethics emerged at a time of disruption and change within anthropology. For some time, at least from the late 1970s, voices had been raised from within the association that the Principles of Professional Responsibility (adopted in 1971, see Appendix C) did not serve the needs of the growing numbers of practicing anthropologists. Subsequently, the AAA Board asked the Committee on Ethics to consider a review of the PPR and an ad hoc committee of five was appointed to prepare a revised statement on ethics. By 1982, a draft document was prepared, which was then reviewed by the board of the AAA, the Committee on Ethics, the Committee on Anthropology as a Profession, and selected members of the AAA general membership.

The Proposed Code of Ethics (see Appendix G) was first presented to the general membership in the October 1984 issue of the *Anthropology Newsletter,* prior to an open discussion at the 1984 annual meeting of the American Anthropological Association. As events unfolded at the 1984 Denver meetings, the proposed changes met substantial opposition. Some of those opposed favored the preservation of the integrity of the PPR. Emotions ran high, with much heated discussion at the general business meeting, and at least one emergency organization, the Action Network for

Responsible Anthropological Professionalism (ANRAP), was put together to mount a national response to any further developments that might threaten the PPR.

The strong reaction to the proposed revision of the PPR resulted in the shelving of the Proposed Code of Ethics at that time. Just over five years later, a new Proposed Draft Revision of the PPR was introduced to the membership of the AAA in the November 1989 issue of the *Newsletter,* and in March 1990 it was sent out to members for their ratification. Continuing concern over the needs of the community of practicing anthropologists is reflected in some new wording regarding anthropologists working for government agencies or private business. All reference to the censure of secret or clandestine research has been eliminated. In the meantime, the National Association of Practicing Anthropologists has generated its own set of guidelines, effective as of November 1988 (see Appendix H). The Society for Applied Anthropology has recently revised its own statement of Ethical and Professional Responsibilities (1983), and the Society of Professional Archaeologists and the Society of American Archaeologists have their own specific sets of ethical guidelines.

Issues Addressed in this Volume

The anthropological professionals who are contributors to this volume, whatever their employment situation, recognize the current difficult and sensitive position of the AAA and of anthropological ethics. They believe in a forthright acknowledgment of our shared contemporary predicament. It is in this framework that the most useful and productive "dialogue for a new era" can take place.

This volume has three major parts that encompass major features of the past and the present situations within the field of anthropology in regard to ethics. Part I, "The Present Crisis and Its Historical Antecedents," contains a historical review by Fluehr-Lobban of issues raised and principles enunciated within the discipline over the past seventy years, as a series of crises involving clandestine research and other examples of questionable action by anthropologists drew attention to the ethics issue. That critical historical review brings us to the "modern" period and the drafting of the Principles of Professional Responsibility, with the efforts to revise it since its introduction in 1971. Gerald Berreman, one of the drafters of the PPR and a member of the Committee on Ethics during the critical Vietnam War period, writes an eloquent defense of the PPR and on the importance of the maintenance of the ethical core of the discipline that is found within the PPR. His revelation of the nature of the involvement of anthropologists in counterinsurgency activities in Thailand is profoundly disturbing and establishes well the context within which the basic principles of the PPR were developed. His description of the decline in ethical standards and concerns during the Reagan years, dubbed "Reaganethics," places the debate over ethics in anthropology in a larger societal context.

David Hakken, whose role has already been described above, takes the dialogue and disruption over ethics from the 1980s into the 1990s, where he posits various options or possible outcomes of the present debate. One of the central points he makes is the need, indeed the necessity, to develop an *effective* ethical culture within the field, such that discussions of ethics take on a positive character rather than the painful, and sometimes embarrassing, exposés that have been a consistent feature of the past.

Part II, "Contemporary Issues of Ethics in the Dialogue within Anthropology," offers several contributions which describe and discuss specific issues that arise within the current research climate and practice of anthropology. Jay Szklut and Robert Reed's chapter reassesses and revises the traditional ethical principle of the protection of community anonymity in research, perhaps one of the few commonly held and widely recognized ethical canons in social science research. They argue that community anonymity is often not obtainable in anthropological research and that frequently it is neither feasible nor desirable. John Halsey's contribution reviews the current situation for the proper ethical and legal practice of archaeology in the state of Michigan, one of the excellent examples today in the United States that can be examined with regard to the protection and management of archaeological data. The contribution by William Graves and Mark Shields represents the only interdisciplinary dialogue, one involving the collaboration of an anthropologist and a sociologist who worked together on a research project. Taking a comparative view, they place the dialogue about ethics in anthropology into a larger professional framework of the social sciences, and in doing so, they reinforce the basic principle of the PPR and other codes, that the rights of the subjects of research override other considerations. The potential retreat from this basic principle is disturbing to them, and, based upon their joint research experience, they make a strong case for the prior negotiation of research procedures and the handling of potential conflicts during the course of research by *all* parties involved in the project.

Part III, "Diverse Voices in the Dialogue for a New Era," offers three chapters written by key personalities of the anthropological associations and others who have raised their concerns in various fora. Like Gerald Berreman, Erve Chambers represented one of the stronger voices to be heard from within the association in the aftermath of the 1984 proposed revision of the code of ethics. His chapter serves to place the current debate within a nonthreatening framework of a dialogue among professionals whose basic concerns about the discipline and the work it carries out spring from a common source. He devotes a special section to the issue of secret research, an issue that has dogged the field since the first crisis in 1919 described by Fluehr-Lobban. The nonappearance of the issue of clandestine research in the proposed revision of 1984 (and also in the 1990 revision) is seen by Chambers as the most powerful and emotional issue, and one that is directly traceable to the drafting of the PPR during the Vietnam War era.

Barbara Frankel and M. G. Trend's chapter offers a straightforward and sensitive overview of the conflicts and complexities of the current period for the anthropological professional. It may be taken as a "Guide for the Perplexed," and it assists the younger professional in sorting out the contemporary issues in preparation for career choices and directions. Various "pressures," intellectual, personal, employment, are described as legitimate sources of tension and conflict for the professional anthropologist today. The contributions by Chambers, Frankel, and Trend are especially valued, from the standpoint of the dialogue offered in this volume, because of their membership and involvement in the Society for Applied Anthropology.

The chapter by Jean Gilbert, Nathaniel Tashima, and Claudia Fishman articulates the specific concerns that have been addressed by one of the newest associations of professional anthropologists, the National Association of Practicing Anthropologists (NAPA), in regard to the difference, in degree and kind, of the issues faced by academic anthropologists and professionals employed outside of academia. The senior author chaired the committee that drafted the 1988 NAPA ethical guidelines, and thus is very well placed to discuss the issues raised, such as the increased visibility of the practicing anthropologist and the numerous employment situations that directly impact the group of people being studied.

*　*　*

These diverse voices reflect a changed discipline of anthropology, one that is struggling to redefine itself in relation to its past and the need to come to terms with a transformed external reality where research is no longer a pure intellectual endeavor, and where increasing numbers of anthropological professionals are earning a living by working for clients rather than for universities. The dialogue represented in this volume is offered as one means of assisting this process of redefinition and, hopefully, regeneration.

REFERENCES

Forman, S., M. Harris, and D. McCurdy
    1987   Impending crisis in general Anthropology affects the future of the association. *Anthropology Newsletter* 28(4).
Helm, June
    1987   From 1902 to 2002: Anthropologists and the AAA. *Anthropology Newsletter* 28(5).
Survey by the AAA
    1987   Doctor rate update. *Anthropology Newsletter* 28(5).

Part I

The Present Crisis and Its Historical Antecedents

Editor's Introduction to Chapter 1

THE SUBJECT OF ETHICS in anthropology may be considered too new to have a proper history, and few professionals may be aware of the integral relationship between the history of American anthropology and issues of ethics. More than a simple history is offered here. Rather, this critical review of ethics and the profession over the past century of anthropology constitutes more of a special political and intellectual history of the field. From the first documentable incident involving Franz Boas in 1919, through the Second World War, to the Vietnam War period, various events and personalities have shaped the way American anthropology has responded to matters of ethics. Certain issues have emerged time and again and are regarded in this chapter as thematic concerns to which the major professional association, the American Anthropological Association (AAA), has responded, sometimes in contradictory ways.

For example, during the 1930s and 1940s the relationship between the anthropologist and the government was considered to be a positive and mutually beneficial one, while the appropriateness of anthropologists working for the government was seriously questioned prior to and during the Vietnam War, with a legacy that taints government-related research until this day. The use of anthropologists as spies, intelligence agents, or individual contractors involved in clandestine or secret research was criticized and vilified repeatedly in the profession in 1919 and again in 1968 and 1970; however, this subject was not mentioned in the proposed revisions (in 1984 and 1990) of the Principles of Professional Responsibility. In the 1971 code, the PPR, the principal and paramount responsibility of the anthropologist was to the people studied, the subjects of research, while in the 1984 proposed revision, the anthropologist's individual moral responsibility is viewed as varied and contextual. The 1971 version was reaffirmed in the 1990 proposed revision.

The relationship between the development of the profession of anthropology and various issues of ethics is demonstrably a close one. The role of the AAA has been both one of leader in the vanguard of needed change within the field and a force that has been conservative and slow to respond to various crises that have arisen over the ethics issue. At times it has reacted in the perceived best interests of the preservation of the organization, but in doing so it has perhaps treated more harshly the individuals who have brought the issues to light than the anthropologists engaged in allegedly unethical behavior. The social syndrome associated with the "whistle-blower" is now well-recognized in government and industry circles, and the fate of anthropological whistle-blowers has been similar to those who have gone to the press with information regarding dangerous or unethical practices in other fields.

This review elucidates the historical patterns in this area so that in our future dialogue and debate over ethics we may utilize the best traditions of the profession regarding moral responsibility and freedom of research.

Carolyn Fluehr-Lobban

Chapter 1 Ethics and Professionalism
A Review of Issues and Principles within Anthropology

Introduction

A MOST INTERESTING HISTORY of the discipline of anthropology could be written dealing with the development of the profession and the painful process of the generation of a set of ethical standards. In fact, beyond the body of knowledge that has accumulated in the century or more of anthropological research, the development of the profession, its real political history, is intimately associated with the process of coming to terms with the ethical issues that have been raised periodically within the discipline. Too often the field has reacted to events rather than anticipating the need for dialogue.

The following remarks are intended to be a critical review of that history of the discipline in which issues of ethics have been discussed, voted upon, resolved, contained, or deferred. This is not intended to be a comprehensive study of the history of anthropological ethics, but a thematic treatment of that history and the issues that have been raised and the principles derived during periodic crises within the discipline. As might be expected, much of that history is informal, unrecorded, and part of the oral tradition of the field, and a wealth of information is yet to be mined by a future historian of anthropology. I will be dealing with the recorded history, where there is sufficient material, for a more formal history of ethics and professionalism in anthropology.

Early Beginnings: The Growth of Professionalism and the First Crisis: 1890 to 1919

As is well known, the beginnings of anthropology in the United States lie with the pursuit of the field as an avocation or passionate intellectual interest, most notably in the case of L. H. Morgan, a man with a deep sense of responsibility to the Native Americans he studied. Later, that group of adventurers who clustered around William A. Powell and the Bureau of American Ethnology (BAE) was forging an identity for anthropology in the American landscape, but it had not yet consolidated a profession. Although these adventurers' research was sponsored by the U.S. government, they had a high degree of freedom of inquiry that we are unaccustomed to associating with government employment in the later part of the twentieth century. Perhaps this is because their mission was to salvage the cultural remnants of already pacified Indian communities and not the more controversial work of later times involving non-Western, non-American populations. While they were aware of the policy implications of their research, there is no evidence that the voluminous BAE reports were ever used in making a single policy decision.

Of course, it was the university affiliation and considerable organizational abilities of Franz Boas that were responsible for creating the foundations of a profession of anthropology in the United States. Boas was the founder of the American Folklore Society in 1888 and he was a founder of both the American Ethnological Association and the American Anthropological Association in 1900. In the early twentieth century, professional anthropology and the name of Franz Boas were inextricably tied, although certain individuals and groups could be said to resent this fact. Boas wrote little in a formal way about professional conduct, but it is clear from the admonitions given to his students and from his public writings as a citizen rather than as a scientist that Boas held to the highest standards of personal and scientific behavior. Boas had a distinguished record as a pacifist during the First World War, despite the virulent nationalism that swept the United States at the time (Harris 1968:292). In 1916 he rebuked the American who "claims that the form of his own government is the best, not only for himself, but also for the rest of mankind; that his interpretation of ethics, of religion, of standards of living is right. I see no reason why we should not allow the Germans, Austrians and Russians, or whomever else it might be, to solve their own problems in their own way instead of demanding that they bestow upon themselves the benefaction of our regime" (quote in Boas's obituary, written by Ruth Benedict, in *The Nation*, 2 January 1943, 15–16).

It was Boas's published letter to *The Nation* in 1919, which expressed his outrage against the wartime activities of four anthropologists who had combined intelligence-gathering with their research, that resulted in the first clear-cut case wherein the issue of unprofessional behavior was raised in the AAA organizational framework. Boas wrote:

> I wish to enter a vigorous protest . . . that a number of men who follow science as their profession, men whom I refuse to designate any longer as scientists, have prostituted science by using it as a cover for their activities as spies. By accident incontrovertible proof has come to my hands that at least four men who carry on anthropological work, while employed as government agents, introduced themselves to foreign governments as representatives of scientific institutions in the United States, and as sent for the purpose of carrying on scientific research. They have not only shaken the belief in the truthfulness of science, but they have also done the greatest possible disservice to scientific inquiry. In consequence of their acts every nation will look with distrust upon the visiting foreign investigator who wants to do honest work, suspecting sinister designs. Such action has raised a new barrier against the development of international friendly cooperation.

Although a founder of the AAA and a scholar with a recognized reputation for accuracy and detail, Boas was censured by a twenty to ten vote of the Executive Council of the Anthropology Society of Washington (ASW). The resolution, moved by Neil Judd, said that the opinion expressed by Franz Boas in the 16 October 1919 issue of *The Nation* is "unjustified and does not represent the opinion of the American Anthropological Association." It was further resolved that a copy of the resolution would be sent to the Executive Board of the National Research Council and other scientific associations having an interest in the matter so that appropriate action could be taken. The Harvard-Cambridge anthropology group sided with the Washington society, while the latter never responded to the question raised by one colleague, "Were Boas' charges true?" (Lesser 1981:17, 19). It is clear from the text of the resolution of the powerful ASW that the council's anger was precipitated by the publicity and wide attention that Boas brought to the matter that "will prejudice foreign governments against all scientific men from this country." As if to spite, the ASW distributed its resolution, even though the resolution or a variation of it had not been passed by the AAA.

Boas's reaction was muted, given his past history, and there is no evidence that his participation in the AAA declined as a result of the controversy. In 1921 he began his employment at Columbia University and the matter was apparently laid to rest. The fundamental flaw of the action taken by the ASW was not so much its harsh judgment of Boas's public stand, but its quashing of this voice of protest and suppression of the issue without debating, at the time, appropriate standards of professional conduct for anthropologists. Instead, the issue was buried, only to reemerge in a dramatic and damaging way fifty years later in the controversy over counterinsurgency research conducted by anthropologists in Thailand.

As a result, the larger issue of the relationship of science to government was also not clarified, and anthropologists concerned with social issues such as racism or world peace found few outlets within the organizational framework of the AAA to express their concerns. Boas himself, with an impressive record of involvement in social issues, devoted the last decade of his life to antiwar activities, not only through his writings but through his militant support for the underground antifascist resistance in Europe. During his last years he chaired the American Council for Democracy and Intellectual Freedom (founded in 1939), a committee with which Ruth Benedict also worked (Mead 1959:348).

Middle Age: Professional Identity Secured— Government Service in a Just Cause

By the 1930s, not only had anthropology in the United States established a scientific identity but increasing numbers of trained students were entering the new professional slots opening up in the academy and seeking professional opportunities in government service. With no impediments or even questions having been raised within the AAA regarding government employment, anthropologists took up government civilian jobs in significant numbers in the 1930s. Agencies other than the traditional hiring places of anthropologists, such as the Bureau of American Ethnology, or National Museum, employed anthropologists in the Department of Interior, Bureau of Indian Affairs (BIA), National Park Service, the Department of Agriculture, and the Soil Conservation Service. Most anthropologists accepted this widening employment pattern as a positive development in the overall recognition of the field and as an expansion of needed employment positions during the Depression.

One dissenting voice was that of A. L. Kroeber, who expressed doubts about the freedom of the anthropologist to maintain his or her independence in research under such employment circumstances (Beals 1969:52). Kroeber's objections extended to his refusal to recommend any of his students for research employment with the BIA. But again, the lack of any wider dialogue within the major professional association prevented such questions from being raised or discussed with respect to awareness of the conditions of government employment and their ramifications for the scholar-scientist. In at least one instance, a major report of a significant study was suppressed for political reasons, and anthropologists employed by the Indian Service found that few reports of their research were published; many left the service when alternative opportunities for employment appeared (ibid.).

The period between the two world wars saw the consolidation of the image of the U.S. anthropologist as one intimately connected with the study of the Native American, but it was also a time when increasing numbers of anthropologists ventured outside of the United States to conduct their research. Robert Redfield and Ralph Beals went to Mexico, Alan Holmberg and Charles Wagley to South America, William Lloyd Warner to Australia, Ralph Linton and Margaret Mead and others to Oceania, while Melville Herskovits pioneered the anthropological study of Africa. Generally excluded were the non-Western areas under European colonialism, where their own nationals were busy conducting studies under the aegis of British or French colonial administration.

With the bombing of Pearl Harbor on 7 December 1941, the United States entered the war, and only twenty-four days later the AAA joined the war effort. At its annual meeting on 31 December 1941, the association passed the following resolution: "Be it resolved that the AAA places itself and its resources and the specialized skills of its members at the disposal of the country for the successful prosecution of the war."

The Committee for National Morale had been organized in 1941 as an effort to mobilize cadre from the behavioral sciences to assist with the war effort. The core of this group was to work with various aspects of psychological warfare and to work on problems of morale; it is in these areas that some of our better-known anthropologists made their contributions. Gregory Bateson and Margaret Mead wrote "Principles of Morale Building" (1941), and the Council for Intercultural Relations sponsored Geoffrey Gorer's exploratory study, "Japanese Character Structure and Propaganda, A Preliminary Survey" (1943). While the interdisciplinary Committee for National Morale stressed the application of social science techniques and data, the Council for Intercultural Relations was more strictly anthropological and it began the study of what came to be known as "national character" in the context of the war effort. Ruth Benedict, working within the Office of War Information, began her work on Thailand and Burma before conducting her famous "study of culture at a distance," research into

Japanese culture that ultimately appeared as *The Chrysanthemum and the Sword* in 1946. Her previous papers were unpublished materials on Thai and Burmese culture and later on German, Dutch, and Polish culture and behavior and analysis of Nazi propaganda films; each paper was written for the Council for Intercultural Relations and several were published after the war. Gregory Bateson, Margaret Mead, Ruth Benedict, and others prepared *Suggested Materials for Training of Regional Specialists, Army Program* (1943). It was the European studies that brought Benedict closest to top-secret conferences and high-level wartime intelligence activities related to support for underground and partisan movements (Mead 1959:353–54). Unlike World War I, this period saw no nasty incidents with the press or image problems for anthropologists, and no public protest within the association of the intelligence-gathering activities of anthropologists was raised. Only slightly more than two decades later, allegations of anthropologists involved in intelligence-related activities in Thailand, the same culture area that Benedict had researched without objection as part of the "war effort," jolted the profession of anthropology and transformed its ethical stance regarding intelligence-gathering by anthropologists.

It was the same period that energized a group of socially conscious anthropologists to form the Society for Applied Anthropology (SfAA) in 1941, focusing their distinctive brand of anthropology on the idea of relating anthropology to a variety of social problems, human relations, and organizational structures. This generally younger group of anthropologists undertook studies for government and private agencies, and it is this same group that formulated the first statement on ethics for a professional anthropological organization, the SfAA, in 1948. It is among the first of such statements in the social sciences and should be recognized for its historic role.

The Postwar Years to the Second Major Crisis: 1946 to 1967

In the post–World War II period, anthropologists continued in a pattern of employment by the U.S. government that was basically a continuation of the war effort. The Office of Naval Research employed some forty anthropologists under the Coordination Investigation of Micronesian Anthropology (CIMA) project, which was intended to conduct ethnographic research to provide cultural information for the U.S. administration of the Trust Territories. This colonial-like relationship between the United States and Micronesia fostered the employment of anthropologists for basic research and is reminiscent of the relationship between British social anthropology and the colonial enterprise. Although the organizers of CIMA believed that anthropological knowledge was essential to the proper administration of the island populations, the research was not directed to this end and apparently had little impact on administration (Beals 1969:61). While opinions vary, there is some agreement that the studies were of an esoteric, technical nature and not readily comprehended by the political administrators. One is tempted to draw comparisons, although the United States operation in Micronesia is dwarfed by the English imperial system; perhaps the better comparison is with the Bureau of Indian Affairs and British colonial administration in Africa and Asia.

Adam Kuper has reflected upon the role of anthropology and the anthropologist by clearly outlining the desire of British anthropology to present itself as useful to colonial administration, and not a small number of degrees at Oxford, Cambridge, and the University of London were justified, in part, as providing training for colonial officers. From the earliest times in the 1920s, Seligman and Evans-Pritchard complained that their consultation or advice was never on a single occasion solicited by the colonial government in the Sudan. By the 1930s, when it was decided to "develop" the colonies economically and politically, the Rhodes-Livingstone Institute and the International African Institute became interested in applied studies and "culture change." But interestingly, this research was perceived as less rigorous and therefore more suited to females, and so Lucy Mair and Monica Hunter achieved their fame with studies of "primitive" law and government, especially in the area of marriage and family law. "The inescapable conclusion," writes Kuper, "is that there was never much of a demand for applied anthropology from Whitehall or from the colonial governments" (1973:143). The functionalist studies produced by this generation of British social anthropologists were a rejection of the colonial model that was evolutionary and chauvinistic that saw the role of Europe as one of uplifting the "savage" cultures. Functionalism, on the other hand, was relativistic and culture-centered, even to the point of ignoring entirely the primary colonial context in which "native" people were studied.

This brief consideration of British social anthropology illuminates the overall discussion of ethics and anthropology and its relationship to governments. When one looks at the examples of the BAE and British social anthropology, it is clear that governments have ignored anthropological knowledge more than they have used it. On the other hand, the charge that anthropology is the handmaiden of colonialism is a powerful reality insofar as anthropologists have been willing to pursue their research within an environment constrained by governments. Academic freedom has been cultivated in the academy, but for all of our history since the 1930s, anthropologists have been seeking work outside of the academy.

Unlike the period before World War II, the 1950s is a decade with which many anthropologists today are familiar, because it is comfortably within the memory of those who were active professionals at the time, or were taught by that generation of anthropologists. It also marks a time of growing public acceptance of the field, which had begun to enjoy its new influence. The dull reputation of the 1950s is somewhat justified insofar as the McCarthy hearings and McCarthyism represented one of the greatest anti-intellectual assaults in the United States in this century. Anthropologists and other intellectuals associated with the peace or antiracist movements were investigated, harassed, removed from jobs, or never securely employed as a result.

A selection of resolutions of the Executive Board of the AAA reflect some of the special concerns of the times. A 1952 resolution expresses its fear of the harm and injustice that may result for Native American populations if certain changes in BIA policy are enacted; a 1962 resolution challenges and repudiates statements of the period that "Negroes" are biologically and intellectually inferior to whites; a 1967 resolution places the organization and its resources at the disposal of those who would counteract the proliferation of nuclear, chemical, and biological warfare (Weaver 1973:43–44).

In the academy, anthropology settled into the task of filling the ever-widening demand for teaching and use of anthropology as more and more subfields emerged. An entire volume on the teaching of anthropology was published by the AAA in 1963; in 611 pages of text, the issue of ethics and professional responsibility, as we have come to understand it in the post-Camelot and post–Vietnam War period, is barely treated. The only discussion of the ethical responsibility of the anthropologist is in connection with the classroom and the professional handling of cross-cultural materials (Mandelbaum et al. 1963:35–36). Ethics is treated only as a feature of the culture concept dealing with societal values and norms and not as a set of moral responsibilities for the anthropologist. Ethel Albert (577) defines anthropology as a field whose subject matter is value-free. She writes:

> As an objective inquiry into human nature and variability, anthropology is not an ethical theory nor does it imply any special ethical or social policy;

however no serious ethical theory can be constructed that ignores or contradicts the results of anthropology.

This view amounts to something of a period piece; it describes a world view that anthropology had shaped for itself prior to the tumultuous events of the late 1960s and early 1970s. After 1967, anthropology could never again see itself so absolutely as "an objective inquiry" with no special ethical or social policy implications. The image of "innocents abroad" abruptly shifted to one of "not-so-innocent abroad," to borrow the phrase Gerald Berreman used (1969:505) when he exposed Department of Defense financing of research in the Himalayan border countries. The profession had emerged and matured; its numbers burgeoned in the 1950s and 1960s with a sharp increase of social scientists employed by the government, and the complexities of the tasks for which anthropologists were solicited or chose to serve had become immensely more complex. .

Project Camelot and the Vietnam War Years: The Second and Third Crises, 1967 to 1973

There is broad consensus that Project Camelot was the turning point, the signal of the beginning of the "modern" era for ethics and professional responsibility within anthropology. It constituted the second crisis in the field and provided the immediate background for the adoption by the fellows of the AAA of the first Statement on Problems of Anthropological Research and Ethics in 1967. The irony of Camelot is that it elicited such a powerful reaction within the social sciences generally, including anthropology, without a single social scientist having been paid to carry out the research. The Camelot idea originated in the Department of the Army's Office of the Chief of Research and Development and was subsequently carried out under contract research to the American University in Washington, D.C. Project Camelot, as described in one of the army's fact sheets, was a "basic social science research project on preconditions of internal conflict, and on effects of indigenous governmental actions—easing, exacerbating or resolving—of these preconditions" (Sjoberg 1967:142). Although the language is ambiguous, it is fair to conclude that the project was addressing the problem of counterinsurgency in Latin America and how increased knowledge, gained through social science research, would assist the army in coping with internal revolutions in the region. With a proposed budget of six million dollars, plans for the project were well advanced by 1964, with a project director named and a large number of social scientists recruited to serve as consultants (ibid.). Interestingly, the bulk of the social scientists recruited were sociologists and psychologists and not anthropologists.

Exaggerated claims of the importance of the research hailed the pioneering Project Camelot as one with the potential of being the Manhattan Project of the social sciences (Beals 1969:6). The project was neither classified nor designed to conceal those who were the sponsors. A Chilean social scientist who was going home for personal reasons was asked by the project head to make unofficial initial contacts among members of the social science community in Chile in preparation for the project. Through this person the story of the project was leaked; a vigorous attack on Project Camelot was published in a left-wing newspaper, *El Siglo,* and then was taken up generally by the press in Chile and, to a certain extent, in the rest of Latin America. The United States ambassador, who was not informed of the unofficial visit of the Chilean social scientist, denied any knowledge and protested strongly to the Department of State. Investigations were launched by the Chilean Chamber of Deputies and by the U.S. Congress, and the army quickly moved to cancel the project, with President Lyndon Johnson issuing a directive requiring the Department of State to review all of the foreign research sponsored or conducted by U.S. government agencies.

So it was not the high crimes of anthropologists involved in Project Camelot that precipitated the second crisis, but the effects that a bollixed operation had for future research in Latin America. In the immediate wake of the Camelot exposé, particular research projects came under closer scrutiny and review. A joint project in Peru with partial financing from the Department of Defense came under sharp criticism, with the result that Peruvian anthropologists formed their first association and made a direct request to the AAA that they be informed of the financing of other projects in Peru. They also inquired about the actions of the AAA regarding the Camelot affair and subsequently received a copy of the first AAA Statement on Ethics in 1967 (Beals 1969:8–9).

The long-term effects were more harmful for researchers in Latin America, especially, but the issue was generalizable beyond South American research. Only a year before Camelot, the "Sanchez affair" broke in the Mexican press over the presentation of the Sanchez family in Oscar Lewis's *Children of Sanchez* (1961), which had just been translated into Spanish and reviewed in the Mexican press. Lewis was pilloried in the press for his portrayal of Mexican life as "degraded and miserable," and his methodology was questioned. The question was asked if a Mexican anthropologist could come and study poor Negro tenant farmers in Mississippi, thus raising, formally, a new ethical matter for anthropologists, that of the powerful studying the powerless. Whatever the merits of Lewis's research and writing, the study, placed in a context of growing mistrust and "imperial Yanqui" researchers, had the same end result as what Camelot had reaped: a politicized research climate and a world of scientific research that was changed fundamentally.

That change is apparent in the 1967 Statement on Problems of Anthropological Research and Ethics. The statement was generated in response to an urgent call from the anthropologists who attended the 1966 AAA meetings in Denver, where they had adopted a resolution calling upon the executive board to "explore the widely ramified issues involving the relationship between anthropologists and the agencies, both government and private, that sponsor their research" (*Anthropology Newsletter,* 1966, 7:1–2). The statement begins with a reaffirmation of its 1949 resolution endorsing "complete freedom to interpret and publish findings without censorship or interference" (*American Anthropologist,* 1949, 51:370). It goes on to say that, except in cases of declaration of war by Congress, anthropologists should not undertake research for exclusive government contracts nor lend themselves to clandestine activities. Anthropologists employed by the government should be given the maximum opportunity to plan research projects. Further, anthropologists engaged in foreign research should be concerned with the possible effects of their sponsorship and sources of financial support. And, fifty years after the Boas affair, the AAA stated that "the international reputation of anthropology has been damaged by the activities of individuals . . . who have pretended to be engaged in anthropological research while pursuing other ends. There is good reason to believe that some anthropologists have used their professional standing and the names of academic institutions as cloaks for the collection of intelligence information and for intelligence operations" (1967 Statement). In terms of basic content, Boas's sentiments of a half century before were repeated and officially sanctioned. Boas was vindicated!

Finally, the appropriate relationship between professional anthropologists and the government was addressed in the following points:

1) it is desirable that social science knowledge be more readily available to the Executive Office of the President

2) when the services of anthropologists are needed in government agencies, it is most desirable that professional anthropologists plan that involvement

3) anthropologists who contemplate accepting government employment should recognize that they will be committed to agency mission and policies and they should seek the clearest possible definition of their expected roles. (*American Anthropologist*, 1967:381–82)

It is fair to conclude that without Camelot no statement regarding ethics and professional behavior would have been forthcoming from the AAA. The political crisis and the reaction to it forced the profession of anthropology to take a hard and critical look at itself. The issue centered on clandestine research and government contracts and the principle generated was the abjuring of secret research, with cautionary words for the anthropologist undertaking research for government agencies. Unaddressed in 1967 was the anthropologist's proper relationship to people studied, to students, to clients, and to fellow human beings.

These issues had been raised and addressed two decades earlier by the SfAA, which revised its Code of Ethics in 1963 and underscored the following points:

1) if an anthropologist has reason to believe that his work will be used in a manner harmful to his fellow men or to science, then he must decline to make his services available

2) to his fellow men the anthropologist owes respect for their dignity—no course of action may be recommended on behalf of a client that would adversely affect the lives, well-being, dignity or self-respect of others

3) to his clients the anthropologist owes the best of his scientific skill and knowledge—a clear understanding must be established with every client as to the nature of his responsibility to his client, to science and to his fellow man. (*Human Organization*, 1963, 22:237)

This simple and straightforward Code of Ethics has stood the test of time and, although revised recently, the essential points summarized above have remained intact.

Had there been the luxury of sufficient time to reflect upon the lessons of Camelot, a decisive policy might have been articulated, however, within a year, the now-famous advertisement placed in the *American Anthropologist* for a research anthropologist for Vietnam touched off another crisis that gripped the discipline for another five years. With respect to the dialogue over ethics, it is perhaps most accurate to see Camelot as a prelude to the Vietnam War period, and the statement of 1967 from the AAA as a necessary background to the production of the first ethical code in the field, the Principles of Professional Responsibility (PPR). To close the Camelot chapter, it is important to say that its greatest effect was the raising of the issue of secret research on a wide scale within the profession and across the social sciences as a whole, and even among the American literati. The principle enunciated was that clandestine research is wrong, that secret research is unethical, and, finally, that both are unprofessional.

The Vietnam War Era and the Principles of Professional Responsibility, 1967 to 1972

The advertisement placed in the August 1968 issue of the *American Anthropologist* (*AA*) gave the appearance that the AAA was not following the very guidelines it had enacted the year before. The position advertised was for an anthropologist to work with the Psychological Operations Headquarters in Vietnam. Duties included research, analysis, and interpretation of findings relative to the effectiveness of "enemy" propaganda and U.S. counter-propaganda on "target audiences," and the evaluation of current and proposed psychological operations. While travel to Vietnam was part of the job, government-supported housing was available only to the anthropologist and not dependents; U.S. citizenship was required; and the ad assured that the government was an equal opportunity employer (*AA,* 1968, vol. 70). The combination of the direct ties to the U.S. military intervention in Vietnam with the clearly classified nature of the research directly contradicted the 1967 statement, "anthropologists should not lend themselves to clandestine activities . . . we deplore unnecessary restrictive classifications of research reports prepared under contract for the government and excessive regulations imposed on participating academic personnel" (Statement on Problems of Anthropological Research and Ethics, 1967). After much protest, the *AA* withdrew the ad and revised its editorial policy such that similar ads would be refused in the future so as not to suggest that the official organ of the AAA would give tacit support to anthropologists engaging in counterinsurgency research.

　　In the society at large, antiwar forces gained tremendous momentum in the period from 1968 to 1970, and the revelations that counterinsurgency work in Thailand had been engaged in by anthropologists must be seen in that light. Eric Wolf, chair of the Committee on Ethics, and Joseph Jorgensen, a member of the committee, received information from the Student

Mobilization Committee in March 1970 regarding six documents dating from 1967 to 1969 that gave evidence of the involvement of anthropologists in war-related research in Thailand. One document, significantly, was entitled "Counter-Insurgency in Thailand: The Impact of Economic, Social and Political Programs." The information shared with Wolf and Jorgensen was published in the 2 April 1970 issue of *The Student Mobilizer,* a national leftist student newspaper, and the newspaper was distributed at the Asian Studies Association meetings, along with the names of the anthropologists allegedly involved. Wolf and Jorgensen wrote to the anthropologists mentioned in the documents, but before the matter could be handled internally within the AAA Committee on Ethics, the public disclosures and growing antiwar sentiment created a furor that politicized all further dialogue on the subject. The AAA did publish the official reaction of Wolf and Jorgensen to the published list of documents, which said: "Since these documents contradict in spirit and in letter the resolution of the American Anthropological Association concerning clandestine and secret research, we feel that they raise the most serious issues for the scientific integrity of our profession. We shall, therefore, call the attention of the American Anthropological Association to these most serious matters" (letter dated 30 March 1970; quotation from personal correspondence with Eric Wolf, 19 December 1988).

As in 1919, the reaction of the AAA was to censure publicly the messengers more severely than those whose professional behavior had been called into question. To this day the names of Wolf and Jorgensen are associated with the "leak," but the names of those who had engaged in the counterinsurgency research are not public knowledge and have been protected. The Executive Board of the AAA reacted first by reaffirming the 1967 Statement on Ethics, and second by citing Wolf and Jorgensen's disclosures as having gone beyond the mandate of the Committee on Ethics and that the two were acting as individuals and not in the name of the committee or the AAA. Similar wording had been used in the Anthropology Society of Washington's censure of Boas. Further, the board instructed the Committee on Ethics to limit itself to its narrow charge and to fulfill this charge without further collection of case material or any quasi-investigative role (Weaver 1973:54). Shortly thereafter, the entire Committee on Ethics signed a letter of concern to the president, president-elect, and members of the Executive Board of the AAA, which stated its grave concern over the relationship between anthropological research and overt or covert counterinsurgency activities in such a way as to threaten the future of anthropological research in Southeast Asia and elsewhere. The individual views of anthropologists regarding such research were not the issue, the letter continued, but such activities generate conflicts between the ethical standards of the association and the personal ethics of individual anthropologists; they polarize the association and downgrade the credibility of social science and social scientists (ibid. 55).

The special Committee on Ethics that had been appointed in 1968 prepared a draft report in the following year that called for an elected standing committee on ethics, and it presented a draft of a code of ethics for the association. The report was tabled, but the standing committee was elected in November 1970, and it published its revised draft code, "Statement of Professional Responsibility," which was subsequently adopted by the membership as the Principles of Professional Responsibility in 1971.

The draft code, prior to its adoption, was the subject of intense debate and controversy, but the mood of the times was one of increased openness, accountability, and responsible professional behavior that would not impair either future research or the well-being of people studied. Some of the signal features of the PPR (written in the male-gendered style of the time) are:

(1) In research the anthropologist's paramount responsibility is to those he studies. When there is a conflict of interest, these individuals must come first.

(2) In addition to the AAA's position on clandestine research, no reports should be provided to sponsors that are not available to the general public, and where practical, to the population studied.

(3) An anthropologist bears responsibility for the good reputation of his discipline and its practitioners. He should avoid even the appearance of clandestine research.

(4) In relation to sponsors, the anthropologist must retain the right to make all ethical decisions in his research. He should enter into no secret agreement with the sponsor regarding the research, the results or the final report.

(5) In relations with one's own and host governments the research anthropologist should not be required to compromise ethics as a condition for the conduct of research; specifically, no secret research or debriefings of any kind should be agreed to or given.

(6) Finally, when an anthropologist by his actions jeopardizes peoples studied, professional colleagues, students or others, his colleagues may legitimately inquire into the propriety of these actions and take such measures as lie within the legitimate power of the Association.

The PPR is a long and impressive document (reprinted here in Appendix C) that speaks to several professional relationships encountered by the anthropologist: (a) responsibility to those studied, (b) responsibility to the discipline, (c) responsibility to the public, (d) responsibility to students, (e) responsibility to sponsors, (f) responsibility to one's own and host governments. It is a document created by a group of thoughtful and concerned colleagues who responded to a crisis in the field and solved the problems that had arisen with a statement of a set of ethical principles. No prior statement of its kind had been generated by the American Anthropological Association.

After 1971, there were no more public revelations of intelligence-related or counterinsurgency work by anthropologists. Either clandestine activities were driven more deeply underground, or the PPR's intended effect was being felt. By 1973, the war's end had been negotiated, and the post–Vietnam War period saw the precipitous decline in employment for younger professionals, not necessarily due to a causal relationship. Academic jobs dropped off sharply after 1975, and a new impetus for employment outside of academia was felt. By the late 1970s concerns began to be raised about certain features of the PPR, especially its alleged academic-centeredness and its lack of appreciation of the various employment situations available to the nonacademic anthropologist. The AAA Board asked the Committee on Ethics to address the problems and propose remedies, which it did in 1980. Several draft documents were circulated discussing these and related issues in 1982, and by 1984, with reorganization of the AAA largely completed, a new code of ethics was proposed and published in the *Anthropology Newsletter* of October 1984.

The new code (entitled the Draft Code of Ethics, reprinted here in Appendix G) bore little resemblance to the PPR of the decade before and controversy stirred anew at the AAA meetings in 1984, with sufficient reaction against the proposed revision to table it. An organization of concerned anthropologists which called itself the Action Network for Responsible Anthropological Professionalism (ANRAP) was formed to respond, and concern was expressed from enough other corners to halt the process of revision.

It is worthwhile to examine the proposed revisions of the PPR since this move was apparently not well understood by the membership. The 1984 proposed code was notable for what it did not say. The preamble states that the code is general, because anthropologists' professional situations are varied and complex, and that it will not address the many ethical responsibilities that anthropologists face either as academics or as workers with government agencies and business firms, where anthropologists may find themselves on opposite sides of an issue. One purpose, then, of the proposed new code was to provide a framework within which disclosures of ethical problems and debate on ethical issues could be conducted within the organizational framework of anthropology. The thirteen statements in the 1984 draft code represent some notable departures from what is contained in the PPR. The statement which outlines the anthropologist's paramount responsibility to those studied is absent, as is any mention of responsibility to the subjects of research. The two points about fieldwork (nos. 5 and 6) say only that the anthropologist should not act in a way that will jeopardize ongoing or future research. While the aims and possible consequences of research should be communicated to the subjects of research (identified as "resource persons," thus eliminating the term *informant*), no ethical statement of responsible field behavior is mentioned. The burden of ethical responsibility shifts to the individual ("anthropologists must consider their own moral responsibility for their own acts"). Nowhere is secret or clandestine research even mentioned, much less reprimanded, and this appears to have been dropped as an issue mandating an ethical statement. There is a remarkable shift in language and terminology from the realm of ethics and principles to one of legal accountability and legal proceedings (nos. 3 and 4). In case of legal action resulting from their research, professionals need to be aware that they may not be able to claim confidentiality. Cautionary notes about government employment are lacking, although they had been strong features of the 1967 statement and the 1971 PPR. And for an entirely new dimension, defined as ethical behavior, anthropologists are admonished to arrange for the proper disposition of their data and materials after death.

After the negative reaction of the AAA membership to the 1984 proposed revision, a new committee was formed during Roy Rappaport's tenure as president that was chaired by Robert Fernea to review the matter of revising the PPR. The committee consisted of both academic and practicing anthropologists and offered a Proposed Draft Revision of the Principles of Professional Responsibility to the membership in the November 1989 issue of the AAA *Newsletter*. Discussion was held at the Open Forum of the AAA meetings in Washington in 1989, and the Revised Principles of Professional Responsibility was sent to the AAA membership in March 1990 for ratification, presumably without further controversy (see Appendix I).

While the new General Principles of Professional Responsibility do not amount to a major revision of the original PPR, as did the 1984 proposed revision, they do reflect some basic changes in the discipline. The principal, first responsibility to the people whose lives and cultures anthropologists study remains the core ethical principle (1.). However, new reference is made to anthropologists engaging in academic or nonacademic research (1.6), thus including the newer group of practicing anthropologists. Likewise, the original section, "Responsibility to Sponsors," has been changed to include the new employment realities that characterize the "new era"; it now reads "Responsibility to Employers, Clients and Sponsors" (5.).

More alarming is the removal of all references to secret or clandestine research, which the original PPR was so clear in censuring (3.a; 3.b). This was a major criticism of the 1984 proposed revision, and its central role in the history of anthropological ethics, as documented here, cannot be denied.

Summary Remarks

Taking a diachronic view of issues raised within the discipline of anthropology and the principles that have been generated in response, we can identify several recurrent themes, which are outlined in Table 1.1.

Other issues have been a part of the discussion of ethical standards, such as the professional responsibility to students, the publication of research materials, and responsibility to the discipline of anthropology, but the issues selected for this critical review are those that have received the widest attention in the field and have generated the most controversy. A key undercurrent, an issue not elevated to principle, is the clear nondesirability of having ethical issues discussed in fora outside of the professional association. The problem with Boas's disclosure, as well as that of Wolf and Jorgensen, is the fact that they "went public" and the journalistic medium raised and discussed the issue, rather than the organizational structure of the AAA. Clearly such a principle could not be formally articulated, for it would violate a much more fundamental principle of freedom of speech and expression, and anthropologists have frequently used the mass media to speak out on other issues. The question might easily be raised, if concerned anthropologists had not chosen the journalistic medium, or had it not been thrust upon them, for airing their grievances, whether the incidents protested would ever have come to light. Indeed, other equally damaging events may be lost to the public record because they were not disclosed. In

TABLE 1.1. Issues and Principles in the History of Anthropology and Ethics (prepared by Carolyn Fluehr-Lobban, Dartmouth College)

Issues	Dates	Principles
(1) Social scientists as spies; intelligence-related research by anthropologists	1919, 1967, 1970	Such activity strongly discouraged for the damage it does to the profession and future research
(2) Secret or clandestine research	1967, 1968	Reports not available to the public are unacceptable
	1990	All reference to clandestine or secret research removed
(3) Appropriate relationship between anthropologist and government	1930s, 1940s	Government work favored and approved
	1967, 1971	Anthropologists cautioned— should retain autonomy
	1984 (proposed)	Government employment neutralized as an issue
(4) Proper relationship to those studied	1971	Paramount responsibility of anthropologist
	1990	"First responsibility to those whose lives and cultures studied" retained
(5) Responsibility to sponsors of research; freedom of research	1971	Sources of funding should be publicly communicated; freedom of research should not be constrained
	1984 (proposed)	Freedom of research may be constrained by certain contractual relationships
		Sources of funding should be reported in publications
	1990	Added to "Responsibility to Sponsors," also responsibility to clients and employers; New reference to anthropologists working for government agencies and private business

personal correspondence, Eric Wolf has said, "As I think back on the matter, I have a strong feeling that we merely touched on a very small segment of an iceberg" (letter dated 19 December 1988).

With respect to the genesis of a code of ethics for anthropology, the relatively late date in which this occurs, 1971, might be surprising, except that comparable developments were taking place within allied social science fields at about the same time, perhaps precipitated by the same or similar events. The American Sociological Association adopted a code of ethics, also in 1971, that preserves the confidentiality of research data and protects the subjects from personal harm, while the American Political Science Association in 1968 adopted its "Proposed Rules of Conduct," which is less concerned with the protection of the subjects of research but assures that research will be conducted with the rights of those whom it affects in mind. The American Psychological Association's code, not surprisingly, is earlier, in 1963, and is concerned with the obvious problems of ethics in the conduct of research and experiments with human subjects.

For psychology especially, the specific principle of "informed consent," as with medical research, has been the focus of the greatest attention. Informed consent has been discussed within anthropology as the responsibility to communicate the aims and possible consequences of research to the subjects of research, but the elaboration of this principle has not extended to the proposed use of consent forms or other formal means of obtaining consent. Margaret Mead argued (1969:361–86) for the possibility of substituting the notion of voluntary participation for informed consent in anthropology, since the former is based on trust and the more collaborative nature of anthropological research.

Joseph Jorgensen (1971) has argued against any normative ethics, "metaethics," for anthropology because context is critical and ultimately determinative of judgments.

No matter what the philosophical view of individual anthropologists happens to be, the ethical dimension of social research can no longer be ignored or submerged in proclamations of objectivity or "pure research." And a uniquely political history of the discipline of anthropology can be discerned by examining closely the issues of ethics and professionalism in anthropology.

REFERENCES
Beals, Ralph
      1969   *Politics of social research*. Chicago: Aldine Publishing Co.

Berreman, Gerald
1969   Academic colonialism: Not so innocent abroad. *The Nation,* 10 Nov.: 505–8.
Harris, Marvin
1968   *The rise of anthropological theory.* New York: Thomas Crowell.
Jorgensen, Joseph
1971   On ethics and anthropology. *Current Anthropology* 12:321–34.
Kuper, Adam
1973   *Anthropologists and anthropology: The British school, 1922–72.* New York: PICA Press.
Lesser, Alexander
1981   Franz Boas. In *Totems and teachers: Perspectives on the history of anthropology,* ed. Sydel Silverman. New York: Columbia University Press.
Mandelbaum, D. G., Gabriel Lasker, and Ethel Albert
1963   The teaching of anthropology, AAA Memoir 94.
Mead, Margaret
1959   *An anthropologist at work: Writings of Ruth Benedict.* Boston: Houghton Mifflin Co.
1969   Research with human beings: A model derived from anthropological field practice. *Daedalus* 98:361–86.
Sjoberg, Gideon
1967   Project Camelot: Selected reactions and personal reflections. In *Ethics, politics and social research,* ed. G. Sjoberg, 141–61. Cambridge: Shenkman.
Weaver, Thomas
1973   *To see ourselves: Anthropology and modern social issues.* Glenview, Ill.: Scott, Foresman and Co.

Editor's Introduction to Chapter 2

WRITTEN BY ONE OF THE FOREMOST ACTORS and spokespersons involved in the dialogue over ethics during the past two decades, the following chapter represents an impassioned defense of the preservation of the core features of the original code, the Principles of Professional Responsibility (PPR). The author was a member of the American Anthropological Association's Committee on Ethics during some of the most turbulent times in the history of the discipline and during an important period for the construction of the first code of ethics in anthropology. As one of the framers and drafters of the original PPR in 1971, Gerald Berreman has unique knowledge of the public ethics debate that occurred within the field, and he possesses an intimate, insider's view of the internal debate over the documents relative to counterinsurgency research that were made known to the Committee on Ethics during the Vietnam War period.

In this article, Berreman reflects upon that time; he includes as part of his discussion selected texts from documents that startle, even today, and remind the anthropologist of the 1980s and 1990s that discussions of ethics are not abstract exercises, but can directly affect the quality and future of human lives. In this regard, Berreman offers an excellent discussion of that special ethical issue of clandestine research, a subject which deserves a fresh examination in the "new era," wherein much anthropological research is subject to contract-client restriction.

The author attempts to capture something of the tenor of the 1980s with the term *Reaganethics,* which he uses to describe a retreat by the Committee on Ethics away from more global, humanistic concerns and toward a greater concern with the protection and preservation of academic careers and reputations through its grievance process. The proposed draft codes of 1984, which responded to the interests of nonacademic anthropologists, carry with them the risk of dividing the profession into academic and practicing moieties, a division the author finds "unnatural, unnecessary, and counterproductive." He finds the 1990 proposed revision more acceptable.

Gerald D. Berreman

Chapter 2 Ethics versus "Realism" in Anthropology

Introduction

AT THE ANNUAL MEETING of the American Anthropological Association in December 1985, I participated as a representative of the Association's Committee on Ethics (COE) during the era in which its Principles of Professional Responsibility (PPR)—the official euphemism for our code of ethics—was drafted and adopted: 1969 to 1971. The situation at the time of that meeting was that a new, draft Code of Ethics (dCoE) had been placed before the membership in the October 1984 edition of the *Anthropology Newsletter*, fundamentally redefining and reformulating the concepts of ethics and responsibility in the profession to accord with what its authors said were the changed circumstances of the time. Discussion of the draft code was invited in the columns of the *Newsletter* and in an open forum, which had been held for the purpose at the 1984 annual meeting, with the goal of revising it and bringing it to a vote in the fall of 1985. If adopted it was to supersede the PPR or, if a vote were to appear premature at that time, further discussion was to be scheduled before holding the vote. The latter course was followed (including the 1985 session, "Ethics, Professionalism and the Future of Anthropology," and a follow-up session at the 1986 meetings). My role in each was to put the draft code into historical context and give my response to it. This chapter is based on those two presentations. The vote, incidentally, was never held.

I will introduce the context for what I have to say simply by asserting that I believe humane ethics in research and scholarship to be practical necessities for anthropologists today, just as human rights and self-interest—social justice and survival—have become inseparable for people everywhere (Berreman 1980:12; cf. 1971c:398–99). Therefore, when I speak of ethics versus realism in anthropology I am not referring to the "consummate realism" that Ernest Becker called "instrumental utopianism" (1971:xi), and that both he and C. Wright Mills before him advocated: the forthright application of reason to the solution of human problems. Rather, the "realism" I contrast ironically with ethics is that referred to by Mills (1963:402) as the boast of "crackpot realists," whom Becker called "hardheaded realists," that is, "the militarists and other bureaucrats . . . [with] their age-old practical nightmares" (Becker 1971:xi). That said, let me proceed to some historical background for the issues of ethics and "realism" in anthropology today.

History: Anthropology and Ethics, 1919 to 1986

The first ethical issue to discernibly attract the attention of the American Anthropological Association was the brief and tragicomical imbroglio of 1919 to 1920, wherein Franz Boas, founder of our discipline in America, became the only member of the association ever to be censured and expelled (Stocking 1968:273). His offense was that he reported in *The Nation* "incontrovertible proof," which had "accidentally" come his way, that "at least four" anthropologists had served as spies under cover of scholarly research during World War I (Boas 1919:729; see also AAA 1920:93–94).

The first serious systematic concern with ethics as such in our profession came about thirty years later, after World War II, when in 1948 the association adopted the "Resolution of Freedom of Publication," urging "all sponsoring institutions to guarantee their research scientists complete freedom to interpret and publish their findings without censorship or interference, provided that the interests of [those] studied are protected" (AAA 1949:370).[1] (That resolution should be borne in mind, I think, as we consider the provisions of the draft code.) But it took the infamous and ill-fated Project Camelot, an American counterinsurgency research plan for Chile in 1965—more than fifteen years after the research freedom resolution—to focus anthropological attention squarely on the issues of ethics and secrecy in research (Horowitz 1967). It was in response to this that the Beals Committee was appointed by the Executive Board of the AAA in 1967, which then produced the ground-breaking report entitled "Background Information on Problems of Anthropological Research and Ethics" (Beals et al. 1967:2–13). As a result of this report, the membership of the AAA voted adoption, in March 1967, of the "Statement of Problems of Anthropological Research and Ethics," based on that report. It is still in effect and is part of the packet of materials entitled *Professional Ethics* (1983), that is available from the Executive Office of the American Anthropological Association. It comprises essentially a draft code of ethics for the association and is a forerunner, both in time and content, of the Principles of Professional Responsibility.

At this point in the history of these matters, we move into what for many members of the association were the glory days (or the gory days, depending upon one's social and political viewpoint) of the late 1960s and early 1970s. The virtuous and the villainous were unambiguously defined no matter which side one was on, with few who were neutral or undecided. To say that is not to belittle the struggle or its importance. It was the good fight and the stakes were high. University and college departments were politically and ethically split (my own, for one), as was the profession. Friendships were severed, even as others were forged that would be strong and everlasting; enemies were made, respect was won and lost, principles were upheld and betrayed. The association was riven. The turmoil was perhaps most vividly displayed during and following the presidential election of 1970, wherein I, a member of the Committee on Ethics (which had confronted the Executive Board on issues surrounding the PPR and the ethics of anthropologists' involvement in mission-oriented activities in Southeast Asia, notably Thailand), was nominated as a presidential candidate. It was the first time that a nomination for association office had come from the electorate, as provided in the constitution, in addition to those candidates provided by the Committee on Nominations (three in the case of the presidency; *Newsletter,* 1970d:1). Shortly before the election, two of the three nominees of the committee withdrew their candidacies in favor of the third, considered the strongest of the three, in order to make it a two-person contest "because of the serious issues confronting the association and the introduction of a new nominee" (*Newsletter,* 1970e:1). The tactic evidently worked, as the committee's remaining candidate, Anthony Wallace, won by a margin of about two to one, although there is, of course, no way to know what might have been the outcome had all four candidates fulfilled the agreement upon which their acceptance of nomination was constitutionally predicated: that they would run and would serve if elected (*Newsletter,* 1971:1).[2]

In any case, in an effort to heal the wounds of these divisive events, at the annual meeting I was asked by the president, George Foster, to give a brief address to the council in my role as the defeated candidate and presumed spokesperson for the dissident minority. In view of the then-recent abolition of the presidential address, mine was the only address delivered before the council that year, an unusual parliamentary event, to say the least, and an opportunity I could hardly decline (Berreman 1971a; 1971b). I doubt that my talk did much to realize the hopes which motivated the request that I speak, but though it viewed the future of the association through what proved to have been a rather clouded crystal ball, it did gratify those who had supported my nomination for the values it represented. The tensions, disagreements, and divisions that surfaced in those days have diminished only slowly and uncertainly at best. The continuing controversy over the PPR, and the possibility of its replacement by the dCoE, are manifestations of that schism, and the heat of the continuing arguments reflects that of the Vietnam era, with some of the same cast of characters generating it. It is still a good fight and the stakes are still high, on both sides, but the substance of disagreement has clearly diminished within the profession, the arguments have become less dramatic, the membership less polarized, and the social and political context less conducive to clear-cut definition and resolution of the issues. Nevertheless, they retain their vital, ultimate importance to anthropology and will continue to trouble it as a discipline and a profession through periods of both apathy and concern.

I have gone through those now rare and yellowed documents, letters, telegrams, pronouncements, minutes of endless meetings, and recaptured some of the vitality I remember from that bygone era—the issues debated, the evidence cited, the strategies planned, the counterstrategies detected— and was reminded of the names and actions of coconspirators, adversaries, and commentators whom I had not seen or thought of for years, as well as those who are oft- and well-remembered. They are all there in the dusty files of the faithful and, no doubt, in those of the faithless as well. They await some energetic chronicler of our profession to bring them systematically to light as an exercise in the sociology (or anthropology) of knowledge, social change, and history.

At the time of these events, American military involvement in Vietnam, both directly and via Thailand, was heavy and rapidly escalating. Chad Gordon put it clearly in a memo to the Cambridge Project advisory board which objected to that involvement: "As the Defense Department's posture in the world becomes increasingly bizarre and dangerous, any participant in such projects will undoubtedly feel called upon to account for his action to colleagues, students and the wider public" (quoted by Coburn 1969:1253). Coburn adds, with renewed relevance today to the proposed dCoE, "It is this issue of accountability that troubles many" (ibid.).

Such concerns were widespread even as those, including anthropologists, whose actions inspired them were running amok with their involvement as advisers and contributors to military adventurism (Student Mobilization Committee 1970; Flanagan 1971).

Committee on Ethics and Principles of Professional Responsibility

At the end of 1968, the Executive Board of the AAA appointed an ad hoc Committee on Ethics, whose mission was "to consider questions of the role of the Association with regard to ethical conduct on the part of anthropologists," and to report the results of their deliberations to the Executive Board (*Newsletter*, 1969:3).

The ad hoc committee was composed of David Schneider, cochairman (University of Chicago), who played a key role in selecting his co-members, David Aberle, cochairman (University of British Columbia), Richard N. Adams (University of Texas), Joseph Jorgensen (University of Michigan), William Shack (University of Illinois, Chicago Circle), and Eric Wolf (University of Michigan). They met on 25–26 January 1969 and wrote a report which included a recommendation for an elected "Standing Committee on Ethics" of the association. Defining in detail the responsibilities of the proposed standing committee, the ad hoc committee outlined "the framework for the issues that the Committee on Ethics must consider." This constituted, in effect, a draft code of ethics for the AAA, and was published in the April 1969 issue of the *Newsletter* (compare: ad hoc Committee on Ethics, *Newsletter*, 1969:3–6, with Principles of Professional Responsibility, *Newsletter*, 1970f:14–16).

That draft code was perhaps too radical for the Executive Board in those turbulent times, for they tabled it and attended only to a second recommendation of the ad hoc committee, namely,

> IMMEDIATE election of an Ethics Committee DIRECTLY responsible to the electorate of Fellows (and of students enfranchised). . . . The Committee urged that the new, elected Committee . . . be independent of the Board. . . . This recommendation was NOT accepted by the Board. . . . It agreed to hold an election for a pro tem Ethics Committee concurrent with the autumn [1969] election of the President-Elect and new members of the Executive Board. (*Newsletter*, 1969:3)

Thus, the two bodies agreed on the principle of an elected ethics committee, but disagreed on whether it should be responsible directly to the electorate or to the Executive Board. This difference of opinion remained a bone of contention for years because, once the elected Committee on Ethics was in place, it defined its responsibility as being directly to the membership of the association, which the Executive Board disputed.

The mission of the new committee was to include consideration of the advisability and nature of an ethics code. The elected committee would consist of nine elected members except that initially, for purposes of continuity, three would carry over for one year from the appointed ad hoc committee, while six would be elected (three allotted terms of three years and the other three, terms of two years). In addition there would be a member of the Executive Board to serve ex officio as a nonvoting liaison member of the committee. Those elected in the fall of 1969 were Norman Chance (University of Connecticut), Robert Ehrich (Brooklyn College, CUNY), Wayne Suttles (Portland State University), Terence Turner (University of Chicago), Oswald Werner (Northwestern University), and I (University of California, Berkeley). Those carried over from the ad hoc committee were Eric Wolf (chair), Joseph Jorgensen, and William Shack. David Aberle, who had been a member of the ad hoc committee, had in the meantime been elected to the Executive Board, which appointed him as liaison member to the pro tem committee.

The newly constituted committee met several times, working primarily toward the preparation of a code of ethics, which it submitted to the Executive Board in May 1970. The board promptly retitled it "Principles of Professional Responsibility" (to soften the blow for members who did not want anyone to subject them to the constraints a "code" seems to imply), and it was published in the November 1970 *Newsletter,* as cited above. After heated debate in the columns of the *Newsletter,* in committees, at annual meetings, in departments, and in private, and after many intervening crises in the Executive Board, the Committee on Ethics, the council, and within the membership, the principles were adopted by vote of the association in May 1971.

The PPR's initial year, spanning the period from its formulation to its adoption, was a stormy one, to say the least. On 30 March 1970, the Student Mobilization Committee to Stop the War in Vietnam (SMC) sent to a number of scholars, including some members of the Committee on Ethics of the AAA, as well as to people in other academic disciplines (primarily people involved in Asian studies of various sorts), materials indicating participation by scholars in what they regarded as clandestine, counterinsurgency research and other activities in Southeast Asia under sponsorship of various United States governmental agencies, including such mission-oriented ones as the Departments of Defense and State and special agencies within them. The SMC planned to release a report on these documents at a press conference they had called for 3 April at the Annual Meeting of the Association for Asian Studies, to be held in San Francisco during the first week of April 1970, and at another press conference scheduled simultaneously, or nearly so, in Washington, D.C. The materials were minutes, letters, reports, financial accountings, publications, and similar contents of the files of an anthropology professor at a major West Coast university, copied by a student employee of the professor from files to which she had legitimate access in the course of her work. She had regarded their contents as alarming, and had taken the liberty of making copies for herself, which she then turned over to the Student Mobilization Committee. The SMC proceeded to publish them in the 2 April 1970 edition of *The Student Mobilizer,* under the edition title *Counterinsurgency Research on Campus Exposed.* At the press conferences arranged to announce these findings and distribute *The Student Mobilizer,* four of the scholars who had been sent advance copies of some of the documents issued statements condemning the work that had been exposed: Eric Wolf, Joseph Jorgensen, Marshall Sahlins (in Washington, D.C.), and I (in San Francisco). Later, others joined in condemning that which had been exposed, while still others condemned the exposure and those who participated in it and those who had decried the activities exposed. Some wrote of "liberated" documents; others of "purloined" ones. Controversy raged, charges and countercharges, insults and counterinsults were traded, lawsuits were threatened (though since no law had been broken, none was ever filed). For vivid and partisan accounts—and all were partisan in this matter, including me—see "Anthropology on the Warpath in Thailand" (Wolf and Jorgensen 1970a:26–36) and "Anthropology on the Warpath: An Exchange" (Foster et al. 1971:43–46).

The Executive Board wrote a stinging (and, I would have to say, ill-informed) letter on 19 May 1970, reprimanding the Committee on Ethics and, specifically, Wolf and Jorgensen for their statements and actions (*Newsletter,* 1970b:1, 10). The letter included these remarks:

> The Board instructs the Ethics Committee to limit itself to its specific charge, narrowly interpreted, namely to present to the Board recommendations on its

future role and functions, and to fulfill this charge without further collection of case materials or by any quasi-investigative activities.

It concluded that "the Board explicitly instructs the members of the Ethics Committee . . . to make clear in individual statements that they do not speak for the Committee or the Association."[3] It was the alleged violation of this last after-the-fact instruction which evidently brought the wrath of the Board down on Wolf and Jorgensen for their joint statement on the SMC revelations, and exempted—at least from explicit condemnation— Sahlins and me. Sahlins was exempted because he was not on the committee, and I was because my statement was made as an Asianist scholar in the context of the Association for Asian Studies meetings, rather than as a member of the AAA ethics committee. Wolf and Jorgensen had identified themselves as members of the ethics committee and indicated their intent to bring "these serious matters" to the attention of the American Anthropological Association, but in no way did they imply that they were speaking *for* the Committee on Ethics. They responded quickly, strongly, and in detail in a letter dated 25 May 1970 to the president and president-elect of the association, the Executive Board (which includes those two officers), and the Committee on Ethics. They concluded the letter with their resignation from the committee, pointing out that

> In its Statement the Board wishes the Ethics Committee to limit itself to its specific charge, narrowly interpreted; but it is not equally specific about its own intention to cope with the issues raised by an applied anthropology which has for its focal concern the internal security of the present Thailand government. In drawing attention to the action of particular members of the Ethics Committee, the Board evidently hoped to avert a threat to the internal harmony of our Association. In not applying themselves with equal diligence to an analysis of the issues which prompted these individual actions, the Board averts its eyes from the real sources of a danger which threatens not only the integrity of the Association, but the fate and welfare of the peoples among whom we work. In view of the failure of the Board to interpret its mandate to the Ethics Committee to include a concern of vital relevance to the profession, we ourselves fail to perceive how the Committee can "present to the Board recommendations on its future role and functions." We therefore tender our resignations as Chairman and Member of the Committee on Ethics. (Wolf and Jorgensen 1970b, which includes not only this letter, but the letter and other documents which the Executive Board found untenable)[4]

Within a week, David Aberle resigned as the board's liaison member on the Committee on Ethics (Aberle 1970:19), while Wolf and Jorgensen encouraged other members to remain on the committee to continue its work.

A month later, in response to demands from both sides of the controversy, David Schneider, then a member of the Executive Board, proposed that a committee be appointed to look into the entire issue, both the activities of the Committee on Ethics and those of anthropologists working in Thailand. Accordingly, the Executive Board quickly appointed the "Ad Hoc Committee to Evaluate the Controversy Concerning Anthropological Activities in Relation to Thailand," consisting of three members: Margaret Mead, chair (Columbia University and American Museum of Natural History); William Davenport (University of California, Santa Cruz); David Olmsted (University of California, Davis); and, as executive secretary, Ruth Freed (New York University and American Museum of Natural History). This ad hoc committee (often called the "Mead Committee") collected documents from a variety of sources, many of them from the Committee on Ethics, and others from principals in the controversy and from other people knowledgeable about Thailand and the issues of the controversy. By this committee's account, "all members of the ad hoc committee and its Executive Secretary . . . examined all of these materials in detail" and in the process "approximately 6000 pages were read, and many reread in order for the ad hoc committee to write this report" (Davenport et al. 1971:2). This achievement was the more remarkable in view of the fact that the committee's chairperson was for much of the year in the South Pacific. The six-page report that resulted was submitted to the Executive Board on 27 September 1971. It totally exonerated all members of the American Anthropological Association of any ethical wrongdoing in the context of this controversy: "1. No civilian member of the American Anthropological Association had contravened the principles laid down in the 1967 Statement on *Problems of Anthropological Research and Ethics* (Beals Report) in his or her work in Thailand" (Davenport et al. 1971:4). It went on to explain seeming offenses as merely misleading claims in research applications and reports made necessary by a climate where defense relevance was required in order to obtain government funding for research. As the committee put it, "The mislabeling or redirecting of scientific projects in order to obtain funds may have seemed necessary: it may also have prepared anthropologists . . . to close their eyes to misuse of their data . . . and . . . talents" (ibid., 4). It was suggesting that "counterinsurgency" may have been merely a buzzword incorporated in applications and reports to release funds for the author's scholarly research, just as earlier buzzwords such as "community development" and "mental health" served this function.

At the same time, the Mead Committee reprimanded the members of the Committee on Ethics who, it said, "acted hastily, unfairly, and unwisely in making public statements . . . without first having consulted the anthropologists named in the purloined documents which formed the basis of their charges, and without having obtained authorization from the Board" (ibid.). The Mead Report was presented to the Council of the AAA in New York at its annual meeting on 19 November 1971, where by vote of the assembled body, and over the vehement objections of its authors, it was divided into three substantive sections and presented for discussion preparatory to a vote on whether to accept or reject each of the sections: part 1 was primarily about the activities of anthropologists in Thailand; part 2 was primarily on the actions of the Committee on Ethics; and part 3 constituted proposed guidelines, recommendations, and resolutions.

The debate, before some four hundred members, focused on the exoneration of those who had been criticized for their work in Thailand. The atmosphere was tense in view of the demands of the chairperson of the ad hoc committee, on behalf of herself and the other authors, that the report not be put to a vote but simply be put in the record as submitted (for the handwriting was already on the wall), and the membership's determination, ratified in short order by its vote, to put each section to a vote. No doubt the most telling moments in the discussion of the report were when two members of the Committee on Ethics, responding to the assertion that no civilian member of the AAA had contravened the ethical principles of the association in their work in Thailand, read from two egregiously unethical projects in which civilian fellows of the association had been directly involved, as demonstrated in documents which the ad hoc committee had had in its hands, provided by the Committee on Ethics. The first was as follows, as reported in its author's own abstract of the project:

AD-468 413 Military Research and Development Center, Bangkok (Thailand) LOW ALTITUDE VISUAL SEARCH FOR INDIVIDUAL HUMAN TARGETS: FURTHER FIELD TESTING IN SOUTHEAST ASIA. By [an anthropologist] 15 June 65, 83 pp. Unclassified. Project description text:
    This report is a detailed study of quantitative information on the ability of airborne observers to sight and identify single humans on the ground. The target background for most of the testing was rice paddy with scattered bushes and trees at the end of the dry season in Southeast Asia . . . [etc., etc.].

The second item read to the membership consisted of excerpts from a forty-four-page proposal in which a fellow of the AAA was involved, titled "Counter-Insurgency in Thailand: The Impact of Economic, Social and Political Action Programs." This was a half-million-dollar social science research and development proposal submitted to the Advanced Research Projects Agency of the Department of Defense by the American Institutes for Research of Pittsburgh in 1967. After introducing the problem, to design preventive counterinsurgency measures for Thailand, and to "pave the way for the generalization of the methodology to other programs in other countries" (p. ii, see below), the proposal went on to state:

> The struggle between an established government and insurgent forces involves three different types of operations: the first is to make inputs into the social system that will gain the active support of an ever-increasing proportion of the population. *Threats,* promises, ideological appeals, and tangible benefits are the kinds of inputs that are most frequently used. The second is to reduce or interdict the flow of the competing inputs being made by the opposing side by installing anti-infiltration devices, cutting communications lines, *assassinating key spokesmen, strengthening retaliatory mechanisms* and similar preventative measures. The third is to counteract or neutralize the political successes already achieved by groups committed to the "wrong" side. This typically involves *direct military* confrontation.
>
> *The social scientist can make significant contributions to the design of all three types of operations.* (American Institutes for Research, 1967:1; all emphasis added)

The proposal continues in this vein for forty-four chilling pages. In the final paragraph of what is termed the "Operational Plan," we read the following: "The potential applicability of the findings in the United States will also receive special attention. In many of our key domestic programs, especially those directed at *disadvantaged sub-cultures,* the methodological problems are highly similar to those described in this proposal, and the application of the Thai findings at home constitutes a potentially most significant project contribution" (ibid., 34; emphasis added).

The proposal was accepted and funded, but its semiannual reports are classified, hence unavailable—for good reason, one suspects. (See Berreman 1981a:72–126, wherein many more examples of ethically questionable and untenable anthropological projects are itemized.)

In that great auditorium where over four hundred anthropologists were seated, there followed a deathly silence. No rebuttal was offered by the Mead Committee or from the membership. The votes were held on the three sections and the report was overwhelmingly rejected, section by section. The *Newsletter* of January 1972 reported it on page 1 under the headline "COUNCIL REJECTS THAI CONTROVERSY COMMITTEE'S REPORT." After introducing the account in general, the article proceeded: "The first part in this division [of the report for purposes of the vote] . . . was rejected by a vote of 308 to 74. The second part was also rejected, 243 to 57. And a final motion to consider the issue of anthropologists' actions in Thailand unresolved and to reject the remainder of the report . . . was carried by a vote of 214 to 14 as the clock moved into Saturday and the Council dwindled away" (*Newsletter*, 1972:1).

In the same issue of the *Newsletter*, two letters were printed as "Replies to the Report of the Ad Hoc Committee to Evaluate the Thailand Controversy," both of which had been distributed to the council at its meeting. One, by Wolf and Jorgensen, gave point-by-point rebuttals to many of the ad hoc committee's assertions and concluded that "we are as much dismayed by the callousness of the report as by its factual and theoretical faults." The other letter was by May N. Diaz and Lucile F. Newman, who challenged the report and concluded that "anthropologists cannot serve both science and war" (ibid., 3–4).

That, then, is the context within which the Principles of Professional Responsibility originated and evolved. It is against this background that we must understand the emergence of the draft Code of Ethics, changes in the role and function of the Committee on Ethics, and even the reorganization of the American Anthropological Association. I think these three changes are symptomatic of common forces at work within the profession, common pressures from without, and common processes at work on the national and international levels. They comprise a shift away from idealism and toward self-interested practicality. It is to the demand for a new code of ethics as a symptom of these broader discontents, and to the implications of that demand and those discontents, that I now turn—or return.

The Draft Code of Ethics: Text and Context

The Principles of Professional Responsibility, having been adopted in 1971 and having served the profession adequately, if not remarkably, for some years as a cautionary and exemplary model more than as an enforcement mechanism or deterrent (although with the potential to serve those functions as well), gradually lost the attention of the membership it was designed to serve, as did the committee which was to sustain and implement it. There had been only three amendments to it since its adoption: one, in 1974, relating to plagiarism (*Newsletter,* 1974:9); and two in 1975, one requiring that informants be apprised of the fact that anonymity cannot be guaranteed against the possibility of accidental disclosure, and the other advising that exclusionary policies against colleagues on the basis of non-academic attributes and the transmittal of such irrelevant factors in personnel actions is unethical (*Newsletter,* 1975:1). The only overall revision as such was the removal of generic use of the masculine pronoun from the document in about 1976.

According to the October 1984 *Newsletter,* "by 1975, active concerns had surfaced about aspects of the PPR and the grievance procedures. The growing number of non-academically based anthropologists held that the PPR was based only on academic considerations. . . . Important inconsistencies and ambiguities were found in the various documents relating to ethics" (*Newsletter,* 1984:2). In short, and in currently popular jargon, the hegemony of academic anthropology, and especially of academic social and cultural anthropology, was challenged. The Executive Board asked the Committee on Ethics to consider these and related problems and to propose remedies. It did so, and its suggestions were circulated to committees and individuals in the association. In 1980, an ad hoc committee was appointed to prepare a new draft code. It was made up of Karl Heider, chair (University of South Carolina); Barry Bainton and Alice Brues (University of Colorado, Boulder); Jerald Milanich (University of Florida and Florida State Museum); and John Roberts (University of Pittsburgh). After the committee members had prepared the draft and it had been circulated, commented upon, and revised, it was finally considered by the Executive Board to be "ready to go to the membership" in 1982 (ibid.). However, in view of the fact that the association was in the throes of reorganization at that time—which process, like the proposed new code, was designed to facilitate and respond to changes in the profession and especially to its members' employment structure—it was thought the membership might be distracted from attending adequately to the ad hoc committee's proposals on ethics. Accordingly, it was decided that the proposed code would be withheld from the membership until the fall of 1984. Therefore, the draft Code of Ethics (dCoE) was first presented to the membership when it was published in the October 1984 *Newsletter* (ibid.).

An "open forum" on the proposed dCoE was held at the November 1984 annual meetings in Denver. These were also the first meetings of the

AAA organized to reflect the reorganization of the association into its five major divisions, now merged with its previously "affiliated" societies. In spite of the chaotic novelty of these changes, there was a lively debate on the ethics proposal—a debate which was reviewed, with discussion invited, by President-elect Helm in the April *Newsletter* (1985:1). Thereafter, the *Newsletter* was sprinkled with letters and commentaries on the subject, displaying a variety of opinions and commitments, in the months leading to the 1985 annual meetings in Washington, D.C., at which the session on "Ethics, Professionalism and the Future of Anthropology" (where the contents of this chapter were originally presented) was held.

These events were in accord with the original declaration in the PPR that it would be "from time to time" scrutinized and revised as the membership of the AAA "sees fit or as circumstances dictate" (*Professional Ethics,* 1983:5).

The 1985 session on ethics was aimed at bringing out key facts, issues, and points of view surrounding the proposed changes in the ethical stance of the AAA in the context of scholarly presentations and intellectual discussion, not to exclude debate and commitment, but with the goal of providing more light than heat.

Ethics versus Practicality: An Interpretation

The remainder of this chapter will comprise my response to the status or condition of ethics in the AAA as it has emerged since 1985. It is an interpretation, therefore, rather than, as above, a historical review. One must be familiar with both the PPR and the dCoE to consider the matter fairly, which is why I have delved into history at such length and why, in addition, these two critical documents are reproduced in this volume.

There are four major changes proposed in the draft Code of Ethics—four deletions from the Principles of Professional Responsibility—which I regard as drastic. These four must be clearly stated and directly addressed in the implications they hold for anthropology and anthropologists to convey why I, and many others, regard the changes as pernicious.

First is the downgrading—the virtual elimination—of the primary and fundamental tenet of the Principles: "1. Relations with those studied: In research, anthropologists' paramount responsibility is to those they study."

Second is the elimination of secret and clandestine activity in anthropological endeavors as constituting violations of anthropological ethics.

Third is removal of the principle of accountability of the anthropologist for violations of ethical principles—removal of any mention of sanctions, or their legitimacy, to say nothing of eliminating all traces of mechanisms for enjoining adherence to ethical principles.

Fourth is deletion of anthropologists' positive responsibilities to society at large, their own and/or those they study: the responsibility to convey their findings and the implications thereof forthrightly to all concerned fully and publicly, to the best of their professional abilities.

I maintain that these omissions have resulted not in a code at all, but a mild statement of intent, and one conspicuously devoid of ethical content. It is in fact, I think, a license for unfettered free-enterprise research, advising and engineering disguised as anthropology, with the intent of employing the ethical reputation of the discipline to enable and facilitate a wide range of mission-oriented activities, including those of dubious ethical and even egregiously unethical nature.[5] To title the draft document "Code of Ethics" is to misrepresent it seriously. It might be better to adopt a title parallel to that of the PPR—this one: Principles of Professional Irresponsibility (PPI). To do so would serve the interests of candor and thereby make at least one contribution to ethics in the profession.

I will briefly discuss these four principles-by-omission, in reverse order.

POSITIVE RESPONSIBILITIES IN ANTHROPOLOGY

To my mind the most insidious, because inconspicuous, deletion from the PPR in the dCoE is the issue of the positive responsibility of anthropologists to let it be known publicly what they have learned and what they believe its implications to be for all concerned. It is stated this way in the PPR:

2. Responsibility to the Public:
    d. . . . . Anthropologists bear a positive responsibility to speak out publicly, both individually and collectively, on what they know and what they believe as a result of their professional expertise gained in the study of human beings. That is, they bear a professional responsibility to contribute to an "adequate definition of reality" [Mills 1963:611] upon which public opinion and public policy may be based.

That is, we acknowledge a responsibility to practice what C. Wright Mills (ibid., and 1959:178–79) called "the politics of truth" for, as he insisted, in the defining instance, truth *is* our politics and our responsibility (Mills 1963:611). If we do not fulfill this responsibility, we are nothing more than human engineers—hirelings in the service of any agency with any agenda that can buy our expertise, as some indeed became during the Vietnam War. This theme has pervaded virtually all discussions of ethics in our profession during the past twenty-five years, including those in this volume (cf. Berreman 1968, 1981).

ACCOUNTABILITY

Now it is proposed that we adopt a code of ethics without accountability. In the dCoE there is no mechanism whatsoever by which individuals can be held to account for their actions, no matter how blatantly and destructively they flaunt their profession's ethical standards and regardless of how bland such standards may be.

Why? Do those who propose and endorse this deletion intend to leave open the opportunity to violate at will the very principles of ethical conduct upon which their profession has agreed? I hope not. Is the statement in the PPR too harsh, too constraining, too dangerous? I think not. Accountability is mentioned in the PPR only in its epilogue, where it is stated:

> In the final analysis, anthropological research is a human undertaking, dependent upon choices for which the individual bears ethical as well as scientific responsibility. That responsibility is a human, not superhuman, responsibility. To err is human, to forgive humane. This statement of principles of professional responsibility is not designed to punish, but to provide guidelines which can minimize the occasions upon which there is a need to forgive. *When anthropologists, by their actions, jeopardize peoples studied, professional colleagues, students, or others, or if they otherwise betray their professional commitments, their colleagues may legitimately inquire into the propriety of those actions, and take such measures as lie within the legitimate powers of their Association as the membership of the Association deems appropriate.* (*Professional Ethics,* 1983:2; emphasis added)

The italicized sentence is a statement of accountability and is the nearest thing in the PPR to a mechanism for its enforcement. Is it too threatening to the new anthropology, to practicing anthropology, to be incorporated into the proposed code? Does it go against the spirit and intent of the dCoE? I think so. It must be remembered that in the Vietnam anthropologist-warriors' case it was accountability that was the issue; it was accountability that was denied by one side and insisted upon by the other. Maybe *that* is the crux of the problem now; maybe *that* is what the draft code proposes to protect future warrior-anthropologists from. Perhaps now all's to be fair in love, war, and anthropology; maybe it is proposed that henceforth there is to be no more honor among anthropologists than has long been claimed to be among thieves. Are we witnessing an attempt to exempt us as scholars, as scientists, as anthropologists, from the principle invoked by the United Nations at Nuremburg after World War II, which held accountable soldiers and bureaucrats who sought to evade being held responsible for their atrocities on the ground that they were only doing their jobs, for their country? Do the anthropologists protesting against accountability not protest too much? If so, again we must ask, why? If, as I prefer to believe is the case (because I am ever charitable in such matters), the aim is simply to forestall the possibility of an ethics witch-hunt, it is misguided—a clear case of the proposed cure being worse than the affliction. There is a striking lack of evidence to even suggest that the PPR is conducive to such an eventuality. In its twenty-year history, the Committee on Ethics has pursued only one case that I know of to the Executive Board, and *no* case went any further than that for, in the balance of power enacted into the "Rules and Procedures" (*Professional Ethics*, 1983:7–9), the Executive Board must agree with the Committee on Ethics that there is a prima facie case of ethical violation for the matter to be pursued further. That has not, to my knowledge, ever occurred. But I believe that the possibility of censure or other measures of accountability within the association, however mild and symbolic, gives credibility to our claims to ethical standards and therefore has a salutary effect in their realization, which a purely and piously advisory "code" would not.

SECRECY AND CLANDESTINE ACTIVITY

We are urged to consider adoption of an ethics for anthropological endeavor which tolerates secret and clandestine activities or, as the president-elect suggested in 1985, which permits secret activity but prohibits that which is clandestine: perhaps she can explain it; I cannot:

> The PPR coupling of "clandestine and secret research" may constitute a *prima facie* condemnation of some anthropologists employed in non-academic settings. In this . . . respect, it appears that the first step might be to set aside the pejorative concept "clandestine" from the consideration of ethical issues arising in employment and research—notably for government, business, industry and special interest groups—that may involve some form or degree of secrecy. (Helm 1985:13)

Yet again, why? Is it, as seems to be the argument, that although "secret" and "clandestine" mean the same they are after all necessary activities in the minds of some practicing anthropologists and "clandestine" *sounds* worse?

It should be noted that the repudiation of secret or clandestine activity in the name of anthropology has been the most long-standing and the most consistently, unequivocally enunciated of ethical principles embraced by American anthropologists. From our earliest expressions of ethical concern as an association and a profession, no secret or clandestine research, no secret reports, have been tolerated among us. In 1948, the association adopted a resolution on freedom of publication and protection of the interests of those studied. It thereby anticipated the PPR by addressing two of its four key principles, now repudiated in the dCoE. That resolution forty years ago stated in part: "(1) that the AAA strongly urge[s] all sponsoring institutions to guarantee their research scientists complete freedom to interpret and publish their findings without censorship or interference; provided that (2) the interests of the persons and communities or other social groups studied are protected" (American Anthropological Association 1949:370). That resolution was reaffirmed by the association in its 1967 "Statement on Problems and Anthropological Research and Ethics," the introduction to which asserted that, "constraint, deception and secrecy have no place in science. Actions which compromise the intellectual integrity and autonomy of research scholars . . . not only weaken those international understandings essential to our discipline, but in so doing they also threaten any contribution anthropology might make to our own society and to the general interests of human welfare" (*Professional Ethics,* 1983:3). The statement went on to quote and endorse the 1948 resolution quoted above and, in order "to extend and strengthen this resolution," added that,

> Except in the event of a declaration of war by Congress [*note:* there was no such declaration in the Vietnam War], academic institutions should not undertake activities or accept contracts in anthropology that are not related to their normal function of teaching, research and public service. They should not lend themselves to clandestine activities. We deplore unnecessary restrictive classifications of research reports . . . and excessive security regulations imposed on participating academic personnel.
> 3. The best interests of scientific research are not served by the imposition of external restrictions. The review procedures instituted for foreign area research contracts by . . . the Department of State . . . offer a dangerous potential for censorship of research. Additional demands [for clearance and the like] . . . are incompatible with effective anthropological research. (Ibid.)

There followed an unambiguous resolution passed at the annual meetings of the AAA in 1969, ratified by mail ballot in the spring of 1970: "Resolution 13 (Karen Sacks), Resolved that members of the AAA shall not engage in any secret or classified research" (*Newsletter*, 1970a; 1970c).

A year later, the issue of secrecy and clandestine activity was addressed directly by the membership of the AAA when it adopted the Principles of Professional Responsibility, which dealt with it in at least six places in the body of the principles and once in an appendix—an indication of the great importance such activity has continued to hold in our profession. It is worthwhile to extract and quote each of these treatments of the issue so that we are vividly reminded of the enormity of the deletion of this subject from the dCoE:

From the PPR:

1. Relations with those studied: . . .
   g. In accordance with the Association's general position on clandestine and secret research, no reports should be provided to sponsors that are not also available to the general public and, where practicable, to the population studied.
2. Responsibility to the public:
   a. Anthropologists should not communicate findings secretly to some and withhold them from others.
3. Responsibility to the discipline:
   a. Anthropologists should undertake no secret research or any research whose results cannot be freely derived and publicly reported.
   b. Anthropologists should avoid even the appearance of engaging in clandestine research, by fully and freely disclosing the aims and sponsorship of all research.
5. Responsibility to sponsors:
   . . . . Anthropologists should be especially careful not to promise or imply acceptance of conditions contrary to their professional ethics or competing commitments. This requires that they require of sponsors full disclosure of the sources of funds, personnel, aims of the institution and the research project, and disposition of research results. Anthropologists must retain the right to make all ethical decisions in their research. They should enter into no secret agreements with sponsors regarding research, results or reports.
6. Responsibility to one's own government and to host governments:
   . . . . [Anthropologists] should demand assurance that they will not be required to compromise their professional responsibilities and ethics as a condition of their permission to pursue research. Specifically, no secret research, no secret reports or debriefings of any kind should be agreed to or given. If these matters are clearly understood in advance, serious complica-

tions and misunderstandings can generally be avoided. (*Professional Ethics,* 1983:1–2)

Appendix C: A Note on "Clandestine"
The 1967 *Random House Dictionary of the English Language,* defines the term clandestine as follows:
characterized by, done for, or executed with secrecy or concealment, especially for purposes of subversion or deception; private or surreptitious.
The [Ethics] Committee construes these definitions to mean that the concealment of research goals from a subject population (including nonarticulation of such goals when they include potentially injurious consequences to the social, economic, cultural and/or physical well being of the population) or other forms of deception of that population with respect to the uses to which the researcher is aware the data he gathers will be put, regardless of whether or not the research program itself is kept secret or whether publications issuing from it are classified, properly falls within the meaning of the term "clandestine" and thus is in violation of the 1967 resolution ["Statement on Problems of Anthropological Research and Ethics"]. (Annual Report of the Committee on Ethics, September 1970, *Newsletter,* 1970f:16)

In thinking back to Helm's suggestion that *clandestine* be distinguished from *secret,* and the former be prohibited and the latter permitted, it seems that *secret* is to be the word for approved clandestinity; *clandestine* will be the word for disapproved secrecy or, as she wrote, the "pejorative" word for secrecy. Whatever the terminology, it is clear that the draft code, in rescuing secret and clandestine activities from the list of unethical practices, is proposing that they be regarded as acceptable, necessary, even desirable (in the case of practicing anthropologists) items in the anthropological bag of methodological tricks. This I regard as abject surrender of principle to a misguided practicality; a sacrifice of public interest to misperceived self-interest: replacing ethics with greed.[6]

I had thought these matters through well before joining the Committee on Ethics or confronting the task of helping prepare a code of ethics. At the risk of offering a surfeit of my own opinions on the subject, I will offer some words of my own, presented in a paper for the presidential panel titled "The Funding of Asian Studies" at the Association for Asian Studies annual meeting in 1970 (the same meeting, incidentally, at which the Student Mobilization Committee held its press conference discussed above):

There is no scholarly activity any of us can do better in secret than in public. There is none we can pursue as well, in fact, because of the implicit but inevitable restraints secrecy places on scholarship. To do research in secret, or to report it in secret, is to invite suspicion, and legitimately so because secrecy is the hallmark of intrigue, not scholarship. . . . I believe that we should make freedom from secrecy an unalterable condition of our research. (Berreman 1971c:396)

So much for secret *and/or* clandestine activity as excusable, much less legitimate, by anthropologists, and so much for an ethics that permits it.

In the new, and otherwise satisfactory (to me) "Revised Principles of Professional Responsibility," prepared after this essay was initially written (published for discussion in the November 1989 issue of the *Anthropology Newsletter;* submitted for ratification to the membership, 15 March 1990), I am alarmed to note that the issue of secrecy is side-stepped. The word does not appear, nor is the matter addressed beyond a single passing mention of a commitment to "open inquiry." This strikes me as odd, to say the least, in view of the centrality of the issue throughout the history of discussions of anthropological ethics in this country. To tolerate secret research is to sacrifice the credibility of anthropology as a research discipline and a humane science.

PRIORITY OF THE WELFARE OF THOSE STUDIED IN ANTHROPOLOGY
Finally, I return to the first of these principles-in-absentia of the draft Code of Ethics, namely deletion from the code of the primary principle in the Principles of Professional Responsibility: that the welfare of those studied is the anthropologist's paramount responsibility. This was anticipated by a second resolution presented to the Council of the Association by Karen Sacks at the 1969 annual meetings, which was passed there and ratified in the spring of 1970:

> Resolution 14 (Karen Sacks),
> Resolved that fieldworkers shall not divulge any information orally or in writing, solicited by government officials, foundations, or corporation representatives about the people they study that compromises and/or endangers their well-being and cultural integrity. (*Newsletter,* 1970a; 1970c)

The Principles of Professional Responsibility stated this point unambiguously at the head of its list of principles. It is worthwhile to repeat a bit in order to remind ourselves:

> 1. Relations with those studied:
>   In research, anthropologists' paramount responsibility is to those they

study. When there is a conflict of interest, these individuals must come first. Anthropologists must do everything in their power to protect the physical, social and psychological welfare and to honor the dignity and privacy of those studied. (*Professional Ethics,* 1983:1)

Contrast that statement with the ambiguous one in the dCoE (bearing in mind that it is perhaps the *least* ambiguous of all the provisions in that document):

1. Anthropologists must seriously consider their own moral responsibility for their acts when there is a risk that an individual, group or organization may be hurt, exploited, or jeopardized physically, legally, in reputation, or in self-esteem as a result of these acts. (*Newsletter,* 1984:2)

Witness the fact that the people we study would be dropped not only from the highest priority (which they held in the ethical obligations specified by the PPR), but would virtually be dropped out of the draft code altogether.[7] And note that people are to be put on a par with organizations. If one were studying the Ku Klux Klan, concern for the well-being of individual informants would evidently be reduced to par with that for the KKK as an organization (or that of the organization would be raised to parity with individuals, as proponents might prefer to put it).

A more fundamental question than the quality of the proposed substitute code is why the change has been proposed—what forces have led to it?

Reaganethics: The Temper of the Times

The history of the Committee on Ethics since 1971 has been one of rapid decline—*transformation* would be a more diplomatic word. It has evolved or devolved from a committee on ethics to essentially a grievance committee; from one concerned with ethical principles and practice to one devoted primarily to personnel matters: fairness in appointments and promotions, issues of plagiarism, priority of publication, and conflict of interest (e.g., AAA 1975:54–55). This parallels a shift in concern and involvement of faculty in a number of universities from issues of academic freedom to issues of privilege and tenure (as the respective academic senate committees are called on my campus), and a pervasive concern in our society with personal well-being at the expense of concern with broader principles of social justice.

I do not blame the members of the Association's Committee on Ethics for this situation. Those are the kinds of cases with which they have been saddled. The grievances are legitimate ones, but they should be the responsibility of a committee constituted for that purpose rather than of an ethics committee perverted to that purpose. The Committee on Ethics, which has evolved in this direction, was largely responsible for the draft code, with additional input from the significantly named "Committee on Anthropology and the Profession." The combination of an ethics committee concerned largely with professional grievances and a committee on anthropology as a profession (and, therefore, presumably focused primarily on nonacademic careers) not surprisingly proposed a code which was avowedly responsive to the "new realities" of a changing profession and, especially, as has been repeatedly asserted, to the circumstances of nonacademic anthropologists: those employed in government and in corporate and consultative agencies. But it was not only these two bodies that constructed the new code. According to the *Newsletter*'s announcement of the draft code, "more than 60 members" of the association had already participated in composing the draft over a period of four years by the time it was first published in October 1984 (*Newsletter*, 1984:2). Everyone knows that a camel is a horse that was designed by a committee, as comedian Allan Sherman was wont to say, and this one was a super-committee. No wonder the result was a super-camel. The PPR was the result of a mere thirteen minds in over a year's time—a bit swaybacked and perhaps even of another color, but definitely the intended horse.

Alexander Leighton has quoted a saying popular in government circles during World War II that "the administrator uses social science the way a drunk uses a lamp post, for support rather than illumination" (Leighton 1949:128). The imperatives are different if one is providing policy support or if profits are the bottom line from a case in which one is seeking understanding. This is where the dCoE differs basically from the PPR, for the former is responsive to the needs of those who provide support; the latter to the needs of those who provide illumination. The letters in the columns of our newsletter make vivid the circumstances and ideologies that underlie both the demand for and the resistance to a revised code. One complains that the PPR

> established a set of standards so narrowly focused on a single environment that it excluded . . . those of us who have chosen to work outside the grove. . . . Many institutions of government are charged with delivering specific services.

The anthropologist can in many cases contribute to making that delivery more effective and humane. But in order to do so . . . he or she . . . must play by the rules of the game. . . .

This is no less the case in the private sector where there are many organizations which exist to *sell* knowledge. . . . Thus, many of us are conducting research the results of which are proprietary . . . they belong to the firm and are simply not available except at a price.

In a similar vein the prohibition of secret research simply fails to take into account the realities of today's world. . . . Anthropologists working in classified areas do so because they wish to influence national policy. . . . I welcome a Code of Ethics which considers such work a matter of personal choice. (Downs 1985:2)

Another correspondence, from a different perspective, notes the increased population of anthropologists and the diminished availability of "'classic' fieldwork experience," which raises critical problems, especially as anthropologists get involved in "the commercial market, and when they begin to reassess their ethical codes." Now that government support is drying up, he continues,

we must seriously question whether or not the accommodation of individual economic incentives and the priorities of employment constitutes an admittedly painful but critical conflict of interest for assessing the ethical directions for anthropology. It is not an oversimplified analogy to note that the wilderness bears of North America have been reduced to garbage dump scavengers. What will a century of private marketing under such priorities do to the ideals and perspectives for the practice of anthropology?

. . . if anthropology does not begin to secure some long-term analysis and planning, its ethical heritage will not sustain itself. (Wyoch 1986:24)

American anthropology has had a tradition of ethical concern and social responsibility of which we can be proud. The revelation of mission-oriented, counterinsurgency, and classified research and consultation undertaken by anthropologists working in Southeast Asia during the Vietnam War does not necessarily contradict this assessment. Such activities may well have been exceptional in the profession. Also, we must avoid the temptation to castigate Southeast Asianist anthropologists as unusually insensitive to ethical issues. I do not think people with that regional specialization were more ready to sell out than others; only that they had unique opportunities and inducements to do so. Had American military adventurism been elsewhere, I am sure that some anthropologists would have stepped forward to do the dirty work there. But I believe such people are in a minority in our profession. The very fact that the ethical issues were raised, the unethical activities exposed and deplored, is evidence of the profession's social conscience. The involvement of anthropologists in deplorable activities was not unusually pervasive, only unusually forthrightly condemned in the discipline. Other social scientists were doubtless equally or more frequently and deeply involved—political scientists, for certain, perhaps psychologists, economists, sociologists, geographers—but their involvement may have been more taken for granted by their colleagues as acceptable professional behavior, for they were not called to account so forcefully, if at all. Thus, the very fact and manner of revelation of anthropologists' involvement reflects an alert professional conscience that is commendable.

On the other hand, we cannot afford to be too self-congratulatory, either. We have had a tradition as well of complicity in colonial and neocolonial activity (Asad 1973; Lewis 1973), of advising exploiters of people and expropriators of their resources. Those who disclaim this have to resort to generalized denial together with claims to extenuating values and behaviors held to be traditional and pervasive in the profession that in fact may prove to have been more often implicit than explicitly manifest. For counterevidence they must rely on a very few individual and collective efforts in opposition to unethical activities, advocating and contributing to the cause of autonomy or emancipation of colonized and otherwise victimized peoples (Maybury-Lewis 1974). Nor can we deny the tendency in our association to overlook or sweep under the rug some of the most egregious of unethical involvements, while seeking to protect our collective reputation, as occurred in the instance described above of the expulsion of Boas by the council, replicated fifty years later by the effort of the Mead Committee to reprimand Wolf and Jorgensen—both instances comprising responses to courageous but potentially embarrassing revelations of unethical behavior by fellow anthropologists. On the positive side, we have the facts that the Mead Report was overwhelmingly rejected by the association and, of course, that the Principles of Professional Responsibility were enthusiastically adopted and seem still to be endorsed by an overwhelming majority of its members.

It is worth remembering, too, that for nearly two years (1972–74), there was a Committee on Potentially Harmful Effects of Anthropological Research (COPHEAR), appointed by the Executive Board at the direction of the membership as a result of a motion passed at the annual meeting of 1971 (AAA 1972:42; 1973:23, 62; 1974:72).[8] When that committee died on the vine in 1974, primarily for want of cooperation and success in collecting information sufficient to carry out its charge, there sprouted a proposal supported by many for a successor Committee on Ethnocide and Genocide to address some of the same issues but without limiting itself to anthropological culpability. This proposal was inexplicably dropped by the Executive Board shortly before the 1974 annual meetings. So far as I am aware, the important issues that it and COPHEAR were to have pursued have not been directly addressed in the association since then, but they did hold our attention for a time, and may again.

Meanwhile, such issues have been the focus of several organizations and collectivities of dedicated anthropologists operating on financial shoestrings outside of the framework of the association. Most notable among them are Cultural Survival, the International Work Group for Indigenous Affairs (IWGIA), and the currently inactive Anthropology Resource Center (ARC).[9] Probably the most useful source of information on these and others of the sort is in the appendix titled "Organizations and Periodicals" in the second edition (and, I understand, the forthcoming third edition) of John H. Bodley's *Victims of Progress* (Bodley 1982:217–20). As an example I would cite Shelton Davis and Robert Mathews (and their Anthropology Resource Center), who advocated and exemplified "public interest anthropology," which seems to be on a most positive track where ethical commitments and practicality are concerned:

> Public-interest anthropology differs from traditional applied anthropology in what is considered the object of study, whose interests the researcher represents, and what the researcher does with the results of his or her work. Public interest anthropology grows out of the democratic traditions of citizen activism rather than the bureaucratic needs of management and control. It is based on the premise that social problems—war, poverty, racism, sexism, environmental degradation, misuse of technology—are deeply rooted in social structure, and the role of the intellectual is to work with citizens in promoting fundamental change. (Davis and Mathews 1979:5)

Closely related to their stance is that of those who use the term "liberation anthropology" (Huizer 1979; cf. Frank 1969) to describe their activist approach to helping achieve the emancipation and autonomy of indigenous and other oppressed peoples—in analogy to the "liberation theology" of certain Christian clergy and lay people in Latin America (Berryman 1987). Bodley (1982:191–216) has proposed a useful typology of activist anthropological approaches and those who employ them: the "Conservative-

64 Gerald D. Berreman

Humanitarian," the "Liberal-Political," and his own commitment, the "Primitivist-Environmentalist." I leave it to the interested reader to pursue the definitions and philosophies of these perspectives and their implications for, and illuminations of, the ethical practice of anthropology.

The recent impetus for redefinition of anthropological ethics comes clearly from those outside of academia who find the Principles of Professional Responsibility to be inconsistent with the demands of their employment. Often calling themselves "practicing anthropologists," they work primarily for corporations, government agencies, and other mission-oriented employers whose priorities, they point out, are not consistent with those confronted by scholar-anthropologists.[10] For them, anthropological ethics as heretofore defined are inconvenient, constraining, even threatening, both to their missions and to their careers. Corporate ends are profits; governmental goals are national political, and international geopolitical, advantage. Anthropologists have something of value to offer in the pursuit of these "real-world" ends, for they know about the peoples and cultures that will provide the work force and customers, the allies and adversaries. They know the populace that will decide the political and economic alignment of its government; who occupies the territory that contains the sought-after resources; and which will be the sites of the military bases and missile silos. As these corporate and national priorities become anthropologists' priorities, no wonder that the subjects of study no longer come first, that secrecy and even clandestinity are no longer condemned, that anthropologists become wary of being held accountable to their colleagues for the ethical practice of their profession, that they do not feel obliged to share with society as a whole the implications of their professional knowledge, and that they view the very concept of ethical standards with anxious skepticism. Anthropologists in these roles are agents of their employers, not advocates for those they study or for the principles of their profession.

It is scarcely surprising, then, that the draft code, arising as it did in response to these circumstances, devotes nine of its new provisions to matters of "professional relations" and only four to the people among whom anthropologists work, whether in practice or in research. This is a major reversal in direction from the focus of the Principles of Professional Responsibility.

Evidently, a code of ethics for the era of practicing anthropology must not subordinate the requirements of the marketplace and realpolitik to mere adherence to principle. The question then is whether this draft code speaks for anthropologists as humane students and advocates of humankind, or as bureaucrats and human engineers. Are there to be two kinds of anthropologists, practicing and humanist; two kinds of ethics, practical and humane; two kinds of anthropology, laissez-faire and principled? I think we should resist such a division as unnatural, unnecessary, and counterproductive. Resistance to it is in the public interest, in our professional interest, and in our individual interests. The demands and opportunities of careers in anthropology, be they in practice or in academia, must not substitute for ethics.

To the extent that anthropologists can remain true to their principles while practicing their profession outside of the academy, I would urge them to follow their career preferences and opportunities. To the extent that they cannot, I believe they must curtail their career choices. There is no place anywhere for unprincipled anthropology or anthropologists.

Conclusion

In conclusion, let me emphasize that I am not opposed to revision of our code of ethics, the Principles of Professional Responsibility. I *am* opposed to the abandonment of the spirit of ethical practice of anthropology which it embodies, and the tenets which codify that spirit. Specifically, I am steadfastly opposed to compromise or elimination of what I believe to be the four fundamental principles of our ethics as anthropologists, all of which are prominent in the PPR and in the history of anthropology, and all of which are conspicuously absent from the draft Code of Ethics which was proposed to replace it. They are well worth repeating:

(1) That "anthropologists' paramount responsibility is to those they study" (PPR 1).

(2) That "anthropologists should undertake no secret research" (PPR 3a) and "should avoid even the appearance of engaging in clandestine research" (PPR 3b).

(3) That anthropologists are accountable for their professional actions: "when anthropologists . . . betray their professional commitments [as set forth in the PPR] . . . their colleagues may legitimately inquire into the propriety of those actions, and take such measures as lie within the legitimate powers of their Association as the membership deems appropriate" (PPR Epilogue).

(4) That anthropologists bear "the positive responsibility to speak out publicly . . . on what they know and . . . believe as a result of their

professional expertise. . . . That is, they bear a professional responsibility to contribute to 'an adequate definition of reality' upon which public opinion and public policy may be based" (PPR 2d).

I see the PPR as structurally analogous to the United States Bill of Rights or the Constitution as a whole: a basic document subject to review and revision by amendment proposed from the membership either directly or through its representatives on the Executive Board, when ratified by vote of the membership at large. But I believe it to be a drastic mistake for a committee to be appointed to create a substitute code, *in toto,* in response to what are said to be the changed realities of the moment—in this case, primarily changes in the anthropological marketplace. This is exactly what was done when the dCoE was proposed just ten years after the original code—the PPR—was drawn up and adopted. At this rate, our ethics would become simply fleeting reflections of the temper of the times, our code a weather vane shifting with every social and political wind, responsive to each economic fluctuation, political fad, or international spasm. If this were to happen, we would not be alone. As the editor of *New York* magazine wrote not long ago, "Ethics in America seem to have dropped to one of the lowest points in history," and "moral lapses blot American history. . . . But," she went on to point out, "today's go-go ethics are in many ways new. For one thing, there's little doubt that idealism is in decline and cynicism on the rise" (Kanner 1986:9). Surely anthropologists, as students of humankind, as practitioners of what Eric Wolf (1964:88) called "the most scientific of the humanities, the most humanist of the sciences," are more principled than to jump on that bandwagon; surely our ethical commitments are more profound, independent, and stable than that; surely those among whom and in whose interests we work deserve better than that.

In short, I believe the draft Code of Ethics constituted an evisceration of the PPR and, as such, betrayed our ethical principles and was unworthy of our discipline and our profession. It proposed to sacrifice the nobility of the politics of truth for the perversity of realpolitik. It seems that the era of Reaganomics spawned the nightmare of Reaganethics. I trust that history will soon be enabled by our profession's collective decision to relegate this episode to the dustbin of other short-lived aberrations of the 1980s.

NOTES

1. The *Newsletter* of the American Anthropological Association (known at various times also as the *Fellow Newsletter* and *Anthropology Newsletter*), from its

inception in 1960 until the present (and especially from 1967 when the "Correspondence" columns became a regular feature), and before that the *American Anthropologist,* are the best, and generally the only, sources for resolutions, votes, and debates. Some of these concerning the issues discussed in this essay have been brought together in Berreman 1973.

2. I can no longer refrain from noting that one of the two candidates who withdrew astounded me a couple of years later, when we were both on the Executive Board, by spontaneously announcing one evening, "I owe you an apology!" He went on to explain that this was because of his role in that maneuver when he acceded to an unexpected late-evening telephone request by the then president of the association to withdraw in favor of the strongest of the three candidates nominated by the Nominations Committee; he was asked, further, that he call the third candidate to persuade him to do likewise, in order to save the presidency from the challenge of "the radicals." He professed having felt guilty ever since.

3. The Executive Board at the time consisted, I believe, of George M. Foster, president (University of California, Berkeley), Charles Wagley, president-elect (Columbia University), Dell Hymes (University of Pennsylvania), David Schneider (University of Chicago), David Aberle (University of British Columbia), Eugene Hammel (University of California, Berkeley), Cyril Belshaw (University of British Columbia), and James Gibbs (Stanford University).

4. Wolf and Jorgensen's observation that in condemning them, "the Board evidently hoped to avert a threat to the internal harmony [and, I would add, the reputation] of the Association," is astute. The action was in this respect reminiscent of the council's action in 1920, hastily condemning and expelling Boas without concerning itself at all with the situation he reported. Both of these instances anticipated the Ad Hoc Committee to Evaluate the Controversy Concerning Anthropological Activities in Relation to Thailand, which concluded its deliberations in 1971 by simply denouncing those who sounded the alarm and thereby threatened the internal harmony and public reputation of the association. The tendency in all three was to close the wagons in a circle to blindly fend off the attackers, principle be damned.

5. " 'Free enterprise scholarship' . . . is scholarship which uses whatever resources are available by whoever has access to them, for immediate payoff without thought to consequences for others. This is a selfish, short-sighted and destructive posture" (my definition: Berreman 1971c:398).

6. The Society for Applied Anthropology has made mention of secrecy-related issues in the 1963, 1973, and 1983 versions of its brief "Statement of Professional and Ethical Responsibilities," although only in 1973 was secrecy explicitly addressed: "2. We should not consent to employment in which our activities and/or scientific data remain permanently secret and inaccessible." That seems to have disappeared in the 1983 version, even as the dCoE of the AAA has jettisoned the issue as well (see: Society for Applied Anthropology 1963; 1973; 1983).

7. The quality of the prose in the draft code fell, relative to that in the PPR, as precipitously as its idealism. To confirm this, one need only compare the preambles to each of the two documents. Alternatively, one might read again the sentences quoted in the discussion above . . . or any pair of paragraphs at random. Better yet,

read the documents in their entirety with this in mind. I would recommend that the draft code be dropped for the dreadful precedent it provides for dull, turgid anthropological prose, if for no other reason.

8. COPHEAR first met in October 1972, and it existed through June 1974. Its members were: Stephen A. Barnett, chair (Princeton University), Norman A. Chance (University of Connecticut), Shepard Forman (University of Michigan), Sally Falk Moore (University of Southern California), Robert J. Smith (Cornell University), and I, liaison member of the Executive Board (University of California, Berkeley) (AAA 1973:23, 62; 1974:72).

Other commitments prevented Sally Falk Moore from serving during the second year of the committee's existence.

9. These three most prominent organizations and their publications are: (1) Anthropology Resource Center (ARC; currently inactive, but publications available through Cultural Survival, Inc.); publications: *ARC Newsletter; The Global Reporter;* a series of occasional special reports and monographs. (2) Cultural Survival, Inc., 11 Divinity Ave., Cambridge, MA 02138; publications: *Cultural Survival Quarterly* (newsletter); occasional papers and special reports. (Also distributor for other publications including those of Anthropology Resource Center.) (3) Although not an American publication, this one is so central to its American audience that I include it here also: International Work Group on Indigenous Affairs (IWGIA), Fiolstraeda 10, DK-1171 Copenhagen K, Denmark; publications: *IWGIA Newsletter; IWGIA Yearbook; IWGIA Documents* (monograph series).

10. For a broader spectrum of points of view than those described here, consult the quarterly journal *Practicing Anthropology: A Career Oriented Publication of the Society for Applied Anthropology* (Box 24083, Oklahoma City, OK 73214). Now in its eleventh year and volume, it began publication in October 1978.

REFERENCES

Aberle, David
    1970   Correspondence: Ethics committee issues. *Newsletter* (AAA) 11(7):19.
American Anthropological Association
    1920   Council meeting, 30 Dec., 4:45 P.M. *American Anthropologist* 22:93–94.
    1949   Resolution on freedom of publication. *American Anthropologist* 51:370.
    1971   Annual report 1970 and directory. April. Washington, D.C.: American Anthropological Association.
    1972   Annual report 1971. April. Washington, D.C.: American Anthropological Association.
    1973   Annual report 1972. Distinguished lecture, proceedings, directory 1973. Washington, D.C.: American Anthropological Association.
    1974   Annual report 1973. Distinguished lecture, proceedings, directory 1974. Washington, D.C.: American Anthropological Association.
    1975   Annual report 1974. Distinguished lecture, proceedings, directory 1975. Washington, D.C.: American Anthropological Association.
American Institutes for Research
    1967   Counter-insurgency in Thailand: The impact of economic, social, and

political action programs. (A research and development proposal submitted to the Advanced Research Projects Agency.) Pittsburgh: American Institutes for Research (AIR International). December.

Asad, Talal, ed.

1973   *Anthropology and the colonial encounter.* London: Ithaca Press.

Beals, Ralph L., and Executive Board of the American Anthropological Association

1967   Background information on problems of anthropological research and ethics. *Newsletter* (AAA) 8(1):2–13.

Becker, Ernest

1971   *The lost science of man.* New York: George Braziller.

Berreman, Gerald D.

1968   Is anthropology alive? Social responsibility in social anthropology. *Current Anthropology* 9(5):391–96.

1971a   Berreman speech to council. *Newsletter* (AAA) 12(1):18–20.

1971b   The Greening of the American Anthropological Association: Address to council, AAA, 69th Annual Meetings, San Diego, 19 Nov. 1970. *Critical Anthropology* (New York: New School for Social Research), Spring 1971:100–104.

1971c   Ethics, responsibility and the funding of Asian research. *Journal of Asian Studies* 30(2):390–99.

1973   The social responsibility of the anthropologist, *and* anthropology and the Third World. In *To see ourselves: Anthropology and modern social issues,* ed. Thomas Weaver, 5–61; and 109–79. Glenview, Ill.: Scott, Foresman.

1980   Are human rights merely a politicized luxury in the world today? *Anthropology and Humanism Quarterly* 5(1):2–13.

1981a   In pursuit of innocence abroad: Ethics and responsibility in cross-cultural research. In *The politics of truth: Essays in critical anthropology,* ed. Gerald D. Berreman, 72–126. New Delhi: South Asian Publishers.

1981b   *The politics of truth: Essays in critical anthropology.* New Delhi: South Asian Publishers.

Berryman, Phillip

1987   *Liberation theology: The essential facts about the revolutionary movement in Latin America and beyond.* New York: Pantheon Books.

Boas, Franz

1919   Correspondence: Scientists as spies. *The Nation* 109:729.

Bodley, John H.

1982   *Victims of progress* (2nd edition). Palo Alto, Cal.: Mayfield Publishing.

Coburn, Judith

1969   Project Cambridge: Another showdown for social science? *Science* 166:1250–53.

Davenport, William, David Olmsted, Margaret Mead, and Ruth Freed

1971   Report of the Ad Hoc Committee to Evaluate the Controversy Concerning Anthropological Activities in Relation to Thailand, to the Executive Board of the American Anthropological Association. 27 Sept. Washington, D.C.: American Anthropological Association.

Davis, Shelton, and Robert Mathews
    1979   Anthropology Resource Center: Public interest anthropology—beyond the bureaucratic ethos. *Practicing Anthropology* 1(3):5.
Downs, James F.
    1985   Proposed code of ethics supported. *Newsletter* (AAA) 26(4):2.
Flanagan, Patrick
    1971   Imperial anthropology in Thailand (AICD Occasional Paper No. 2). Sydney: K. J. Mcleod.
Foster, George M., Peter Hinton, A. J. F. Köbben, Eric Wolf, and Joseph Jorgensen
    1971   Anthropology on the warpath: An exchange. *New York Review* 16(6):43–46.
Frank, Andre Gunder
    1969   Liberal anthropology vs. liberation anthropology. In *Latin America: Underdevelopment or revolution,* Andre Gunder Frank, 137–45. New York: Monthly Review Press.
Heller, Scott
    1988   From selling Rambo to supermarket studies, anthropologists are finding more non-academic jobs. *The Chronicle of Higher Education,* 1 June: A24.
Helm, June
    1985   Commentary: Ethical principles, discussion invited. *Newsletter* (AAA) 26(4):1, 13.
Horowitz, Irving Lewis, ed.
    1967   *The rise and fall of Project Camelot: Studies in the relationship between social science and practical politics.* Cambridge, Mass.: MIT Press.
Huizer, Gerrit
    1979   Anthropology and politics: From naiveté toward liberation? In *The politics of anthropology,* ed. Gerrit Huizer and Bruce Mannheim, 3–41. The Hague: Mouton.
Kanner, Barbara
    1986   The ethics pendulum swings: Idealism's out, cynicism's in. *San Francisco Examiner-Chronicle* (This World section) 10 August: 9, 12. (First published in *New York* magazine.)
Leighton, Alexander
    1949   *Human relations in a changing world: Observations on the use of the social sciences.* New York: E. P. Dutton.
Lewis, Diane
    1973   Anthropology and colonialism. *Current Anthropology* 14(5):581–91.
Maybury-Lewis, David
    1974   Don't put the blame on the anthropologists. *New York Times* (Op-Ed section) 15 March: 13.
Mills, C. Wright
    1959   *The sociological imagination.* New York: Oxford University Press.
    1963   *Power, politics and people: The collected essays of C. Wright Mills,* ed. I. L. Horowitz. New York: Ballantine Books.

Newsletter (AAA)

    1969   Report of the ethics committee. 10(4):3–6.
    1970a   Resolutions to be ratified. 11(1):7.
    1970b   Board statement on ethics issue. 11(6):1, 10.
    1970c   Resolutions ratified. 11(6):1.
    1970d   Candidate information. 11(7):1.
    1970e   Spaulding and Spuhler withdraw candidacies for president-elect. 11(8):1.
    1970f   Annual report of the Committee on Ethics, September 1970. 11(9):10–16.
    1971   Wallace voted president-elect. 12(1):1.
    1972   Council rejects Thai controversy committee's report. 13(1):1.
    1974   Council to vote on amendment to PPR. 15(7):9.
    1975   COE proposes two additions to PPR. 16(2):1.
    1984   For discussion: Proposed code of ethics would supersede Principles of Professional Responsibility. 25(7):2.
    1989   Proposed draft revision of the Principles of Professional Responsibility 30(8):22–23.

Professional Ethics (AAA)

    1983   Professional ethics: Statements and procedures of the American Anthropological Association. Washington, D.C.: American Anthropological Association.

Society for Applied Anthropology

    1963   Statement on ethics of the society for applied anthropology. *Human Organization* 22(4):237.
    1973   Statement on professional and ethical responsibilities. The Society for Applied Anthropology (circulated to the membership).
    1983   Proposed statement on professional and ethical responsibilities. The Society for Applied Anthropology (circulated to the membership).

Stocking, George W., Jr.

    1968   *Race, culture, and evolution: Essays in the history of anthropology.* New York: Free Press.

Student Mobilization Committee to End the War in Vietnam

    1970   Counterinsurgency research on campus exposed. *The Student Mobilizer* (April) 3(4).

Wolf, Eric R.

    1964   *Anthropology.* Englewood Cliffs, N.J.: Prentice-Hall.

Wolf, Eric, and Joseph Jorgensen

    1970a   Anthropology on the warpath in Thailand. *New York Review* 15(9):26–36.
    1970b   Correspondence: Ethics Committee issues. *Newsletter* (AAA) 11(7):2, 19.

Wyoch, Bruce

    1986   Anthropology: Corporate tribe or market commodity. *Newsletter* (AAA) 27(1):24.

Editor's Introduction to Chapter 3

DAVID HAKKEN is another author who has assumed an activist role in the most recent round of the debate over ethics. As a founder of the Action Network for Responsible Anthropological Professionalism (ANRAP) in the wake of the presentation of the 1984 proposed revision of the original PPR, the author brings a unique passion and commitment to the exploration of contemporary issues of ethics and professionalism. As a professional socialized during the Vietnam War era and the period of the events leading to the first code of ethics in anthropology, Hakken relives and revives the deep concerns that were a part of this era. And as an activist, he has argued for the creation of a positive ethical culture within the discipline of anthropology. He sees this as a part of a broader view that includes the effective handling of ethical issues as a natural part of what it means to be an anthropologist.

Hakken has been an active voice for the preservation of the PPR and sees the current debate over the ethics issue as stemming from several differences that are inherent in the history and definition of anthropology. One problem is that a single ethical code is meant to cover diverse field and practical situations that arise in anthropological work; moreover, the philosophical bases of the code and the profession are neither clearly enunciated nor understood. That a revision in the code of ethics might be seen as a solution to the employment problem underscores this confusion. The only real solution, Hakken argues, is the development of a renewed ethical culture within the discipline, one that is based on a shared vision of what anthropology is and what it is for.

Hakken is critical of the recent leadership of the American Anthropological Association for not promoting and organizing a dialogue within the discipline on ethics, noting a tendency to avoid the issues. An ethically conscious anthropology would act *proactively,* instead of reacting and responding to crises in the field.

David Hakken

Chapter 3 Anthropological Ethics in the 1990s
A Positive Approach

Introduction

THE DILEMMAS EXAMINED and events described elsewhere in this volume illustrate the significant challenges faced by anyone who wished to practice anthropology ethically in the 1980s. What are the sources of the ethical impasse at which we find ourselves? As it currently functions, can we depend on our professional organization, the American Anthropological Association (AAA), to lead us effectively in dealing with these issues, or is some additional initiative required?

I argue here that, to an important extent, our ethical difficulties are conceptually self-inflicted, a consequence of inappropriate notions of what we can expect ethics to accomplish. We need to change and develop a different notion of what to expect from ethical thought in our discipline, to clarify the language we employ in our discourse over such issues. I show how we can get help in doing this; first, through locating our discourse in the context of current philosophical discussion of ethics, and second, by locating our conceptual problems within the substantial contemporary distress over the identity of U.S. anthropology. This distress is a result of the major changes which have taken place in the social practice of our discipline over the last twenty years. To respond effectively to this distress, manifest in both employment and legitimation crises, we need to resolve our ethical impasse.

While making this critique, I also describe what an "anthro-ethic" appropriate for today would look like. I argue for an "engaged" approach, one that strives to resolve our ethical impasse by finding ways to resolve the other problems of our profession. My overall aims are to present an alternative way of thinking about ethics and to encourage a positive ethical culture. The ethics advocated maintain continuity with the humanistic, critical bent that attracted many of us to anthropology in the first place, and, at the same time, react to the substantial changes that have taken place recently in our discipline. I conclude by illustrating what I advocate by applying it in a particular case, that of culture-centered computing.

Action Research on Anthro-ethics

My views about the problems of ethical practice in U.S. anthropology have been shaped by my experience. This experience over almost twenty years has convinced me that dealing effectively with ethics is essential to resolving the broader issue of what it means to be an anthropologist. An important aim of my contribution to this volume is to argue for an anthro-ethics that relates more directly to the specifics of our individual experiences. It is often in the quandaries we face as individuals that our collective ethical failures are most clearly revealed. It is thus appropriate that the following is more autobiographical than most anthropological writing.

Since 1978, I have been active in the AAA, trying to convince others to join in particular scholarly projects and courses of professional action. I have often used ethical argument to justify placing particular issues closer to the center of disciplinary concern by taking particular actions in relation to them. From 1979 to 1985, as the chairperson of the Council for Marxist Anthropology (CMA) I participated in several attempts to get anthropological organizations to take positions on various (often controversial) issues. Also, as one of the cochairs of the Action Network for Responsible Anthropological Professionalism (ANRAP), with Carolyn Fluehr-Lobban, I tried to create a framework to identify and debate the fundamental aims of and issues of concern to ethical thought within the association. As fieldworkers, we anthropologists value the reflective thoughts of active participants; indeed, practicing anthropologists have come to pay particular attention to the experience and perspective of those whom we call "brokers." Of equal value are the experiences and thoughts of those who try to organize action.

Further, in my current research on computerization and culture change, I have found myself examining the ethical practice of other professionals, those who develop information systems. This activity has given me a new perspective on the ethics of my own profession. Finally, the career I have experienced since the time I applied to graduate school is broadly reflective (in both its promising and everyday, even tawdry, moments) of the experience of nonelite, "journeyperson" U.S. anthropologists. We make up the bulk of the membership of the discipline today.

The Current Ethical Impasse

In 1984, the leadership of the AAA proposed replacing the existing professional statement on ethics, the Principles of Professional Responsibility (PPR), with a narrower draft Code of Ethics (dCoE). In her introduction to this volume, Fluehr-Lobban has described some of the major differences between the two documents. In my opinion, the draft Code differed substantially from the PPR, the dCoE effecting a rethinking of anthropology, away from a broadly humanistic science and toward a narrowly individualistic technology. As one who was actively critical of the dCoE, I helped organize the Action Network for Responsible Anthropological Professionalism to defend the spirit of the PPR. I was pleased when the AAA leadership abandoned the dCoE, and I am pleased that the PPR remained the formal standard of professional conduct in anthropology through the 1980s.

Those of us who defended the PPR may have won the battle over the dCoE, but the war over anthro-ethics is far from over. Indeed, despite our efforts, a number of U.S. anthropologists still talk as if the dCoE actually is the association's current standard. The curious outcome of the PPR/dCoE episode suggests something about why it is that professional issues discussed below, issues such as "communicating, appreciating, and linking" (Helm 1987), get posed but not addressed. Before they can be dealt with successfully, we need a shared analysis of the nature of our ethical practice, the sources of our difficulties in binding together, and what will be necessary if we are to revitalize these aspects of our discipline. The following propositions summarize my approach to our current professional ethics:

(1) that there is too great a diversity over the purpose of, proper form of, and expectations about ethics within our profession;

(2) that our difficulties with ethics derive at least in part from philosophical confusions over ethics similar to those recently addressed by philosopher Bernard Williams;

(3) that our difficulties in handling other professional issues, such as employment and relegitimation, are reciprocally related to our problems over ethics; and

(4) that we must develop a renewed ethical culture within the discipline, one based on a shared vision of what the discipline is *for*, if we are to resolve our difficulties.

PROPOSITION #1: THAT THERE IS TOO MUCH DIVERSITY OVER ETHICS
WITHIN OUR PROFESSION

Our problems in binding together have to do with our difficulties, despite considerable discussion (e.g., Cassell and Jacobs 1987), achieving consensus about ethics within the profession.[1] Indeed, one of the dominant impressions I have as a consequence of my work with ANRAP is of the diversity regarding basic points, such as what the content of our ethical practice should be and what kind of standards and machinery for enforcement, if any, we should have.

There are various ways to conceive of the appropriate level of and functions to be served by a professional concern with ethics. For some, ethics is primarily a kind of talk, (1) an *ethical dialogic technology,* or a medium whose essential purpose is to sharpen particular analytic skills. There is implicit hope that, in the process of developing such skills, the appropriate resolution to ethical dilemmas will become clear, but this latter result is not a necessary part of ethical practice so conceived. This approach to ethics is similar to what Williams calls (2) *"ethical egoism"* (1985:12). This is the philosophical position that the best ethical rule is for individuals to act always and only in their own self-interest, a kind of philosophical counterpart to laissez-faire economics. In a professional context, this apparent contradiction in terms may mean viewing ethics as a way to minimize the interference of others' methods, politics, or religion in one's own professional practice. Even such relatively anti-interventionist views of the functions of professional ethics can result in development and publication of (3) *written ethical statements.* A profession might choose to depend exclusively upon the development of such written statements or codes to provide the requisite ethical framework. Alternatively, codes can also be used more actively, as the basis for (4) *collective structures* to protect the profession from conduct that tends to threaten an interest perceived to be shared by those who identify with the profession. A range of views about such structures is possible; this range can also be arrayed in terms of increasing levels of intervention. A profession might design its ethical structures to concentrate primarily on (5) *articulating explicitly* what the shared interest is. Alternately, a profession might emphasize positive mechanisms to (6) *encourage appropriate, and discourage inappropriate, identification* with the articulated interest. Finally, the structures might primarily administer negative procedures to (7) *sanction individuals and groups* whose conduct is perceived as threatening, or (8) *pursue public policies*—for example, legislation—to accomplish its ethical goals.

Manifestations of each of these views of appropriate ethical concern can be found within U.S. anthropology. The *Anthropology Newsletter*'s ethical dilemmas are examples of the "dialogic technology" conception, in that they clearly aim to sharpen analytic skills more than to develop organizational policy with regard to issues of substantial concern. We also have examples of "ethical egoism." In the discussion of the dCoE, for example, it was argued that the PPR was wrong to argue against covert research because this argument limited the opportunity of individual anthropologists to work for the CIA and similar governmental agencies. (Without apologies to Richard Nixon, this argument was used to explain why we needed to "de-Vietnamize" the PPR!)

The PPR is an example of a written ethical statement addressing the behavior considered appropriate for a U.S. anthropologist. In the discussions surrounding the dCoE, some of those active in the development of the PPR argued that what we should hope for in ethics was to make such statements as explicit as possible, but that more interventionist ethical activities would inevitably fail. Yet the older AAA structure of fellows and general members, and the similar structure proposed for the new Society for Cultural Anthropology, are examples of attempts to establish different degrees of identifiability with the field. These structures, as well as the various associational awards, were and are justified in at least quasi-ethical terms, terms which link quality, prestige, and "distinguished service."

The development of explicit statements of shared interest continues within the various organizational groupings of anthropologists both inside and outside the AAA. The existing procedures of the Society of Professional Archaeologists are examples of sanctioning structures; some individuals in the National Association of Practicing Anthropologists (NAPA) have developed a similar code. Finally, there has also been periodic discussion of legislation, some of which has been implemented with regard to areas of federal and state policy—for example, with regard to cultural resource management.

We are clearly not of one mind about the appropriate manifestation of ethical concern within our profession. Anthropology is a diverse set of activities, including but going beyond the professional "enterprise" to which a presidential article (Helm 1987) recently alluded. It is not necessary for a discipline to have a singular notion of the function of ethics. For example, the practice of an ethical dialogic technology could be designed to feed into articulation of a written code or the administration of sanctions against individuals. The breadth of the current diversity of view on ethics, however, interferes with the relegitimation of our profession which, I argue below, is necessary. We should be cognizant of the frustrations encountered by our colleagues who have pursued consistency in disciplinary ethics, especially the frustration of their attempts to enforce existing standards. When we examine the diversity described above, however, we see that it is really more about what we can reasonably expect from anthro-ethics than about what we would like from them.

PROPOSITION #2: THAT OUR DIFFICULTIES WITH ETHICS DERIVE FROM
PHILOSOPHICAL CONFUSIONS

As I have talked with my colleagues about ethics, I have realized that there are substantial problems in the way we think about ethics as well as what we want from our ethical practice. Conversations about ethics with professional philosophers have led me to understand that, to an important extent, our problems are conceptual, connected to but at least somewhat distinct from the employment and legitimation difficulties, and antecedent to the dCoE and even the PPR.

I wish to make an ethnographic argument that a substantial portion of our ethical wounds are self-inflicted, due to inappropriate expectations from ethics. I wish to critique the *terms* within which the anthropological discussion of ethics usually takes place. My approach will be to outline some of the ideas contained in Bernard Williams's recent (1985) analysis of the history of moral philosophy, *Ethics and the Limits of Philosophy.*

Williams argues that moral philosophy begins with the Socratic question, How should one live? He describes moral philosophy as, in general, the discussion of the extent to which answers to this question should involve a particular kind of consideration, one involving both longer- rather than shorter-term perspectives and relatively abstract values like "the good life." These answers are what philosophers tend to call "ethical thought." Moral philosophy may be considered the attempt to develop a consistent ethical theory, some firm philosophical ground on which to base "strong" forms of ethical thought.

Williams's book is a critique of moral philosophy as such. He is suspicious, because of "the limits of philosophy," of the general prospects for attaining the goal of a precise foundation for a universal ethics. His grounds for suspicion are appealing to anthropology, since they have a great deal to do with cultural relativity.

Williams is particularly hostile to one kind of moral philosophy, "morality," which in his view has enslaved ethical thought since Kant. Like slavery, he brands morality "The Peculiar Institution." Based in Kant's search for a categorical imperative, morality "is distinguished by the special notion of obligation it uses," and by "one especially important kind of deliberative conclusion," moralism (1985:174, 175). The deliberative conclusion of moralism is the belief in and search for objectively grounded laws of appropriate behavior, laws which apply to all persons irrespective of their personal situation or cultural background; for example, "Moral obligation is inescapable."

Williams makes a convincing case that moralism is a philosophical chimera. He also identifies several negative consequences of a preoccupation with moralism, such as the promotion of a culture of guilt and blame and the inevitability of ethnocentrism, which follows from a sense of moral superiority. Williams traces the extent to which the Kantian heritage continues to dominate contemporary moral philosophy, including the recent "linguistic turn."[2]

The confusions over ethics in moral philosophy which Williams illuminates seem to be manifest in anthro-ethics. This is particularly clear in the futile search for a morality of transcendent obligation, a technology of ethical enforcement. The failure of our disciplinary ethical mechanisms is at base due to a confusion of appropriate ethical culture with moralism. Inaction on the most difficult issues we face is the source of the confusion over how best to promote "binding" within our association.

According to moralism, binding is accomplished by development of transcendent rules. Our (according to Williams, inevitable) failure to develop a satisfactory moral code leads beyond immobility in particular cases to despair about ethics in general. From Williams's perspective, the frustration of those like David Aberle, who have grown weary trying to create tighter ethical machinery in the discipline, is interpretable as the consequence of yet another failure of the moralist paradigm. The dCoE described above by Fluehr-Lobban is revealed to be a predictable overreaction, a step toward dumping any ethical life within the discipline.

Yet as Louise Lamphere argued in a 1985 panel sponsored by the AAA, we in anthropology "still want ethics." One reason we have failed to find a satisfactory ethics in U.S. anthropology is that we have not adequately understood what ethics can reasonably be expected to accomplish. If Williams is correct, we are not alone in this, but instead share in the general ethical failure of Western industrial civilization. Indeed, through his clearly Geertzian notion of "thick ethical constructs," Williams suggests the West has much to learn in the area of ethics from the peoples many of us study.

Thick ethical constructs, concepts that interweave notions of value and fact, "is" and "ought," are in his view characteristic of community. To describe an individual as courageous or honest, for example, is both to say something descriptive about what they do and evaluative of what they are.

PROPOSITION #3: THAT ETHICAL CONFUSION IS RELATED
RECIPROCALLY TO OUR CURRENT PROFESSIONAL DISTRESS

I wish to argue now that there is a direct link between our problems over ethics and our difficulties as a profession in adjusting to the changes of the 1960s, 1970s, and 1980s. In barest outline, my case is that our discipline's specific history has required a recasting of our ethical thought, but inappropriate notions of what ethics are for have gotten in the way. As a result, we are functioning more or less without sufficient ethical coherence, caught between an ethics of engagement inadequately anchored in the discipline on the one hand, and the search for a sanitized "techno-ethic" profoundly inappropriate to humanistic endeavor on the other. To see how we came to this pass, one must examine the characteristics of our current disciplinary predicament, especially its employment and legitimation aspects.

Beginning in the 1970s and throughout most of the 1980s, new M.A. and Ph.D. anthropologists had increasing difficulty in finding professional employment, particularly the academic employment which had been characteristic of the field since the end of the Second World War. At one time, we had the worst record for placing new Ph.D.'s in U.S. academe (*Anthropology Newsletter* 1983). These labor market difficulties may have lessened somewhat recently, but they are not likely to disappear completely, given the forces that fostered them. First, there was the slowdown in the expansion of higher education, particularly in the public sector; we may have been hit particularly hard by this because anthropology, beginning from a smaller base, expanded proportionately more in academia than did other social sciences. Even those of us lucky enough to find work within the academy in this period have often had our attitudes readjusted rather brutally. When I was being introduced to my colleagues at my first faculty meeting, my college president blurted out, "An anthropologist? What the hell do we need an anthropologist for? This is a college of technology!"

Next came an actual contraction of professional employment in higher education, due to the deliberate strategy of universities of hiring part-time faculty to teach. There was also an assault on higher education, particularly its humanistic components, by the Reagan administration and its right-wing supporters (Cole 1984). As an obvious target for the "scientific" creationists, anthropology is particularly susceptible to such attacks. Our contention that non-Western cultures should be taken as seriously as Western ones was a suspect idea in the Bennett U.S. Department of Education. The notion of "cultural relativity" is attacked explicitly by those who advocate "cultural literacy." In the mid-1980s, there was a dramatic decline in enrollment in anthropology courses (Whitney 1985), although declines were unevenly distributed across subfield, type of course, and level of instruction.

Partly for these reasons, new colleagues (and retrenched older ones) have had to find work outside of academe, and there they have confronted work conditions which often differ to a substantial degree from what their educational experience had led them to expect. Among the negative characteristics of such conditions are short-term contracts, "soft" money, and no presumption of academic freedom.

Similarities between the experience of anthropological colleagues in other countries (e.g., Britain) and differences from the experience of other academic colleagues (e.g., psychologists) suggest the possibility of a crisis specific to anthropology. As some departments disappeared and we lost our separate federal listing, it appeared that anthropology might be losing its status as a profession.

The sociology of professions in capitalistic social formations suggests that, once attained, the maintenance of professional status involves two things: first, an occupation must maintain collective control over access to practicing the trade (e.g., credentialing); and second, its professional ideology must remain legitimate. To the extent that anthropology is a profession in this sense, what control over access to the field we have has been obtained by integrating anthropological training into institutions of higher education, especially graduate education in the arts and sciences. This was a good strategy in a growth market, but it has been less successful in the recent past, and it is even less effective in a technicist, anti–liberal arts age. These are among the reasons why anthropologists in the AAA were asked in 1987 to consider steps to certify the practice of anthropology, "because of the move toward certification requirements in nonacademic positions and the initiatives of other disciplines in meeting the demand" (Helm and Rappaport 1987:5).

Maintaining professional standing in a shifting and shrinking labor market is difficult; it is almost impossible if the profession's ideology is no longer sufficiently persuasive. One part of our original legitimation had to do with "salvage anthropology," the perceived value of maintaining for

posterity a record of the customs and beliefs of peoples who were understood to be disappearing in the face of "advancing" civilization. Anthropology's "founding myth," tied to notions of humanism and the broadest
forms of noninstrumental scientific enquiry, was in essence an ethical one:
that an understanding of other cultures will contribute to our ability to be
fair as well as effective in our interactions with them. Gradually, our legitimation came to include the claim that study of such peoples had relevance
to modern times as well. We claimed that our knowledge would help us deal
with our own, internal difficulties.

I submit that this ideology, whatever its truth value, no longer has
sufficient social legitimacy. Curiously, our public "brand identification"
may be at an all-time high. Witness the popularity of the anthropologist as a
role in television programs, movies, and popular science fiction, and the
continuing spread in application of "culture," the major theoretical construct of U.S. anthropology, and the use of our primary method, participant observation, in many new areas. Even my business colleagues at
SUNY College of Technology write pamphlets with titles such as *From
Scientific Management to Corporate Culture* (Hall 1984). Yet our popularity
has come at a time when our disciplinary "stock" in terms of employment is
down. We appear to have succeeded in convincing U.S. power elites of the
importance of "culture" but not of the necessity of anthropology to its
understanding. While Americans find other cultures "fascinating," they
appear no longer to accept the notion that knowledge of them should be
applied to improve our relations with them or own social process, or that
anthropologists are the ones who should do the applying. (The professional problems of U.S. anthropology may be connected to the general
decline in the influence of liberalism in politics, politics intimately supported by and supportive of earlier Americanist anthropology.)

At this point it is useful to consider another of Williams's notions, that
of the importance of thick ethical constructs to the maintenance of an
ethical culture. U.S. anthropology no longer has enough of these. Those
we used to use are no longer satisfactory, and attempts to develop new
constructs have yet to succeed; indeed, on occasion they have been undermined.

Our older ethical constructs, and the public legitimations associated
with them, were tied intimately to the professional ideas and practices of
previous scholars, especially Margaret Mead. Historical particularist ethics
no longer satisfy us, for a number of reasons. Partly it is the result of the
built-in tension between what Murray Wax calls "humanist" and "ortho-

dox" views of cultural relativity (1987:4). The development of ethno-history has undermined much of the methodological justification for historical particularism, while the resurgence of evolutionism undermines its theory. James Hill describes how the classical anthropological humanism and its main living proponent, Mead, failed U.S. anthropology in its moment of greatest crisis in the early 1970s (1987:14).

I submit that Meadian anthropological humanism was flawed by its inability to account for anthropology itself. Its Olympian view of our own practice, as outside of the cultural processes we studied, was perhaps maintainable in an age of anthropologists with independent wealth, elite associations, and entry into the field with the support of forty native bearers. It is not tenable in an age of the academic assembly line, covert activity by our government throughout the world, and fierce competition for contracts and academic positions. In Williams's language, our ethical practice has foundered on the lack of transparency in our ethical institutions.

Similarly, the elitism of Meadian anthro-ethics is corrosive of "binding," especially for those of us in decidedly nonelite employment circumstances.[3] I am, of course, quite aware that envy and resentment may have something to do with my feelings about the centrality of elitism in our discipline, but it is important to consider recent fluctuations of the employment opportunities in the discipline before dismissing a critical view. I have in mind the rapid increase in academic jobs in anthropology after the war, followed by the equally rapid contraction of opportunities for those like myself who finished graduate school in the late 1970s and early 1980s.

I see the connection between delegitimation and elitism in the following way. As Williams presents it, the "moralistic" approach to ethical culture involves an abstraction from the particular situation in which the ethical actor is found. As a nonelite, I often feel overwhelmed by my particular circumstances, including a heavy teaching load, little support for research, absence of a scholarly community, and a hostile, powerful, anti-intellectual management. Consequently, I am marginalized by a moralistic ethics.

An effective ethical dialogue requires a community of at least roughly social equals, yet elitist AAA structures are constantly suggesting that, as Orwell aptly expressed it, some pigs are more equal than others. The interaction between a moralistic conception of ethics and a hierarchical conception of prestige within U.S. anthropology exacerbates the difficulties of a profession already in crisis. If a discordant view, or a noisy demand that the profession "go on record" against this or that atrocity, is threatening to the professional interest of the discipline, it is precisely because our existing ethical constructs are stretched to the breaking point by relatively minor contradictions.

The Problem with Ethics in Our Discipline: An Illustration

The elected leadership of the AAA has on various occasions recognized the ethical issue, but it has a hard time finding ways to address it effectively. The presentation of the issue in a 1987 article in the *Anthropology Newsletter* by the then president of the AAA, June Helm of the University of Iowa, is typical. The aim of the article was to analyze the history of the AAA in relation to the broader activity in which anthropologists participate—the creation, reproduction, and/or transformation of an academic discipline. The AAA is presented as having three basic functions: "To foster anthropology as an *enterprise* of research and scholarship; to serve all anthropologists as professionals in all lines of work . . . ; and to bind us together as a body of communicants for our mutual intellectual and professional benefit" (emphasis added). Helm argues that there is reason to be concerned about how well the AAA binds us: "The grand unifying vision of holism that we share . . . does not impinge daily upon us in our workaday lives." Further, she says that there is an "*imperative need* to strengthen communication, appreciation and linkages among all anthropologists both intellectually and organizationally" (1987:1; emphasis added).

Unfortunately, the article gives little attention to where the "binding as a body of communicants" problem comes from, nor does it offer suggestions about how to meet the "imperative need" identified. Instead, when the president takes up "the charge to the Association, now and in the coming years," only the "enterprise" and "profession" functions, not the "binding" one, are dealt with.

Indeed, the history presented avoids analysis of several significant controversies and developments within the discipline. It does not address events that might have complicated "communicating, appreciating, and linking," such as the decisions of important groups within the profession to remain outside the AAA when it reorganized in 1983. Comments on controversy—references to "intellectual bloodletting," or labeling positions as "deliberately sectarian postures" without identifying the sects involved—tend rather to be dismissive. According to *The Chronicle of Higher Educa-*

tion, anthropology is a leader among U.S. social sciences in regard to ethics. However, reference to the considerable and continuing debate within the organization over ethics, as well as the development of entities like the Principles of Professional Responsibility (PPR) or the AAA Ethics Committee, is strangely missing.

There is surely a place for ceremonially "presidential," unity-building activities within any profession, and it is typical for such activities to stress what is shared and avoid difficult and/or controversial matters. Yet if this were Helm's purpose, I still feel it significant that she thought our problems as "communicants" important enough to label dealing with them "imperative." Further, the failure to connect our ethical practice with "communicating, appreciating, and linking" suggests that ethics has nothing to do with "binding." Conversely, it may mean that ethics and being communicants should be connected but that it has not worked out that way in our discipline.

Structures Impeding a Response to Current Ethical Dilemmas

I intend the foregoing illustration to indicate why we anthropologists cannot simply wait for our current leadership structures to solve these problems for us. Other illustrations of our organizational difficulties addressing binding and ethics could also be given. These difficulties have been exacerbated by several recent developments. The new professional structure of U.S. anthropology described above, which was created by the reform of the AAA in the mid-1980s, decentralizes control to various subdisciplinary organizations. However much these reforms may have been required for other reasons, they make rigorous analysis of the predicament of our discipline as a whole and its general ethics even more difficult. Decentralization mitigates against shared ethical thinking.

The recent reorganization has made it harder for several kinds of anthropology with which I identify to function within the association and in the broader discipline. The Council for Marxist Anthropology (CMA), for example, was founded in part in order to raise political issues within the discipline. The AAA changes made this much more difficult, and the CMA, having a harder time functioning within the organization, collapsed. The Society for the Anthropology of Work (SAW) also found the new structures an obstacle. In part, this follows from SAW's desire to cultivate discussion about work among all those interested in it, irrespective of subdiscipline (or academic field). SAW has not been interested in the elaboration of a proprietary anthro-technique for study of work or its self-promotion as an enterprise in capitalist society. Subsequent loosening of the new structures encouraged SAW to join the AAA, however.

Reprofessionalization Options

The ethical diversity, employment crisis, and the delegitimation of U.S. anthropology have prompted a variety of responses. Two main approaches to reprofessionalization can be perceived. One is a broad, vigorously public defense of the discipline and its continued relevance to humanistic concerns, the strategy of the "engaged" anthropologist. This approach includes the use of our organizational forms to foster disciplinary consensus and involvement, to project anthropology as a vital and relevant part of modern social process. The several analyses of creationism, such as that published by the Northeast Anthropological Association, could be taken as representative of this approach.

The PPR itself can be seen as an early manifestation of this strategy, in essence an attempt to provide a new set of ethical constructs for U.S. anthropology. The potentially most powerful notion in the PPR is that, wherever we may be located in society, anthropologists have a positive responsibility to search out ways to participate *effectively* in the public policy dialogue over matters that fall within areas of professional expertise. While having continuity with the idea that the holistic comparative perspective has something of unique relevance to say to our contemporaries, PPR ethics also recognize our actual place in the reproduction of the employment-based social formations in which we participate. To be ethically effective, we must involve ourselves in, rather than stand above, the actual activities of the social groups attempting to affect this reproduction. How to do this most effectively, however, depends on our situation.

In the crucible of the late 1960s and early 1970s, the era of Project Camelot, Vietnam, and Thailand, the ethics of engaged anthropology did not become firmly enough embedded in the discipline to replace those of historical particularism. The moralistic perspective on ethics, combined with elitism, was incompatible with the political, generational, ethnic, and prestige conflicts manifest within the discipline at this time. The result was a retreat from trying to deal effectively with ethics on the part of the organization.

The decline in the number of "big" ethical issues brought before the AAA's Committee on Ethics is not, as Hill would have us believe, due to a change in the kinds of problems which confront anthropology. Rather, it is a consequence of the inability of moralistic ethical machinery to deal adequately with the issues raised in the 1960s and 1970s. If, as implied by the PPR, the important ethical demand on the engaged anthropologist *as anthropologist* was to develop appropriate professional policy, then the AAA's popular policy bodies, such as the annual business meeting, were more appropriate loci of ethical practice than the Ethics Committee was.

It is in the arena of the business meeting that the confrontation between engaged, humanistic anthro-ethics and the second approach to relegitimation, anthro-tech, has been most evident. Anthro-tech, as suggested above, fosters such a narrowing that it is more a reconceptualization of the field rather than a relegitimation of the existing one. One version of anthro-tech, derived from a misunderstanding of the natural science model, projects an anthropology based on elaborate, almost impenetrable techniques; a field focused on arcane issues of immediate interest primarily to specialists. (This is the view of anthropology that emerged, for example, from the bulk of the "Odyssey" series on public television.) Another version would model anthropology on literary criticism. Whether approached from the "science" or the "humanities" perspective, anthropology is perceived as a discipline for which involvement in public controversy is of dubious value, appropriate only on occasion and after considerable contemplation. The dCoE itself is perhaps the clearest example of the narrow, anthro-tech approach to relegitimation.

Several events in the 1980s suggest that this second reprofessionalization strategy is the dominant one, albeit perhaps more by default than design, within the AAA. On the legislative side, there was the passage in 1984 of a ballot initiative which severely limited the use of the AAA business meeting as a place to respond to issues of general public concern. While the AAA Board originally presented itself as in opposition to this initiative, it took no steps to reverse the effects of its passage. Indeed, the board itself introduced a "Legislative Steering Committee" and gave it the job of ruling on the appropriateness of legislation. The standard to be applied was so narrow that, in 1984, a resolution on the dangers of nuclear war was ruled "not relevant to the purposes of the AAA." The lack of participation at subsequent AAA business meetings suggests that anthro-tech has triumphed in the legislative domain.

Williams believes that a common consequence of the frustrations of treating ethics moralistically—that is, as a matter of absolutes—is the development of organizations based primarily on "administrative ideas of rationality." The recent history of the AAA, on balance, manifests preoccupations with administration much more than a substantive "binding together of communicants." The General Section can only be understood as an administrative rather than substantive solution to the need for discussion of general issues in the discipline. The editor of the *American Anthropologist* continues to argue adamantly that the general can only be found in the particular, a view that effectively diverts the journal away from those things that anthropologists share across subdisciplinary boundaries.

I seriously doubt that there are many anthropologists who find in anthro-tech an appealing image of their profession. Rather, its influence has grown by default, out of the rejection, led by Mead, of engaged anthropology and unthinking conservative reactions to the job crisis. Both of these responses were made more likely by an inappropriate view of the role of ethics. I doubt that anthro-tech can provide an adequate answer to the predicament of U.S. anthropology. For example, former president Helm drew attention to the "holistic" view of anthropology as a "grand, unifying vision," but she does not draw attention to the downside of the four-field definition of anthropology in the U.S., its abstractness. This downside means that our profession is vulnerable to centrifugal processes, like those to which Eric Wolf (1980) drew our attention: "They Divide, and Sub-divide, and Call it Anthropology." The new AAA structure may succeed in stemming the membership decline, but it is evident from the *Newsletter* that the real activity within the discipline is now devolved to various hyphenated anthropologies. Some of them feel strong enough to operate outside of the AAA completely. In this professional world, "anthropology" may come to have as much (or as little) content as other words revered within the academy, like "liberal education." I doubt strongly whether the new structure is adequate in itself to address the legitimation crisis in which we currently find ourselves.

In general, instead of actively promoting a dialogue within the discipline over ethics and organizing a constituency for it, there is a tendency for our leaders to avoid the kinds of issues raised elsewhere in this volume and opt for a sanitized presentation of the discipline and its history. Instead of seeking out those who put effort into fostering debate on substantive ethical issues, they continue to make safe, elite nominations for leadership positions.[4]

As I talk with other anthropologists of my professional age, we often find ourselves expressing ambivalence about the field. We desire to be part of anthropology as an intellectual practice, but we feel marginalized in relation to it because of our employment and we are annoyed by its professional stodginess. Like me, my anthropological age-group mates, especially women and minorities, have had to fight to establish whatever employment security and intellectual space we have within our institutions. Whether academic or nonacademic, our employers are often indifferent or even hostile to the insularity of elite anthropology. In our marginal positions, we feel little benefit from the organized profession and its elitist structures; indeed, we often feel our attempts to participate are rebuffed. At such points, we begin to question our desire to participate even in the intellectual practice of anthropology, driven as we are by the necessity to justify our careers in terms of the "applicability" of the discipline. We are asking if, at the core of U.S. anthropology, there is more to attract us than an abstract holistic humanism, one with which we can identify without belonging to the AAA.

I do not wish to denigrate the association's activities in the areas of scholarship and professionalism to which Helm draws attention, but I wish to suggest that more needs to be done in the third area of "binding" if the anthropologists I describe above are to remain active participants in our association. Our ethical diversity at the moment suggests a humanistic science without an ethical center.

PROPOSITION #4: THAT WE MUST DEVELOP AN EFFECTIVE ETHICAL
CULTURE WITHIN THE DISCIPLINE
We need to rediscover such an ethical culture if we are to be successful in maintaining a unified profession in terms of both employment and re-legitimation. Instead of searching for a transcendently grounded ethical theory, Williams argues we should strive to construct an ethical life out of our current cultural circumstances, a practice that recognizes the extent to which such a life lies outside the individual. In language similar to Habermas's discussion of discursive redemption (1975), Williams locates ethical life in a deliberative community to which participants have roughly equal access. (Anthropologists might prefer to think in terms of conscious cultural discourse.) He is adamant that the institutions of such a community be "transparent"; that is, open to clear understanding of how they function. More fully developed ethical constructs provide guides for how to behave in various situations, notions which, after careful collective scrutiny of their implementation, are taken as important models of and for action. How

such concepts and institutions are to be combined, and how to promote in a particular context a situation where "there will be individuals with dispositions of character and a life of their own to lead," can only be answered through living reflectively, not unilaterally by philosophy (1985: cf. chapters 9, 10).

I submit that there is within the legislation adopted by this association in business meetings and referenda over the last twenty years a general, if not completely coherent, core of ethical thought. This core is something we should study, periodically celebrate, and expand, rather than ignore.

Let me illustrate, in one area, the kinds of ethical goals I believe our association should be pursuing. Considering culture-centered computing is a useful way to show how the association might bind to itself younger anthropologists in diverse employment contexts. This is because computerization is the kind of problem with which journeyperson anthropologists typically find themselves concerned.

In the process of carrying out research on the cultural implications of computerization for working people in Sheffield, England, my research partner and I encountered widespread criticism of the "normal" practice of information system development. Typical machine-centered procedures often resulted in oppressive work for data entry clerks and the rigidification of preexisting faulty organizational procedures. Consequently, machine-centered systems often just do not work. Even the alternative "human-centered" or "ergonomic" approaches to system development treat people physically and individually rather than culturally and collectively. Systems based on such approaches also fail, because of lack of understanding of organizational culture or the dynamics of the class cultures in which system operators participate.

In Sheffield, we met a number of people striving to develop an alternative approach which took such factors into account, one which they were happy to have us label as "cultural" or "culture-centered." Among the more difficult issues they found themselves addressing was the problem of identifying the goals of such systems. To do this, they needed to go beyond usual institutional imperatives and establish broader legitimations. They tended to articulate these in terms of a notion of "socially useful," as well as efficient and profitable, production. Their problem, then, became the construction of persuasive arguments about how criteria of culture, society, profit, and efficiency were to be balanced, as well as how to create a social base powerful enough to have an impact on system development decisions.

In light of this ethnography, consider the various ways that anthropological ethics might be related to how we study computerization. As an association, we could wait to address the issue of computing until it was presented to us in the form of an ethical dilemma. Perhaps it would be the case of an anthropologist employed by a computer company which is thwarting his or her professional desire to develop culture-centered approaches. Unfortunately, chances are that the thwarted colleague would see little point in raising his case with the Ethics Committee, since there is no reason to believe they could do anything about it. Similarly, we could also wait until an AAA unit on culture-centered computing formed and organized a symposium on the ethics of computer system design. Again unfortunately, such a group is unlikely to develop on its own, since the majority of those who share such an interest (e.g., the Conference on Computer-supported Cooperative Work, Computer Professionals for Social Responsibility, Computers for People) are more likely to gather in some other context. Most likely, we would continue to take an opportunist approach to computing and the range of social futures held to be implicit within it. We would continue to address computerization primarily in the way the association has done so, as a nifty, socially neutral technique to add to our methodological armamentarium. In other words, we would ignore computers' social correlates.

Alternatively, an ethically vibrant anthropology could act proactively, recognizing in computerization an area which uniquely combines ethical problems, the special expertise of anthropologists, and substantial issues of social policy. We could ask, how can we promote discussion of such issues within our profession, and how should we change our AAA structures so that we address how, as a profession, we might help increase the abilities of disadvantaged peoples throughout the world to influence computerization? How could we build, within our association, a consensus over the kinds of approaches to computerization that are consistent with an engaged anthropology? What kind of campaign to promote these makes most sense, given our membership, the state of the association, and the present moment in the reproduction of human social life?

I am not arguing that computerization is the most important terrain on which to pursue a proactive ethics. Rather, I am trying to sketch out a vision of an active association, one seeking out ways to demonstrate both the professional and the ethical relevance of anthropology. This would be an association which recognized the necessity of encouraging development of its ethical constructs. There would clearly be difficulties in transforming the AAA into such a more activist organization; it might be argued, for example, that the identification and development of these issues is the job of the affiliated societies, sections, special interest groups, and so forth, of the AAA. Ultimately, however, if there are no arenas in which it is more appropriate for anthropology as a whole, as opposed to one of its appendages, to take ethical initiative, then there really is no need for anthropology.

NOTES

1. It is formally true that U.S. anthropology is in a relatively advanced ethical position within the U.S. social science establishment, in that its association has a specific code of professional ethics, the PPR, and that application of this code is the focus of periodic formal discussion. This much emerges for those of us who have been following Karen Winkler's discussion (e.g., 1986) of academic professional ethics over the years in the *Chronicle of Higher Education*. Our formal mechanisms for addressing ethical questions include an ethics committee, periodic committees to draft revisions to the PPR, and the long series of ethical dilemmas published in our *Newsletter*. Yet as I argue subsequently, the existence of such documents and procedures should not be taken as indicative of a high level of substantive consensus over ethics.

2. In an analysis of a similar "linguistic turn" in anthropology published shortly before his tragic death, Bob Scholte commented along similar lines that "no scientific method or ethical stance can guarantee the truth of [anthropological] images. They are constituted—the critique of colonial modes of representation has shown at least this much—in specific historical relations of dominance and dialogue" (1987:37).

3. It is, of course, difficult to separate one's feelings about elitism from one's experience. Having been educated at Stanford and the University of Chicago, I have some notion of the benefits of elitism. My Ph.D. is not from such an institution, and I now teach at a branch of a state university where I am the only anthropologist. I also once had a reviewer recommend against an article, because he or she felt it was a "think piece," and "an inherent difficulty with think pieces is that unless the author is a person of distinction, no one cares what he thinks. Is this author a person of distinction?" This implies to me, at any rate, that my article was to be evaluated in terms of my status in the field rather than in terms of its intrinsic merits.

4. For example, despite an active campaign on her behalf and despite being active as cochairperson of ANRAP, Carolyn Fluehr-Lobban was not selected for nomination for a position on the AAA Ethics Committee. Also, in order to participate in a panel on ethics at the annual meeting, one must relinquish one's right to give a presentation on one's research.

REFERENCES

Anthropology Newsletter
  1983   Award for highest % of unemployed Ph.D.s goes to—anthropology. *Anthropology Newsletter* 24(6):4.

Cassell, Joan, and Sue-Ellen Jacobs, eds.
> 1987   *Handbook on ethical issues in anthropology.* Washington, D.C.: American Anthropological Association.

Cole, John
> 1984   The political economy of the academy. Presented to the 86th Annual Meeting, American Anthropological Association, Denver, Colo.

Habermas, Jürgen
> 1975   *Legitimation crisis.* Boston: Beacon.

Hall, Allen
> 1984   *From scientific management to corporate culture.* Utica, N.Y.: SUNY College of Technology.

Helm, June
> 1987   From 1902 to 2002: Anthropologists and the American Anthropological Association. *Anthropology Newsletter* 28(5):1, 36, 37.

Helm, June, and Roy Rappaport
> 1987   Long-range planning and development. *Anthropology Newsletter* 28(6):1, 5.

Hill, James
> 1987   The Committee on Ethics: Past, present, and future. In *Handbook on ethical issues in anthropology,* ed. Cassell and Jacobs, 11–19.

Scholte, Bob
> 1987   The literary turn in contemporary anthropology; review article. *Critique of Anthropology* VII(1):32–47.

Wax, Murray
> 1987   Some issues and sources on ethics in anthropology. In *Handbook on ethical issues in anthropology,* ed. Cassell and Jacobs, 4–10.

Whitney, James
> 1985   Results of the 1985 survey of departments. *Anthropology Newsletter* (October): 1, 15, 17.

Williams, Bernard
> 1985   *Ethics and the limits of philosophy.* London: Fontana Press/Collins.

Winkler, Karen
> 1986   Anthropologists debate the ethical propriety of keeping research results secret. *Chronicle of Higher Education,* 17 December.

Wolf, Eric
> 1980   They divide, and sub-divide, and call it anthropology. *New York Times,* 30 November.

Part II

Contemporary Issues of Ethics in the Dialogue within Anthropology

Editor's Introduction to Chapter 4

Protecting informants and their communities has become a canon in anthropological research; it is probably one of the few ethical principles taught during professional training. Traditionally, the identity of informants and communities is concealed by the use of pseudonyms. Critics have often pointed out, however, that this approach lends itself more to the study of complex societies rather than traditional small-scale, non-Western communities. While acknowledging this criticism, the authors take a step back to examine the more fundamental issue of using pseudonyms as an automatic, perhaps even perfunctory practice.

Individual field researchers may raise the question of community identity privately with other professionals. Curiously, however, a more open dialogue within the profession has not taken place. The authors use this opportunity to open this issue for discussion. They argue that anonymity is no more ethical than identification; both involve costs and pose problems. Separating the use of pseudonyms for individuals from the similar practice for communities, they examine the rationale underlying community pseudonym practices. Their discussion points out that a concern for informant confidentiality is not identical with the decision to conceal a community's identity.

The use of pseudonyms is not without its own set of scholarly, technical, and ethical consequences. Heading this list may be the mistaken belief that community anonymity can be achieved easily. In reality the standardization of this practice has resulted in an easily penetrable facade. While they do not advocate the indiscriminate identification of field sites, the authors, likewise, do not endorse the traditional, and perhaps unthinking, use of community pseudonyms. What they stress is the complexity of the issue, and that the preference for community anonymity is not inherently more ethical, though it is frequently the easier choice (especially given the common belief that a simple community pseudonym insures confidentiality). In writing this piece, the authors hope to encourage anthropologists to make more informed and reflective decisions regarding the use of community pseudonyms in future anthropological research and writing. Indeed, the 1990 revision of the PPR reflects this thinking in its new position on informant anonymity—"the right of those providing information to anthropologists either to remain anonymous or to receive recognition is to be respected and defended" (A.I.).

Jay Szklut and Robert Roy Reed

Chapter 4 Community Anonymity in Anthropological Research
A Reassessment*

THE ISSUE OF RESEARCH ETHICS has reemerged recently as a focus of anthropological attention. The increasing percentage of professionally trained nonacademic anthropologists who question the utility of the profession's Principles of Professional Responsibility (PPR) has sharpened this debate. As with previous concerns over ethical behavior (e.g., Wax and Cassell 1979), however, most of this attention has focused on the ethical foundations of research and the moral dilemmas encountered during fieldwork. Seldom addressed are the ethical dilemmas that arise from the demands of publication: what to publish and where, how, and for what audience?

The ethics of publication is a complex topic, but avoiding it can lead to problems ranging from unwelcome publicity for the subject community to informants' exposure to legal sanctions or other harmful consequences (Cassell 1979). Responding to such dilemmas, the revised PPR admonishes anthropologists to assess both the positive and the negative consequences of their activities and the *publications* resulting from these activities and to take steps to assure the safety of their informants (1990, Section I.A.5, emphasis added). The "steps" taken by anthropologists has been the use of pseudonyms to protect the community and its residents.

But should researchers always conceal the location of their research sites? This question is often discussed in private, though seldom in public (but compare, Gibbons 1975).[1] Barnes (1979), in his book on social science ethics, devotes only ten pages to the topic, though he mentions many issues that weigh upon that decision. Reynolds (1979:180) justifies the use of

*This chapter is a collaborative effort and the order of the authors' names has no special significance.

community pseudonyms by concluding that "a serious attempt to disguise locations is tangible evidence of concern for the rights and welfare of the participants."[2] This chapter expands on these works and addresses some additional concerns arising from research that the authors have conducted (separately) in the United States and Europe.

We do not advocate the indiscriminate identification of field sites, but neither can we endorse the unthinking use of pseudonyms. We contend that community anonymity is not inherently more ethical than identification, and it certainly is not a panacea for ethical dilemmas. Either choice invokes costs and poses ethical and technical problems that must be confronted by researchers.

The History and Practice of Pseudonym Use

Most formal guidelines, such as the instructions on "Protection of Human Subjects" found in the Code of Federal Regulations (title 45, part 46) and the American Anthropological Association's Principles of Professional Responsibility only indirectly address the question of field site anonymity. The PPR offers these words of advice: "Informants have a right to remain anonymous. This right should be respected both where it has been promised explicitly and where no clear understanding to the contrary has been reached" (section 1-C). Note that the issue being addressed is the individual's right to confidentiality; this is not a prescription for community pseudonyms. The revised PPR highlights an individual's right to remain anonymous or to receive recognition, but again fails to address directly the issue of community anonymity.

The common assumption remains that informant confidentiality and community pseudonyms are simply different labels for the same phenomenon—the ethical imperative to protect our sources of information. However, the connection between an informant's right to confidentiality and the use of a community pseudonym is much less substantial than this common assumption posits. In fact, the connection is founded more on historical circumstance and a discipline's particular ideological or methodological perspective than on substantive identity. Although there are occasions when decisions in the one sphere affect the other, it is only by largely unexamined supposition that the argument for individual confidentiality has been extended to communities.

Today, the motivations for the use of community pseudonyms are significantly different from those of some forty or fifty years ago. Probably the two most well-known early investigations to use pseudonyms were the community studies of Middletown (Lynd and Lynd 1929) and Yankee City (Warner and Lunt 1941). Careful examination of these works, however, reveals that their use of pseudonyms was sociologically inspired. Thernstrom (1964:193), addressing the work of Warner, observes that a "latent function of the pseudonyms he applied . . . was to lend an aura of typicality: 'Yankee City' is manifestly a place of more universal significance than Newburyport, Massachusetts." These were studies of a *society* and not of a *single community*. Thus, it made sense to use a generic name, something representative of the wider sociological essence. It was not the community-as-object that was under study, but the community-as-sample (Arensberg 1961). Anthropologists often followed a similar practice without using pseudonyms; they lived in specific communities, but their study was of an entire society. For example, Evans-Pritchard did not live among all the Nuer, although his study was of Nuer society.

The use of field-site pseudonyms to augment informant confidentiality, that is, the ethical rather than sociological justification for pseudonyms, is a practice that arose with the awareness of how anthropological information might be used by governments or other agencies that did not share the discipline's goals. The publicity surrounding the Project Camelot affair (cf. Horowitz 1965) highlighted the need for a closer examination of the possible uses and abuses of field research. Questions arose regarding ethical problems involved in anthropological research and the need for a voluntary code of professional conduct.[3] The cornerstone of this code was the recognition that anthropologists had a debt to the people they studied and part of this debt was a grant of individual privacy. But fulfilling this grant proved to be difficult.

> Even though we do not publish an informant's name, height, weight, or serial number, the interested reader can identify the revolutionary in the Santiago squatter settlement, the reformer among the Northern Ute, the Lebanese trader in central Ghana, or the patrón on the upper Rio Ucayuli. (Jorgensen 1971:331)

Implicit in this statement is the common assertion that it is impossible to disguise an individual's identity without also disguising his or her residence. The modern anthropological practice of disguising both informants and communities follows from this and, as a result, informant and community anonymity are conflated into one issue.

Other sciences, however, have not confused these issues. The separation of informant and community anonymity receives support from practices in the biological and medical sciences, including our colleagues in biological anthropology. These disciplines have strict ethical guidelines for establishing informed consent and maintaining individual confidentiality. But they have no explicit policies regarding community anonymity. The separation of these issues is obvious from the fact that field sites are not disguised in most of these studies. For example, in epidemiological research it is common practice to specify the research location in order to allow for verification and comparative studies.

Perhaps even more striking, considering the revised Code of Ethics' silence on the issue of community pseudonym use, is the following statement taken from the Code of Ethics of the American Sociological Association:

> Organizations, large collectivities such as neighborhoods, ethnic groups, or religious denominations, corporations, governments, public agencies, public officials, persons in the public eye, are not entitled automatically to privacy and need not be extended routinely guarantees of privacy and confidentiality. (part 1, section E, paragraph 1)

Thus, sociology recognizes a distinction between community anonymity and individual confidentiality, whereas anthropology conflates the two. Why this difference in ethical considerations? We suggest that the difference arises because of the two disciplines' distinct conceptual approaches (see Herzfeld [1987:66–67] on the case of anthropology and folklore).[4] Anthropology has focused on personal studies of powerless peoples. Participant observation, the hallmark of anthropological methodology, involves the anthropologist with individuals first and societies second. Sociology, on the other hand, has traditionally focused on the more abstract social structure: the family, the neighborhood, and the community. Sociology's reliance on survey methodology and a more quantitative approach leads it to emphasize the social system first and the individual second.

Common Justifications for Community Pseudonyms

Maintaining informant confidentiality and using a community pseudonym are not identical issues, nor are they as closely related as is commonly thought. While we recognize the primacy of the individual's right to confidentiality, we also feel that this right does not always demand the use of a community pseudonym. Therefore, we would like to query some of the justifications used for community pseudonyms. These questions address both the alleged advantages of disguising the field site and the hidden costs of doing so. We begin by examining the assertion that the use of a pseudonym indicates respect for informant's rights. Second, we examine the notion that a community pseudonym enhances individual confidentiality.

Paul Davidson Reynolds, a sociologist, discusses the use of community pseudonyms in his analysis of Arthur Vidich and Joseph Bensmen's (1958) study of Springdale. In that case, residents were so incensed with the published study of their community that they lampooned the book and its authors in their Fourth of July parade (Whyte 1958). "The participants obviously felt they had not been treated with respect and dignity in the monograph that reported the study" (Reynolds 1979:181). Reynolds finds that the Springdale study is marked by a condescending and patronizing tone as well as by the authors' casual attributions of motives and attitudes to community members. It is clear that this mixing of personal evaluations and objective descriptions enhances the possibility that participants will feel demeaned. Reynolds (1979:184) concludes that the study of Springdale shows "that reports of fieldwork can have significant negative effects for the participants—effects that could be mitigated considerably if the same information were provided in a different *form*" (emphasis added). Thus, it is not the use of a pseudonym which has the greater impact on informants' feelings of being treated with respect and dignity, but instead how the information is presented; ideally there should be a clear separation of descriptive data, interpretations, and participants' personal evaluations of one another and their community.

Have we really increased informant confidentiality by extending pseudonym use from the individual to the community? Informant confidentiality can be divided into two aspects: concealment from those outside the community and concealment from individuals within the community itself. What information we gather and from whom is easier to conceal from those outside the community than is the location of the field site itself. It is doubtful if governments and other agencies, which caused our original concern with confidentiality, are so powerless as to be unable to identify fieldwork locations. Proposals commonly specify the research site, letters home carry postmarks and, typically, the researcher must register himself and his place of residence with the host government when initiating a prolonged study. Thus, an informant's protection from outside agencies is seldom reinforced by attempts to conceal where the information was gathered. On the contrary, the use of field-site pseudonyms may falsely lead us to believe that we have established anonymity when, in actuality, none exists. This false confidence can lead to the publication of information which may have severe consequences for the individuals we originally sought to protect.

Additional factors may also arise which contravene attempts at creating field-site anonymity outside the community. In a study by one of the authors, the physical location of the town being studied is significant. The fact that it has both a northern and southern harbor, thus making it a convenient location for the trading of goods, cannot be ignored in an anthropological examination. The town's central location in the region also provides an important index to its subsequent development. These facts, along with population figures and statistics on its economic base, necessary for a study of social organization, will inevitably reveal the location. Yet, the social organization of the community and many other social facts cannot be understood without reference to all of the above.

Protecting the community from external agencies, such as governments, is very difficult—though with careful planning it is possible. Still, there remains the belief that community pseudonyms protect the field site from internal conflict, for example, it protects informants from community reprisal. Attempts at granting this type of protection present us with a much more complex issue. The first question which needs to be addressed is: Do our informants wish to conceal the name of their community? Because of anthropology's expansion into industrially developed societies and due to the spread of education throughout the world, many "natives" are now literate. Quite often they have some knowledge of anthropology, or folklore, and wish to read the final product of the field study.[5] Indeed, many are proud that their community was chosen for study. While conducting his fieldwork, one of the authors found that people were highly insulted by the idea that a pseudonym would be used for their community, though they did concede the wisdom of disguising personal identities.

At times, it seems that the anthropologist is the only one with a concern for protecting anonymity of informants. In the preface to the second edition (1964) of *Village in the Vaucluse*, Laurence Wylie reveals the true name of his field site. He did this after learning that not only had the first edition of his book found its way into the village, but also that a local café owner had ordered copies to sell to tourists. Furthermore, in some copies, villagers signed their photographs that were labeled with their pseudonyms. Obviously, Wylie had a pleasant, and lucky, field experience. But, his experience illustrates that anonymity may not be desired by the people themselves.[6]

In other cases the decision for or against anonymity is more problematic. During research, anthropologists inevitably discover information that is potentially embarrassing within the context of the community. Yet there are situations that are significant only because of the social positions of individuals in a specific community; that is, significance is due to the fact that it is these particular individuals in this particular community who are interacting. For example, within a given community, a statement about the quality of life takes on a particular meaning if it is uttered by a local environmentalist as opposed to a local developer, though both statements are valuable. In order to disguise these individuals we change their names and the name of the community.[7] The second practice, the use of field-site pseudonyms, is deemed necessary because some individuals, such as environmentalists and developers, can be recognized by their social position within the community. But the specificity of the community and the individuals is exactly what gives the interaction its meaning.

Some might argue that the above situation is easily handled by using vague identifiers: "a local environmentalist/developer." Typically, however, the meaning of a particular interaction can be understood only through an understanding of the history of interactions between the specific individuals. The more this history is detailed to create ethnographic accuracy, the greater the *definition* of individuals. This is a familiar dilemma to all social scientists. At what point does the obscuring of data, necessary for anonymity, interfere with the accurate description of social processes? How can the researcher maintain analytical rigor and protect the rights of informants?[8]

The possibility of an individual's embarrassment owing to identification within the community presents a delicate problem. If we name the community and then state that the town moderator, a pseudonymic "Mr. Smith," said such and such, then Mr. Smith's true identity is revealed to any resident of the town or, indeed, to anyone who bothers to inquire as to the identity of the town moderator. Does this discovery, or at least the easy possibility of discovery, necessarily constitute an ethical failure to preserve individual confidentiality? What if Mr. Smith's opinions were known already, or reported in the local press, or gossiped about at the local bar? We here are dealing with public information, information readily available to any member of the community. Certain individuals are public figures and *in that capacity* they make public statements. Our identification of them to other local residents is not a loss of confidentiality within that community. (Intercommunity relations, however, present a different situation. We deal with this possibility below.)

The ethical problem for the researcher working with public figures is in differentiating information gathered from a person using his or her public figure persona—that is, information supplied by Mr. Smith speaking as the "town moderator"—and information supplied by Mr. Smith speaking as the researcher's "friend." The first source provides information for public consumption: "The town moderator says Smithburg is booming." The latter source is providing private or privileged information that almost certainly should remain anonymous: "All the development in town benefits only a few people." The distinction between private and public personae may impel the researcher to use different pseudonyms for the same individual. In most cases, we believe that this would not affect the analysis.[9]

Two reasons are commonly given for community anonymity: (1) the need to protect the community, and (2) the need to protect the researcher. But who or what are we protecting the community from?

> The protection of participants is the value invoked, though it is not always clear what they are to be protected from—annoyance, risk, invasion of personal privacy, or the intrinsic discomfort of learning that they have been deceived, at least, uninformed about having been observed or studied. (Riecken 1983:8)

Indeed, there are situations where the information in an anthropological report could be detrimental to the community and its citizens. In these instances, clearly, our duty is to protect those who have given us that information.

Yet, even when our information is not harmful, we often persist in using pseudonyms. Are we protecting ourselves from the community or from accusations of libel? Certainly, we neither write maliciously nor try to distort facts. Perhaps we are afraid that the citizens will not like the way they are portrayed. This possibility, however, should not influence the portrayal. Otherwise, we are merely local boosters and not professional anthropologists.[10] Furthermore, why should we fear that informants will not like our report? Is there a fear of rebuttal from the studied themselves? Reactions from the community, however, can alert the researcher that perhaps the study is somehow inaccurate, or they can open doors to other avenues of research, or, in the best of all worlds, even support the initial study.

Are we afraid that we will not be allowed to restudy the community at a later date? In some communities this may be the case, but the use of a pseudonym does not guarantee against such a possibility, as Vidich and Bensmen's (1958) study of "Springdale" demonstrates. Is there fear of a restudy done by one of our own colleagues? Are we deliberately vague about where we have worked in order to avoid professional controversy?[11] Regardless of how these questions are answered, they obviously focus on professional advantage and have little to do with using pseudonyms to protect informants.

There is a disturbing underside to the manner in which community pseudonyms are employed in anthropology. While preserving field site anonymity is the norm for studies of social systems in Europe and North America, as we move from these areas there seems to be an increasing lack of concern for anonymity (cf. Barnes 1963:127). Anthropologists have rarely seen the need to conceal the location of their communities when studying non-Western societies. The urban studies of the Manchester school (cf. Epstein 1958), David Jacobson's (1973) study of Mbale, Abner Cohen's (1969) study of Ibadan, and John Gulick's (1967) study of Tripoli did not require anonymity. Why do the home societies of anthropologists inevitably invoke the veil of confidentiality while foreign research sites are left bare? Is this ethnocentrism in disguise or is there some other reason for this seemingly two-sided approach?

Thus far we have looked at anonymity in terms of concealment from some individual or some group. There is also the issue of using a pseudonym because of the nature of our findings, that is, concealing the community because of an uncomplimentary portrayal in the research report. There is no simple answer here. The anthropologist cannot, and probably should not, be the only one to decide whether publishing certain information is harmful. If he or she feels that the report will generate negative consequences, the residents of the community should be consulted. Most likely, this negative information, if it can be exploited by a faction within the community or by another community, will eventually be discovered anyway. For the anthropologist, exploitation by some other group is the key. Where the possibility of exploitation exists, the use of a field-site pseudonym may be advisable to allow time for the community to act on the anthropologist's observations. (Here again, the community will recognize itself in the report.) But if no foreseeable possibility of exploitation exists, then there is a strong case for the benefits of accuracy, replicability, and truth outweighing the embarrassment of a negative portrayal. To use a pseudonym simply because a report is uncomplimentary is not a reasonable justification.

Still, exacerbating local problems by the naming of the community remains an important issue. As significant as this issue is, however, we find that over time the actual names of nearly all pseudonymic communities are revealed. This is partially due to curiosity and also due to the fact that often today's burning local issue, which may necessitate anonymity, is not even an ember five or ten years later. Along with these practical considerations, we also hold that eventually most communities are revealed due to the ethical belief that science is better advanced through openness than through secrecy.[12]

The use of pseudonyms incurs costs and, at times, creates its own scholarly and ethical dilemmas. For example, as anthropologists move into literate cultures, they have access to materials (historical documents, local histories, newspapers, etc.) that pose special problems. Obviously, these materials should be used, if they are fitting. The researcher who uses them, however, soon confronts the dilemma of speaking of a pseudonymic Jonesburg in the text while his bibliography bristles with references such as *The Story of the Town of Smithburg*. Should we disguise our bibliographies, as some might advocate? As social scientists, we are all aware that documents may be interpreted differently. The use of such a tactic would challenge the criteria of validity and replicability in anthropological research. Such a practice runs counter to the belief that "we have an obligation to make systematic comparisons and exercise systematic controls in our research to ensure that our generalizations are valid" (Jorgensen 1971:333). In order to conceal the name of the research site, do we disguise our sources behind such clumsy circumlocutions as "the local newspaper" and "the town's history," or, even worse, omit necessary or pertinent data? How can we justify making these materials unavailable to other scholars and still call our studies scientific?

If secrecy is truly necessary, then painstaking efforts must be made to disguise and protect the community. These efforts must go beyond the current practice of casually applying a pseudonym. This "formality" mocks a real consideration for confidentiality while simultaneously calling into question the scientific quality of our studies. If secrecy is necessary, then far greater effort must be expended in creating a genuine anonymity.

Some Considerations for Informed Decisions

Once again we stress that the concern for community anonymity is not unjustified. Our genuine concern for this question was aroused not only by our fieldwork dilemmas, but also by our dilemmas in reporting that fieldwork. This problem admits of no pat solution. Even the authors of this chapter are not in complete agreement. One feels that each anthropologist needs to consider the use or nonuse of a field-site pseudonym and, given that no ethical norms are violated, neither choice is necessarily preferable on moral grounds. The other takes the stronger position that identification of the community should be the standard except in those cases where harm will clearly result. Still, we both agree that a conscientious decision must be made.

Admitting that a decision must be made, what are the criteria for making it? We do not aim to create a set of rigid rules for the anthropologist making this decision. The variety of field situations and fieldworkers makes this impossible. We must also admit that our suggestions are guided by the laws (both the Code of Federal Regulations and libel statutes) of the United States. As Maurice Punch (1986:19–21) recently pointed out, European social scientists operate in a much different legal environment. Because of these constraints, our suggestions are tentative and, admittedly, grounded in our own society. Still we would be remiss in not putting them forward.

Our first suggestion is obvious: ask the people.[13] Of course, this advice should be tempered by the researchers' belief concerning their understanding of the situation. Yet, we should not elevate ourselves to a position of moral superiority by deciding what is best for "our natives" based on some neocolonial conception of The Anthropologist's Burden. They may make the wrong decision, but then so may we. After all, the innocents abroad may very well be us and not them. Furthermore, as Bell (1959) has noted, the understanding of a social structure was markedly improved and inaccuracies removed when participants reviewed and commented on a draft of a research report.

Our second suggestion may surprise those who believe that we advocate full identification of all field sites. We suggest that researchers consider their future publications about the community. Jacobs (1987) reports on an interesting case wherein anonymity was invoked by the researcher, against the wishes of the community, in order that the researcher might later publish more sensitive information about the community. This case underscores the fact that once a site has been identified it cannot be subsequently hidden. Today's decision for field-site identification might foreclose the possibility of future publications that would require anonymity. The contrary also holds; once a site has been hidden, future publications must be abandoned when they require materials that would identify the site. Except for extraordinary situations, once a decision has been made, it must be maintained.

A third, again obvious, suggestion is to consult with colleagues. Consultation can be especially helpful when the writer is trying to decide if some information, which by its nature would demand or destroy anonymity, is necessary to the published analysis.

Fourth is the especially vexing problem of working with public figures. We have suggested that the researcher isolate information gathered from an informant in his or her public figure persona from information supplied by the informant speaking as a private citizen. This suggestion, however, is only tentative. Dealing with public figures presents special problems. The identities of public figures are difficult to disguise and the repercussions of identification often are especially dangerous for these people. On the other hand, some information is significant because, for example, the mayor said it, not just some anonymous private citizen. Furthermore, we must be especially sensitive to possible ethnocentrism in our final decision. Westerners, and Americans in particular, believe that public figures have less right to anonymity than private individuals. Indeed, this point of view is enshrined in the Code of Federal Regulations: "All research involving survey or interview procedures is exempt [from these regulations], when the respondents are elected or appointed public officials or candidates for public office" (45 CFR 46.101, 3[iii]). We must be sensitive to the possibility that the societies we work in might not share in the belief and grant public figures the same rights afforded private individuals.

Our final suggestion is, we believe, the most important. Think about the implications of hiding or revealing the research site during the period of data collection as well as afterward. Many times information which gives the researcher important insights into the community cannot be published because it would reveal a particular informant. This possibility is of critical importance when community pseudonyms are not used. Community identification greatly increases the importance of maintaining individual confidentiality. If the researcher is aware of this problem in the field, then other publishable sources of the same information can be sought out. This procedure, typically used to verify information, can be a very effective method of protecting an informant's privacy. It also should be noted that when a community pseudonym is deemed necessary, other sources of information may need to be abandoned or heavily edited, for example, census and voting records. This, of course, hampers or even negates the possibility of certain types of research where community anonymity is judged necessary. The issue here is that the choice for or against anonymity affects the information that can be used in a published report. Therefore, the restrictions imposed by a particular choice should be considered and appropriate remedial action taken while the anthropologist is still in the field.

The reader should not mistake the elementary nature of the above suggestions as being indicative of a trifling issue. The use of community pseudonyms needs to be discussed prior to, during, and after research. Each of these phases presents its own problems. Those individuals who do not seriously consider this issue can easily find themselves in moral and ethical quandaries at a later date. For example, a researcher who has promised informants that their community will not be named may find years later that this promise was unnecessary. In attempting to publish the research findings, editors may concur and request a full disclosure to strengthen the general applicability of the conclusions. The researcher is now faced with the personal moral dilemma of whether to break a promise and the professional ethical concern for advancing the discipline.[14]

To state the problem succinctly, our research and our obligation to communicate our findings leave us facing problems that range from the ethical to the technical, from informants' right to privacy to citation problems. The above concerns raise many questions about the use of field-site pseudonyms. We believe the fundamental question is, What is being hidden from whom and for what purpose? We understand and wholeheartedly support the concern for anonymity when investigating sensitive topics.[15] Sometimes, to accomplish this goal, the community must remain anonymous, in addition to the individuals. But, to create anonymity how much important data is left out? And how much of that data is now lost because anonymity was created when it was not imperative?

Our purpose in this chapter has been to inaugurate an open forum in which the question of field-site anonymity, and its consequences, can be discussed publicly. We hope that such a forum will aid anthropologists in making more informed decisions concerning the use of anonymity. We do not presume to have exhausted or even to have raised all of the issues involved. We do hope, however, that we have underscored the complexity of this decision and have shown that the choice for community anonymity over identification is not inherently more ethical; it is simply easier. If this matter receives more thoughtful scrutiny in the future, then we will have accomplished our task.

ACKNOWLEDGMENTS
A preliminary version of this paper was read at the symposium "Appropriate and Inappropriate Secrecy in Anthropological Research: Dialogue for a New Era," 85th Annual Meeting of the American Anthropological Association, 3–7 December 1986, Philadelphia, Pennsylvania. We would like to thank the symposium's organizers, Carolyn Fluehr-Lobban and Arnold R. Pilling. A revised version of this paper appeared as a commentary in the *American Anthropologist*. We thank the anonymous reviewers for their input and suggestions. Finally, there are many individuals who contributed to this work and who, unfortunately, cannot be singled out for thanks. To all of these people, whether they agreed with our views or not, we express our appreciation for their time, comments, and opinions.

NOTES
    1. Exceptions to this observation are illuminating, especially those which ground themselves in specific publications. For example, John W. Cole (1975) notes in his review of John Davis's *Land and Family in Pisticci* that Davis did not disguise his field site or the names of many of his informants. Musing on this, Cole states, "We had better *assume* that the identities of all individuals and places that we refer to in our ethnographic accounts will become common knowledge, and write accordingly. We only delude ourselves if we think that a pseudonym will maintain anonymity" (Cole 1975:90, emphasis in original). More recently, Norman Whitten (1988) has taken serious exception to Stephan Beckerman's (1987) review of Whitten's book *Sicuanga Runa*. Beckerman accused Whitten of inventing false informants and field sites. Whitten replied with a blistering rejoinder pointing out that wherever possible he used the actual names of people and places. Only in those instances where clear harm would result did he disguise individuals. The thrust of Beckerman's review is that Whitten's book is unscientific. Whitten's rejoinder stresses the factual nature of his work, epitomized by its use of the actual names of people and places.
    2. Note that he does not maintain that community pseudonyms actually enhance individual privacy, but only that they evince a *concern* for this right.
    3. For a concise history of the AAA's Committee on Ethics and the formulation of PPR, see Hill (1987).
    4. There is obviously a great deal of overlap between the two disciplines. It is not our intent to minimize these similarities, but only to note the more general and historical differences in their theoretical approaches.

5. Max Gluckman (1967:xvii–xviii), referring to Barnes (1963), points out that this development can have serious theoretical implications for the collection of field data. Once people become aware that what they say and do may appear in a form available to others, especially others they know or others who can affect their lives, people have a vested interest in providing some data while obscuring or distorting other information.

6. Since the second edition of his book Wylie has gone on to make a film (1983) that includes interviews with the town's residents. This raises the difficult problem of informant confidentiality and ethnographic film. Unfortunately, this important topic is beyond the scope of this chapter.

7. See Fay Cohen (1976) for an exception to both these practices.

8. Harrell-Bond (1976:119) discusses her similar ethical dilemma and notes that "much rich illustrative material had to be discarded in the final writing of my research for publication. The rights of privacy had to take precedence over the claims for well-documented data." Interestingly, however, she did not see that privacy would be bolstered by the use of a community pseudonym and therefore revealed her research site.

9. Even in cases involving public information we suggest that researchers still consider substituting pseudonyms for personal names. This procedure can protect other individuals who are not public figures but who have become publicly associated with the investigator. By consistently not using personal names these individuals can state, for example, that someone else supplied a particular piece of information; that is, they can use confidentiality as they see fit. In any case, assuming the study has made its way back to the community, the use of a pseudonym for the community will not add to the anonymity of local informants.

10. Boosterism, of course, is not limited to advancing a specific community. John Messenger (1983:113–34) has provided a detailed account of Irish nativists' and others' furious reaction to his description of the island culture of the pseudonymic "Inis Beag." While many of Messenger's critics did not deny the truth of what he said, they took great exception to his saying it.

11. Compare, for example, the Oscar Lewis (1951) and Robert Redfield (1930) confrontation over Tepoztlan; Fredrik Barth's (1965) and Akbar Ahmed's (1976) differences about the Pathans; and, recently, Derek Freeman's (1983) questioning of Margaret Mead's work in Samoa.

12. We are concerned in this article with the use of secrecy (pseudonyms) as it pertains to published materials. The view that science is better advanced through openness than through secrecy, however, is applicable to the research activity as well as the publication of those activities. It is well worth considering the relationship between the advancement of science and secret research. Unfortunately, this important topic is beyond the scope of this chapter.

13. For an interesting case study on this point see Jacobs (1987:25–26).

14. We lean toward the position that the anthropologist's word should be his or her bond. In this situation the only ethical solution we see is for the anthropologist to revisit the site and try to gain permission to disclose the community.

15. As much as we support the use of pseudonyms for informants and field sites when publishing some types of research, we would like a clearer definition, or at

least a fuller discussion, of what constitutes "sensitive" topics. Does this include information that only might be embarrassing to the community, for example, the existence of a drug community in a small town, while not relating any information about individuals? Of special concern is the legal use of the term in the Code of Federal Regulations, title 45, part 46, subpart a.46.101, 3.

REFERENCES

Ahmed, Akbar S.
  1976 *Millennium and charisma among Pathans.* London: Routledge and Kegan Paul.

Arensberg, Conrad M.
  1961 The community as object and as sample. *American Anthropologist* 63:241–64.

Barnes, J. A.
  1963 Some ethical problems in modern field work. *British Journal of Sociology* 14:118–54.
  1979 *Who should know what? Social science, privacy and ethics.* Cambridge: Cambridge University Press.

Barth, Fredrik
  1965 *Political leadership among Swat Pathans.* London: Athlone Press.

Beckerman, Stephan
  1987 Review of *Sicuanga Runa* by Norman E. Whitten, Jr. *American Anthropologist* 89:485–86.

Bell, Earl H.
  1959 Freedom and responsibility in research: Comments. *Human Organization* 18:49.

Cassell, Joan
  1979 Regulating fieldwork: Of subjects, subjection, and intersubjectivity. In *Federal regulations: Ethical issues and social research,* ed. M. L. Wax and J. Cassell, 129–44. Boulder, Colo.: Westview Press.

Cohen, Abner
  1969 *Custom and politics in urban Africa.* London: Routledge and Kegan Paul.

Cohen, Fay G.
  1976 The American Indian movement and the anthropologist: Issues and implications of consent. In *Ethics and anthropology: Dilemmas in fieldwork,* ed. Michael A. Rynkiewich and James P. Spradley, 81–94. New York: John Wiley & Sons.

Cole, John W.
  1975 On the origins and organization of South Italian poverty. *Reviews in Anthropology* 2:84–91.

Epstein, A. L.
  1958 *Politics in an urban African community.* Manchester: Manchester University Press.

Freeman, Derek
 1983   *Margaret Mead and Samoa*. Cambridge, Mass.: Harvard University
        Press.
Gibbons, Don C.
 1975   Unidentified research sites and fictitious namés. *American Sociologist*
        10:32–36.
Gluckman, Max
 1967   Introduction. In *The craft of social anthropology,* ed. A. L. Epstein, xi–
        xx. London: Tavistock.
Gulick, John
 1967   *Tripoli: A modern Arab city*. Cambridge, Mass.: Harvard University
        Press.
Harrell-Bond, Barbara
 1976   Studying elites: Some special problems. In *Ethics and anthropology:
        Dilemmas in fieldwork,* ed. Michael A. Rynkiewich and James P. Sprad-
        ley, 110–22. New York: John Wiley & Sons.
Herzfeld, Michael
 1987   *Anthropology through the looking-glass: Critical ethnography in the mar-
        gins of Europe*. Cambridge: Cambridge University Press.
Hill, James N.
 1987   The Committee on Ethics: Past, present, and future. In *Handbook on
        ethical issues in anthropology,* ed. Joan Cassell and Sue-Ellen Jacobs, 11–
        19. Washington, D.C.: American Anthropological Association.
Horowitz, I. L.
 1965   The life and death of Project Camelot. *Transaction* 3(1):3–7, 44–47.
Jacobs, Sue-Ellen
 1987   Cases and solutions. In *Handbook on ethical issues in anthropology,* ed.
        Joan Cassell and Sue-Ellen Jacobs, 20–36. Washington, D.C.: Ameri-
        can Anthropological Association.
Jacobson, David
 1973   *Itinerant townsmen: Friendship and social order in urban Uganda*. Menlo
        Park, Cal.: Cummings Publishing Company.
Jorgensen, Joseph G.
 1971   On ethics and anthropology. *Current Anthropology* 12:321–33.
Lewis, Oscar
 1951   *Life in a Mexican village*. Urbana: University of Illinois Press.
Lynd, Robert S., and Helen Merrell Lynd
 1929   *Middletown: A study in contemporary American culture*. New York:
        Harcourt, Brace and Company.
Messenger, John C.
 1983   *An anthropologist at play: Balladmongering in Ireland and its conse-
        quences for research*. Lanham, Md.: University Press of America.
Punch, Maurice
 1986   *The politics and ethics of fieldwork*. Beverly Hills, Cal.: Sage Publications.
Redfield, Robert
 1930   *Tepoztlan: A Mexican village*. Chicago: University of Chicago Press.

Reynolds, Paul Davidson
    1979   *Ethical dilemmas and social science research*. San Francisco: Jossey-Bass Publishers.
Riecken, Henry W.
    1983   Solutions to ethical and legal problems in social research: An overview. In *Solutions to ethical and legal problems in social research,* ed. R. F. Boruch and J. S. Cecil, 1–9. New York: Academic Press.
Thernstrom, Stephan
    1964   *Poverty and progress: Social mobility in a nineteenth century city.* Cambridge, Mass.: Harvard University Press.
Vidich, Arthur J., and Joseph Bensmen
    1958   *Small town in mass society.* Princeton: Princeton University Press.
Warner, Lloyd, and Paul Lunt
    1941   *The social life of a modern community.* New Haven: Yale University Press.
Wax, Murray L., and Joan Cassell, eds.
    1979   *Federal regulations: Ethical issues and social research.* Boulder, Colo.: Westview Press.
Whitten, Norman E.
    1988   Savagery in general anthropology. *American Anthropologist* 90:153–55.
Whyte, William F.
    1958   Freedom and responsibility in research: The Springdale case. *Human Organization* 17:1–2.
Wylie, Laurence
    1964   *Village in the Vaucluse*. Revised edition. New York: Harper Colophon.
    1983   *Laurence Wylie in Peyane* (film). Bernard Petit.

Editor's Introduction to Chapter 5

This contribution, dealing with the protection and management of archaeological data, is written by the archaeologist for the state of Michigan. He is one of the full-time, practicing anthropologists who have contributed to this volume. The case, although taken from a particular state, nevertheless has a high degree of general application for the issues that it raises. The extensive federal legislation mentioned in the chapter, especially over the past few decades, attests to the increased level of national consciousness over the need to protect archaeological resources.

While the legislation is a welcome source of legal protection, the author describes jurisdictional disputes with the state's Department of Natural Resources, and he relates a certain suspicion and tension that has existed between the state's professional staff of archaeologists and the university-based archaeologists. Compilation and control of site-location information was one issue that became moot once a computerized state file of sites was created. Then the issue shifted to control and regulation of access to site information, with both state and university professionals concerned about protecting the sites from illegal collectors, at one time referred to in anthropological jargon as "pot hunters." In practice, requests for information from individuals obviously on "fishing expeditions" were consistently denied, while requests from archaeologists, engineers, and developers were handled routinely.

An important factor included in Halsey's discussion is the reaction of the Native American community in Michigan. For the most part, he reports, Native American leaders have expressed no interest in archaeological and site preservation, except in those few cases where burials have been excavated in emergency salvage operations. Professional archaeologists have had a moratorium on the excavation of burials for at least fifteen years, and this is one of the controversial issues in the current period involving the conflicting interests of the scientific community and native peoples. This issue is discussed more fully in chapter 10.

Ironically, given the suspicion that surrounds anthropologists working for governments in recent decades, Halsey claims that state archaeologists have, in fact, no secrets to keep. The state never involves itself in an agreement between a client and an archaeological contractor unless it is a party to or beneficiary of the contract, and all such bids are subject to public disclosure. So, the state appears to be a more open and accessible source of information than the private contractors for whom other, nonacademic anthropologists are working.

John R. Halsey

Chapter 5 "State Secrets"
The Protection and Management of Archaeological Site Information in Michigan

WITH THE PASSAGE OF the National Historic Preservation Act of 1966, the federal government set in motion a series of actions that have revolutionized the practice of archaeology in the United States. This act and its later amendments, plus Executive Order 11593, the Archaeological and Historic Preservation Act of 1974, the National Environmental Policy Act of 1969, the Archaeological Resources Protection Act of 1979, and the volumes of regulations implementing these laws, have altered not only how, when, and where archaeology is done, but increasingly, who does the work. Employment opportunities for professional archaeologists vastly increased in the 1970s and 1980s in universities, colleges, junior colleges, and museums. Additionally, thousands of people who did not go on in archaeology have had a chance to experience real field archaeology as field crew members, field school students, or volunteers. They have been able to make once-in-a-lifetime discoveries *and* experience that special kind of boredom that only comes in a sterile pit in an open bean field on a cloudless, windless one-hundred-degree day! Institutions that once had little power, or perhaps did not even exist prior to 1970, now are major forces in directing the course of American archaeology as it approaches the twenty-first century. Millions of dollars have been spent on archaeology, and tens of thousands of new archaeological sites have been discovered nationwide. Cataloging information on these sites, creating site data bases, protecting sites and site information, and the growth of contract fieldwork have created ethical problems on a scale commensurate with the explosive growth of North American archaeology as a whole. As an object lesson on how some of these ethical dilemmas have been handled, I propose to use Michigan's experiences as an example.

Today the Archaeology Section, Division of Museums, Archaeology and Publications, Bureau of History, Michigan Department of State maintains Michigan's official archaeological site file. This was not always the case. Before 1980 the keeping of site records and the assignment of site numbers was the responsibility of the University of Michigan Museum of Anthropology. As the home of Michigan's first "professional" archaeologist and the state's first regular archaeological program, it also published an early compendium of archaeological site information, Wilbert Hinsdale's "Archaeological Atlas of Michigan" (1931). Hinsdale assembled the data in this pioneering document from published reports, personal communications from amateur archaeologists and landowners, Government Land Office maps, and his own personal research. The information conveyed in Hinsdale's atlas was vague, and precise presentation of site locations was impossible given the scale of maps used (1/4 inches = 6 miles). Taking Arenac County for example, Hinsdale reported:

> Along or in the vicinity of the Bay shore there were a few settlements. It is not impossible that the fort-builders, who were very active in Ogemaw County, also had sites upon the Rifle River toward its mouth, but no evidences of them have been found. Sites identified: Villages—5; Burying grounds—7; Mounds—2. (1931:15; Map 12)

Even today it is nearly impossible to use the Atlas without Hinsdale's original documentation and there are very few specific report references in the text. All in all, the Atlas compromised the integrity of very few sites while conveying a great deal of compiled general information. It was clear to all who read the Atlas that Michigan, while not as rich in, let us say mounds, as Ohio or Wisconsin, had a considerable aboriginal past.

Although it was not the obvious intent of Hinsdale to conceal or obscure precise site locations, he did so rather effectively. Later publications in the 1930s expressed no particular concern with concealing site locations (Greenman 1937; 1939). Site locations in reports from this period, even for excavated sites, are frustratingly vague by contemporary standards, but this vagueness would not deter a serious searcher if he were in the site vicinity and determined to find it.

From the late 1930s up until especially the mid-1970s (and indeed even to this day) those individuals most concerned with the exact location of sites have been the private collectors. In their newsletters (most now defunct), sites were described only in evasive terms such as "about two miles north of the Thunder Bay River on a little sand ridge" or, if the site was known to several collectors, by its common name or amateur-designated site number. The cooperation of amateur archaeologists with professional archaeologists was a relatively rare occurrence (e.g., Brose and Essenpreis 1973) until the late 1970s and early 1980s. This lack of cooperation apparently represented a deep-seated fear that professional archaeologists would come and entirely "dig up" or otherwise dispossess the amateurs of "their" sites. By the early 1980s it had long become obvious that professional archaeologists did not have the time, money, students, or interest in examining any more than a handful of the enormous number of known sites. In any case, there was no guarantee that the sites that attracted collectors, sites with many surface artifacts, would be the same ones, necessarily, that would be attractive to professional archaeologists.

The University of Michigan Museum of Anthropology continued through the 1970s to maintain the "official" state sites file, with sites being entered and numbers assigned by graduate students. Other universities kept their own files, usually maintaining primary documentation at home and sending only the briefest sort of site information to the University of Michigan. The system proceeded more or less as it always had except that in the early 1970s, the Michigan History Division (MHD) of the Michigan Department of State became active in archaeology. The arrival of the MHD (now the Bureau of History) created no small disturbance in Michigan's archaeological community. This agency, which could trace its antecedents back to 1828 and could count among its ancestors Lewis Cass, Father Gabriel Richard, and Henry Rowe Schoolcraft, had a broad mandate in the field of history. The powers of the Michigan Historical Commission, the Michigan History Division's parent created in 1913, were

> to collect, arrange, and preserve material, including books, pamphlets, maps, charts, manuscript, papers, copies of domestic and foreign records and archives, paintings, statuary, and other objects and material illustrative of and relating to the history of Michigan and the old northwest territory; to procure and preserve narratives of the early pioneers, their exploits, perils, privations and achievement; *to collect material of every description relative to the history, language, literature, progress or decay of our Indian tribes;* to collect, prepare, and display in the museum of said commission objects indicative of the life, customs, dress and resources of the early residents of Michigan, and to publish source materials, and historical studies relative to and illustrative of the history of the state. (Public Act 271 of 1913; Michigan Compiled Laws Annotated 399.4; emphasis added)

Despite the scope of these powers, in 1973 the MHD found itself involved in a series of jurisdictional disputes with the Michigan Department of Natural Resources over the control of history within the state bureaucratic structure. Supported by legislative budget decisions and an attorney general's opinion, the MHD took full control of state historical programs, including the position of State Historic Preservation Officer (SHPO) and management of the federally funded historic preservation program (Bigelow 1974).

One of the responsibilities of the SHPO was maintenance of a body of information officially referred to as the "State Survey Data." The State Survey Data were supposed to include, but not be limited to, the following:

(1) data on properties listed in or determined eligible for listing in the National Register of Historic Places;
(2) data on properties nominated to the National Register, but not yet finally approved;
(3) data on properties that may potentially meet National Register criteria;
(4) data on properties that are ineligible for listing or specific geographical areas that have been surveyed and do not contain significant properties other than those already identified;
(5) predictive statements concerning the probable distribution of sites in different areas of the state based on systematic background research and sample fieldwork;
(6) specification of those areas of the state for which inadequate survey data are available and about which no reliable predictions could be made.

Furthermore, in addition to maintenance, these data were to be continually updated and reevaluated and placed

in an accessible location and . . . be kept up-to-date so that the information is readily available to Federal, State, and local planners during the decision-making process. The State Survey Data need not be published, but shall be physically organized and/or indexed in a manner to provide for easy access. Availability of State Survey Data may be limited to the general public if, in the opinion of the State Historic Preservation Officer, such availability might result in damage to historic properties. (National Park Service 1977:47660)

The federal government had handed a major record-keeping responsibility to the SHPO, along with the funding and staff to take care of it. Some archaeologists in the state continued to maintain that, funding, legislation, and procedures notwithstanding, the site file should be maintained by universities rather than the state. Such state/university jurisdictional disputes have certainly not been limited to Michigan (Kent et al. 1985).

When it quickly became clear that the SHPO and its staff were not going to go away and there were in fact plans to create a computerized state file, professional concern began to take a different tack, one no longer directed at the legitimacy of the state's site file-keeping activities. Site file maintenance as an issue of professional concern disappeared as soon as most of the active archaeologists in the state began to participate in the review and compliance and grant-funded archaeological survey activities of the State Historic Preservation Office. They created data which by law had to be reviewed by the state. Now the general concern was about the security of site locational information and who would have access.

Almost as soon as the state began assembling its own site file, the then state archaeologist, James E. Fitting, prepared an explanatory document describing the proposed computerized site file and outlining the archaeological objectives of the Michigan History Division as a response to a series of questions raised by the Conference on Michigan Archaeology, the state organization of professional archaeologists (Fitting 1973). These questions included: (1) To what individuals or institutions would site location data be released? (2) What kinds of data would be released to individuals or institutions? (3) What kind of enforceable restrictions on the release of site data are legally available?

As a response to the third question, an informal opinion from the attorney general's office was appended, stating that a closed site file was legally defensible under state law. The answer to the first question was that precise site locations would be available to recognized research institutions and individuals with genuine research and planning interests. It would be available, in a processed form, for environmental impact statements.

The answer to the second question was that individuals and institutions requesting information for research and planning purposes would need to include the types of information they were seeking in their requests for permission to use the file. Requests for planning information would be screened by MHD and only such information as was deemed essential for the project would be released. No information submitted to the file on a privileged basis would be released without permission of the contributor.

This system worked well, and through regular correspondence with the University of Michigan Museum of Anthropology concerning sites in their files, the state was able to establish a smooth-flowing review and compliance process and at the same time build up its own site file. Funding from the Department of State and the Department of Natural Resources even allowed some institutions to review and correct their own site location data and produce documents of broad general utility such as *The Distribution and Abundance of Archaeological Sites in the Coastal Zone of Michigan* (Peebles and Black 1976). No absurd requests were made; no raids on the site file were attempted by collectors seeking new areas to work; no political pressure was applied to staff members of the MHD.

In 1976, however, the development of Michigan's "Freedom of Information Act" (Public Act 442 of 1976; Michigan Compiled Laws Section 15.231 et seq.) made both university and state archaeologists nervous. Archaeological site files at the MHD and in the various state universities were unquestionably public records as defined by this legislation, that is, "a writing prepared, owned, used, in the possession of, or retained by a public body in the performance of an official function, from the time it is created." How could site-location information be protected in the face of this perceived threat? The answer proved to be very simple. We worked through the Department of State's legislative liaison branch and requested that an amendment be drafted allowing the department to exempt site-location information from release under the legislation. The need and motives for this request were explained to the bill's sponsors and the requested exemption was included in the original legislation which became law on 13 April 1977.

Were we justified in seeking a legislative remedy to this perceived problem? Before I give my answer, we should briefly reprise the nature of archaeological sites. Prehistoric and historic archaeological sites exist on and beneath the surface of the ground and on the bottomlands of lakes and rivers. They are best understood only through scientific excavation, which unfortunately is also a destructive action. It is not yet possible to understand more than a little about most sites through remote sensing technologies. Lacking any kind of test information, each site must be assumed to contain unique data with the potential to inform us about certain aspects of past human life.

Archaeological sites are the only places where certain kinds of information exist: for example, prehistoric human skeletons, the remains of plants and animals used by people, and so forth. This is not to say that all sites contain important or significant information or that we should preserve all currently extant sites forever. However, excavation of archaeological sites is very expensive and labor-intensive. In Michigan in the 1980s salvage excavations averaged about one hundred thousand dollars per site, so that substantial excavation of a large number or perhaps even just a representative sample of sites will not be possible. In order for archaeology to continue to exist and grow as a profession, it is important that as many sites as possible be preserved and assessed before they are destroyed.

We also have a responsibility to the private landowner who generously allows us on his land to discover archaeological remains that are his property and for which we need his permission to remove. The vast majority of landowners have no adequate understanding of the extent of the "real property" rights in their land and artifacts. Yet, it is often the owner of a significant site who has been the most vigorous defender of the site's integrity once someone has taken the time to explain the significance of a site to him.

The forces of destruction are numerous and implacable and our legislative armaments are useful against only a very limited number of offenses. As King Canute could not command the tides to roll back, neither can we force the Great Lakes to stop rising and wasting their site-laden shorelines. Nor can we stop the landowner from building a new house on his private plot or even the plunder of ancient cemeteries if local authorities will not support existing statutes.

However, it was against the hard-core collectors that all of the secrecy and protective mechanisms were directed: the thousands, perhaps hundreds of thousands, of pot hunters, treasure hunters, coin shooters, shipwreck salvagers, and bottle collectors who have only the artifact or valuable cargo as their goal. Did we succeed?

We never did receive the expected rush of letters requesting information on all the good places to find arrowheads or bottles, but as a result of the new law, major changes were made in site-file management. Formal responsibility for site number assignment was turned over to the MHD by the University of Michigan and we developed a set of procedures and site-file imperatives governing the release of archaeological information. Thus, we were able at last, under color of law, to implement our longtime practices; namely, that information would be released to:

a) qualified professional archaeologists, including members of the Conference on Michigan Archaeology and/or individuals who meet the professional standards of the Society of Professional Archaeologists;
b) individuals, agencies, firms, etc. who are involved in land use and development or other activities which might affect archaeological resources and who are consulting with professional archaeologists regarding the interpretation and assessment of those data;
c) other individuals, if, in the opinion of the State Historic Preservation Officer and the State Archaeologist, such information would contribute to

the scientific assessment or preservation of the site or sites in question. (Michigan History Division 1981)

We responded to the few requests from individuals who were obviously on "fishing expeditions" with denials and there was no further correspondence. Requests from archaeologists, engineers, and developers were handled routinely. An informal survey of state archaeologist colleagues in Massachusetts, New Mexico, North Carolina, and Wisconsin revealed that only in Massachusetts had there been a serious effort by a collector to gain access to the state site files. The experience of the other states mirrored that of Michigan. They also had sought protective legislation or administrative procedures and, curiously enough, at the time when they were beginning to mechanize their site files, just when it was becoming obvious that a whole lot of information *might* be had just for the asking. A common archaeologist's nerve had been struck from one end of the country to the other!

Pressure to deliver politically expedient decisions on site locations or site significance by superiors has been an insignificant ethical factor in the Michigan SHPO office and in most others with which I am familiar. There is always a certain "background" level of pressure exerted by local politicians and project sponsors, usually because they are unfamiliar with and fear the review and compliance process, but large municipalities and major federal agencies in most cases routinely carry out their legally prescribed roles. In those cases where a determination of eligibility must be sought from the Keeper of the National Register of Historic Places, the SHPO archaeologist's opinion is only one of three opinions being expressed on the significance of the site, the other two being those of the contracting archaeologist who discovered, analyzed, and presented the site in a report to the client and the SHPO and the archaeologist at the National Register. Each of these archaeologists is somewhat insulated from pressure because it is not his opinion alone that determines whether or not a site is significant and therefore whether or not it will require mitigation. I am not aware of any state where the SHPO archaeologist also performs contract work which he would then have to review.

What has been the Native American reaction to archaeological site preservation in Michigan? In the main they have expressed no interest in archaeology or site preservation except in those very few cases where burials have been excavated in emergency salvage excavations. Professional archaeologists in Michigan have had a moratorium for at least fifteen years on the excavation of burials except those discovered accidentally or during construction. For a number of years I represented the Department of State on the Interagency Advisory Council to the Michigan Commission on Indian Affairs. It was clear from the attitudes and opinions expressed that, while Native American history and culture were of great importance to them, archaeology and historic preservation ranked very low as concerns or as perceived sources of useful information to contemporary Native American groups. Active attempts to involve Native Americans with the interpretation and preservation of sacred sites such as pictographs and petroglyphs have had only lukewarm success. George Cornell summarized an educated Native American's point of view on archaeology when he stated:

> The existence of Native American populations in the Americas has always been of interest to European and contemporary scholars. It should be clearly stated, however, that native peoples do not always subscribe to academic interpretations of their respective histories and beliefs. For centuries scholars have been attempting to theoretically explain the origins of American Indians. In contrast, it should be remembered that native peoples have formalized traditions which describe their existence in diverse regions. American Indians explain their life and past as an act of creation rather than as a stage in evolutionary theory. All peoples have the undeniable right to spiritual interpretations of life and purpose. These beliefs are the very core of Native American societies and must be considered as viable alternatives to continually changing "scientific" explanations. (Cornell 1986:v)

In retrospect, we appear to have erected a legal Maginot Line which, as was the case with the original, could be easily outflanked, in this case, by site looters. Many of these individuals never would have thought of coming to us in the first place. They did not want us to know where sites are! They got their starts as hobbyists walking plowed fields looking for artifacts. They simply developed their own information bases and cultivated sympathetic landowners, in much the same way that professional archaeologists have done. Some collectors will even pay landowners for the right to collect on their land.

Much information was already available in the form of site reports, surveys, and even old history books. The Matthews site, an early nineteenth-century aboriginal cemetery in Clinton County, Michigan, was discovered and excavated by a collector armed only with local history books and a metal detector (Cleland 1972).

Shipwrecks, a distinctive kind of archaeological site common in Michigan's Great Lakes, pose a special problem. Although they are legally state property (Halsey 1985), they hold a fascination for divers and nondivers alike. Shipwrecks of any age also are very difficult to protect (Halsey and Martindale 1987). There are countless books devoted to tales of ships and their losses, and such works often come complete with locational information, for example, *Lake Superior's "Shipwreck Coast"* (Stonehouse 1985). The Midwest Explorers League publishes dive charts for each of the Great Lakes, with shipwreck locations marked and thumbnail sketches given of each wreck. The chart for Lake Superior notes, for example, in its description of the USS *Essex,* "Divers are fond of her copper spikes" (Ackerman 1983).

Shipwrecks, unlike land sites, are almost entirely the province of sport divers because there are few practicing underwater archaeologists in Michigan or the Great Lakes area as a whole. There has been a very interesting evolution in sport diver attitudes over the last twenty years. In the 1960s, wrecks were viewed as sources of nautical memorabilia or personal mementos of having dived on a particular wreck. Eventually, it became obvious that wrecks stripped to the bare hull of all removable equipment were much less interesting places to visit. By the 1970s many divers and charter-boat operators were willing to support legislation restricting salvage and, by 1988, were demanding legislation which made it a felony to remove artifacts from wrecks in certain protected areas. Without significant input from the professional archaeological community, divers, charter-boat operators, and state officials crafted a state law recognized throughout the United States as one of the toughest and most protective of the shipwreck resource (Halsey 1989). At the same time, it guarantees public access to the sites for recreational and other nondestructive uses.

Since archaeologists seldom conceal the locations of sites they publish in monographs or journal reports, it appears that state law is really only protecting new, often very small and sometimes deeply buried sites discovered during review and compliance surveys. It is a rare site these days that is on or near the ground surface and is significant, but was not previously known to collectors. In reality, we have only been fending off persons too lazy to do their own research.

Besides site locations, does the Bureau of History have any other archaeological/anthropological secrets to keep? Surely you might think, there are all sorts of details relating to contracts and bids for archaeological fieldwork. This is not the case. The bureau has never involved itself in the details of agreements between a client and an archaeological contractor unless the state itself was to be a party to or a beneficiary under the contract. This happens only on such state-funded projects as highways or fieldwork on state-owned archaeological or historical sites. Information on bids or proposals is exemptible from disclosure only until the time for the public opening of proposals or until the time for receipts of bids or proposals has expired. Moreover, the law has specifically stated that information in a bid, such as an archaeologist's hourly service rate, cannot be considered some sort of financial trade secret (Public Act 442 of 1976; Michigan Compiled Laws Annotated 15.231).

Similarly, all correspondence relating to the bureau's review and compliance activities are public documents. As long as a requester can identify a describable document, we will have to provide it. For example, Contractor A could write to our office and say, in effect, "I want copies of all letters in which you have required a municipality, consultant, etc., to perform an archaeological survey or be allowed to examine such letters." We would have to comply, but are not obligated to provide his competitors with this information unless they ask for it. Neither would we be obligated to tell competitors that Contractor A has requested these documents. The important thing to remember is that the law requires the release of existing *documents,* rather than mere information (Bozen 1984). In other words, we are not obliged to respond to informational requests, or to create a document to satisfy a Freedom of Information request, but we must furnish those documents we already have.

This examination of the history of the archaeological site filed in Michigan has touched on some, but certainly not all, of the major ethical problems examined at length in a volume edited by Ernestene L. Green, *Ethics and Values in Archaeology* (1984). It has revealed that many traditional university-based archaeologists found it difficult, at least at first, to work with archaeologists in nontraditional (that is, nonteaching) positions in government and private industry. There have been times when each side has retreated to stereotyped visions of one another: ivory tower academics unable to adapt to the demands of contemporary archaeology; unimaginative, rule-bound, nine-to-five bureaucrats; private contractors who do cut-rate, low quality archaeology. Fortunately, in Michigan the archaeological community is small enough and the good will is strong enough to allow us to air these false images and, occasionally, even to punch some holes in them with laughter. Unfortunately, like the racist words we learned as children, we never seem able to entirely dispense with them. Contemporary archaeology has grown so large that it needs representatives in many places where archaeologists did not previously exist. The archaeologist is an adaptable creature and has found many new niches.

The relationship of archaeologists to the Native American community is similar to that found in many states. Few Native Americans will publicly admit that archaeologists contribute anything worthwhile to the understanding of their recent or distant ancestors. Few archaeologists have undertaken to learn specifically of contemporary Native American questions about their past and provide specific useful or interesting answers to these questions. The conflict over repatriation of artifacts and reburial of human skeletal remains has yet to reach the level in Michigan that it has in California, Nebraska, and South Dakota. Proposed legislation in Michigan addresses these problems among others. Of course, we recognize that legislation is not a panacea for what is essentially a conflict of different world views between Native Americans and archaeologists. Nevertheless, it is heartening, for the purposes of this presentation, to note that Wisconsin's burial site protection law, nationally acclaimed as a model for dealing with burial site issues (W. Green 1987), has at its core, a burial site catalog, a site file. In the end, archaeologists and Native Americans in Wisconsin came to agree that it was essential to have a detailed, accurate, and professionally maintained record of burial places if the interests of both were to be served. I hope that this will also be the case in Michigan.

REFERENCES

Ackerman, Paul W.
> 1983   *Lake Superior dive chart: Shipwrecks located and identified.* Chicago: Midwest Explorers League.

Bigelow, Martha M.
> 1974   Activities of the Michigan History Division during 1973. *Michigan History* 58(1):54–96.

Bozen, Nicholas L.
> 1984   Access to state agency records—the myth of secret law. *The Michigan Bar Journal* 63:1030–32.

Brose, David S., and Patricia Essenpreis
> 1973   A report on a preliminary archaeological survey of Monroe County, Michigan. *The Michigan Archaeologist* 19:1–182.

Cleland, Charles E.
> 1972   The Matthews site (20CL61), Clinton County, Michigan. *The Michigan Archaeologist* 18:174–207.

Cornell, George L.
> 1986   The prehistoric roots of Michigan Indians. In *People of the Three Fires: The Ottawa, Potawatomi and Ojibway of Michigan,* by James A. Clifton, George L. Cornell, and James M. McClurken, iii–v. Grand Rapids, Mich.: The Grand Rapids Inter-Tribal Council.

Fitting, James E.
    1973   *The Michigan History Division computerized site file*. Memorandum to the Conference on Michigan Archaeology, 26 December.
Green, Ernestene L., ed.
    1984   *Ethics and values in archaeology*. New York: Free Press.
Green, William
    1987   Wisconsin's burial site protection law. *The Wisconsin Archaeologist* 68:75–85.
Greenman, Emerson F.
    1937   The Younge site: An archaeological record from Michigan. *University of Michigan, Museum of Anthropology, Occasional Contributions* 6.
    1939   The Wolf and Furton sites, Macomb County, Michigan. *University of Michigan, Museum of Anthropology, Occasional Contributions* 8.
Halsey, John R.
    1985   Michigan's underwater archaeology program. In Proceedings of the Sixteenth Conference on Underwater Archaeology, ed. Paul Forsythe Johnston, *Society for Historical Archaeology, Special Publication Series* 4:143–46.
    1989   Nine years before the mast: Shipwreck management in Michigan since 1980. In *Underwater Archaeology Proceedings from the Society for Historical Archaeology Conference*, ed. J. Barto Arnold III, 43–48.
Halsey, John R., and James L. Martindale
    1987   Sacking the inland seas: Shipwreck plundering in the Great Lakes. *Michigan History* 71(6):32–38.
Hinsdale, Wilbert B.
    1931   Archaeological atlas of Michigan. *Michigan Handbook Series* 4.
Kent, Barry C., Stephen G. Warfel, and Kurt W. Carr
    1985   Archaeological site survey and recording in Pennsylvania. *Pennsylvania Archaeologist* 55:54–56.
Michigan History Division
    1981   *Archaeological site file policies*. Lansing: Michigan Department of State.
National Park Service
    1977   National register of historic places and comprehensive statewide historic survey and plans: Criteria, determinations of eligibility and plans. *Federal Register* 42:47658–47668.
Peebles, Christopher S., and Deborah Bush Black
    1976   *The distribution and abundance of archaeological sites in the coastal zone of Michigan*. A limited distribution planning report by the Division of Great Lakes, University of Michigan Museum of Anthropology for the Michigan Department of State, and the Michigan Department of Natural Resources.
Stonehouse, Frederick
    1985   *Lake Superior's "Shipwreck Coast": A survey of maritime accidents from Whitefish Bay's Point Iroquois to Grand Marais, Michigan*. Au Train, Michigan: Avery Color Studios.

Editor's Introduction to Chapter 6

This chapter is jointly authored by an anthropologist, William Graves, and a sociologist, Mark Shields, and thus their contribution possesses a valuable interdisciplinary perspective. The chapter is, as the coauthors phrase it, "an unintended consequence" of two years of collaborative research on several different projects.

In an introduction that raises serious and profound questions regarding the intent and purpose of codes of ethics, the authors speak, perhaps, from the perspective of academic professionals who have spent more time in the field than in the classroom. They criticize the current codes that emphasize certain key words of "ethics talk" (to use Chambers's phrase), such as *control, harm,* and *protection.* Rather, they contend, the actual conditions of fieldwork and the often unanticipated consequences of research reveal the fundamental inadequacy of codes of ethics because they presume the absolute power of researchers.

A basic reconsideration of the contemporary character of social science inquiry and the role of the researcher is in order as a necessary first step in the rethinking of our professional codes of ethics. This is the challenge of the current era, to achieve a "more dialogic conception" of the character and function of social science research, one that rejects the traditional view of the omnipotence of the researcher in favor of more egalitarian values.

Throughout their provocative essay, the authors challenge us with such questions as, Can we protect the subjects of research?, even though that is a principle about which there is considerable consensus. They discuss a poorly known Supreme Court case involving political scientist Samuel

Popkin wherein the social scientist's right to protect his data was stripped away and he was rendered powerless to "protect" anyone, thus making canons of ethics talk such as "anonymity" and "confidentiality" apparent legal nonentities.

Graves and Shields discuss two separate research projects they worked on; in both cases they ask the question of whether the relationship between client and researcher is fail-safe and whether unanticipated outcomes of research *on both sides* are not only possible, but quite probable. Too much past discussion of ethics has involved attempts to assess harm and assign blame, and the authors see the need for a reformulation of research ethics that encompasses the relations that exist among researchers, sponsors, informants, and the general public. This is the needed "dialogue for a new era."

William Graves III and Mark A. Shields

Chapter 6 Rethinking Moral Responsibility in Fieldwork
The Situated Negotiation of Research Ethics in Anthropology and Sociology

> Thus dualism of social experience [being "controlled" vs. being "in control"] is central to our very existence in modern society. It is, therefore, central to all the forms of thought and work which articulate our experience of that society.
>
> —Alan Dawe 1978:365

Preliminaries

IN THE 1980S, there has been a resurgence of widespread interest in ethics, moral values, and accountability that, once again, raises difficult questions about the relationship between professional codes of ethics and actual research practices within the social sciences. As Donald Warwick's study shows (1980), most social scientists today will agree that attention to moral values and responsibility is an integral part of our collective professional identity. Furthermore, the sustained serious assaults on positivism, value-neutrality, and objectivity have shaken the epistemological foundations of all the social sciences, underscoring the importance of making the issues of value and the moral consequences of research central to our disciplines (cf. Asad 1973; Said 1978; Haan et al. 1983; Marcus and Fischer 1986).

But the matter is much more complicated than this. Among many social scientists there also appears to be a high degree of wary indifference to those who show a strong interest in ethics (Warwick 1980:37 and passim). Warwick found a fairly pervasive fear that too much attention to ethics both discourages practitioners from undertaking many types of research and legitimates the proliferation of questionable legal and political constraints on social science inquiry (Warwick 1980:39–40).

Such concerns are not at all new. They have been voiced since the first serious discussions of the institutionalization of our professional codes of ethics. In the early 1960s, Howard Becker was opposed to professional codes of ethics on the grounds that they could provoke premature and artificial closure of crucial issues that he felt should be openly debated on the same intellectual grounds as any other theoretical or substantive issue in the social sciences (1964). Becker feared that we were giving up debatable conceptual ground too easily. He warned that concepts of ethics should remain as much a puzzle to any serious social scientist as any other concept—ethics should not be defined by bureaucratic fiat.

On a more apocalyptic note, Robert Friedrichs (1970) argued that codes of ethics were little more than defensive and cosmetic responses to external legal and political attempts to control social science research and, perhaps, to undermine social science inquiry totally by denying researchers access to crucial resources. Friedrichs feared that we were all too willing to be sanctioned and that legal and political problems might result. He argued that we needed not codes of ethics but a radical theoretical overhaul of our conception of subjects of research.

In a painfully emerging post(neo?)-colonial world marked by myriad new challenges to entrenched systems of authority and control, both Becker and Friedrichs felt deeply that social scientists were gradually losing their voice; both felt that only a vigorous and open reconsideration of the nature and character of social science inquiry would resolve this problem. The passage of time has only served to sharpen the relevance of these types of objections to our codes of ethics. In spite of the fact that the social sciences have expressed a clear concern for moral responsibility by instituting professional codes of ethics, we have been since the 1970s in an increasingly weaker position to define and protect our own rights and interests in research—our voice—vis-à-vis our subjects, funders, sponsors, and the general public.

In spite of (or, perhaps, because of) all of our work to create mechanisms for guiding researchers and holding them accountable, the world beyond our disciplines continues to take its own defensive measures. Our own established systems of professional authority and control can no longer be taken for granted. It is not unusual for researchers to be denied access completely to certain research settings, to be held strictly accountable by nonprofessionals, or to have their credibility stiffly challenged on all fronts and at all levels. More than ever before, researchers are now subject to a much wider range of external constraints and sanctions than most of us clearly understand (cf. important discussions by Edsall 1975; Wax and Cassell 1979; Chambers 1980; Deloria 1980; Fetterman 1981a and 1981b; and Toulmin 1981).[1]

We have chosen Alan Dawe's quotation as our epigraph because it seems to characterize aptly a pervasive contemporary view of social life that informs much of our theory and practice. Indeed, we believe that our professional codes of ethics are based on, and our typical discussions of ethics reaffirm, a conceptualization of social life as a game of control, thus contributing to the growing influence of the view that conflict is an inevitable consequence of differences.

As commonly expressed in the domain of social science research ethics, this pervasive game of control *necessarily* entails the infringement of someone's "rights": "One person's rights limit the freedoms of others, and the more others are free to do what they wish, the narrower is the protection of rights" (Beauchamp and Pinkard 1983:2). As influential as such common-sense views may be, we find such conceptualizations of social life troubling. Furthermore, we have not found such orientations to *social research* to be either productive or desirable in routine practice. Therefore, we will attempt to make the case that the key ethical issue for social scientists today is the need to redirect our professional thinking and practice to definitions of moral responsibility that are based on a much more positive set of ideas than control, harm, and protection.

Drawing on the literature and on our combined past and present research activities, we will first argue that professional codes of ethics in the social sciences are founded on questionable presuppositions about the power and authority of researchers and the pragmatics of social science inquiry. We will contend throughout that both the "unacknowledged conditions" and the "unanticipated consequences" (Giddens 1979) of social science research chronically reveal the fundamental inadequacy of our professional codes of ethics because these codes presume unlimited powers of control by researchers.

Having argued that researchers have no privileged basis for presuming authority and control in field research, we will then suggest that the prevailing conditions, constraints, and sanctions on social science research should compel us to rethink questions of moral responsibility within the context of a more general reconsideration of the role of the researcher and the character of social science inquiry.

We will examine the practical and theoretical reasons for our claims and argue that both codification of professional ethics and critical discussions of "ethical dilemmas" should be recast within a broader, more dialogic conception of the character and functions of social science inquiry. By a "more dialogic conception" we mean a theoretical and methodological definition of social science inquiry that rejects traditional, dominant presuppositions of authority and control in favor of explicitly egalitarian values.

The Foundations of Ethics in the Social Sciences

Since the late 1960s, each of the social science disciplines has instituted a professional code of ethics covering research activities. Although each particular code of ethics reflects the specific character of its own disciplinary concerns, it is well-known that all professional codes of ethics in the social sciences, as well as the closely related federal regulations governing human subjects research, have been developed on the basic model of experimental, biomedical research (cf. Kelman 1978; Cassell 1980).

At the heart of the biomedical research model is a basic concern for the nature and consequences of the relationship between researcher and research subject. As Cassell (1980), Kelman (1978), and others have pointed out, in biomedical experimentation the research paradigm gives researchers both maximum control over subjects and maximum potential to harm them irreversibly. For this reason, "control," "power," and "harm" are the key concepts that have provided the explicit grounds for bioethical discourse, a discourse that is self-consciously concerned with protecting the subjects of research.

The same key concepts of control, power, and harm have provided the foundations for ethical discourse in the social sciences, too, for our persistent concern with such fundamental issues as deception, anonymity, confidentiality, and informed consent reveals a basic sense of duty to protect. As the newly minted Code of Ethics of the Association of Social Anthropologists (ASA) of the Commonwealth phrases it, "Anthropologists have a responsibility to anticipate problems and insofar as is possible to aim to resolve them without damaging the research participants or the scholarly community" (ASA 1988:523). However, the cautious tenor of this statement of ethical responsibility—"insofar as is possible" and "to aim to resolve"—its studied vagueness in identifying those who would be "damaged" ("research participants" and "the scholarly community") and the essential indeterminacy of the term *damaged* all reveal the crux of our dilemma. In contrast to the biomedical model of research, it is not at all clear in most forms of social science research who we are protecting, how we are protecting them, what we are protecting them from, or what constitutes the limits of our capacity to protect.

Ethics by Moral First Principles: Can We Protect the Subjects?

In the early days of fieldwork, serious pursuit of the "truth" required a little arm-twisting now and then. In the honest pursuit of truth, the Bureau of American Ethnology's Mathilda Cox Stevenson could bully her way into any kiva with the help of her sense of moral right and her trusty umbrella (Cushing 1979). Paul Radin was known to use privileged information obtained from one informant to coerce another into telling the truth (Radin 1970). Bronislaw Malinowski himself spoke of "socking a recalcitrant informant on the jaw" (Malinowski 1967). And James Clifford has cited Marcel Griaule at length to the effect that fieldwork was a process of digging out "secrets" from the "guilty" in the manner of the "police inspector" (Clifford 1988).

Of course, there have been worse cases of abuse than these; nevertheless, such anecdotes nicely illustrate the extent to which many researchers have subordinated the rights and interests of the peoples they studied to the rights and interests of science.

We live in markedly different times now. The great majority of social scientists today would find such an overtly manipulative and adversarial approach to research unacceptable. Furthermore, the rest of the world has found it unacceptable, too, so those who find such approaches acceptable employ them at their own risk. There are a number of well-publicized cases on recent record of researchers who have been made to pay in various ways for violating the rights of their subjects of research. In short, it would appear that the earlier authoritarian pragmatics of research has been reversed today in favor of a general ethic of "subjects first; science second."

Our codes of ethics in the various social sciences have been founded on this radical reversal of priorities. In an important overview of the basic principles of ethics in contrasting models of research, Cassell explicitly locates the focal point of ethical decision-making in the researcher's individual responsibility to preserve the autonomy and power of the subjects of research (1980). And even in the more recently formulated ethical guidelines, where complex contingencies are acknowledged and where explicit recognition is given to conflicting interests and perspectives in research, it is still assumed that the researcher alone must ensure that "subjects" are "protected" (cf. ASA 1988; National Association of Practicing Anthropologists [NAPA] 1988).

Thus, the message of our various professional codes of ethics is very clear—the rights and interests of science must never override the rights of the subjects of research, and it is the researcher's responsibility to ensure that they do not. Although there have been notable contemporary dissenters who argue that such a position entails shielding those who should be unmasked by "objective" social research (cf. Douglas; Galliher, in Bulmer 1982), we believe that the great majority of researchers are in agreement with this position.

However, the major difficulty with this ethical commitment to the subjects of research is that the researcher is often in no position to "protect" the subjects of social science research. Since the 1970s we have seen an increasing number of discussions that suggest that we can never know with certitude whose rights and interests are being served or whose are undermined when we undertake basic research (cf. Everhart 1975; Platt 1976; Deloria 1980; Punch 1986). These discussions emphasize the subordinate role the researcher often finds him- or herself playing vis-à-vis sponsors, funders, the legal system, and the media.

More profoundly, there has been a steady stream of recent critiques that the traditional research relationship and the authoritative perspective it entails can directly undermine the rights and the interests of the subjects of research (Asad 1973; Said 1978; Fabian 1983; Clifford 1988). These discussions focus on the dangers inherent in authoritatively "objectifying" and "representing" the people with whom we work and who serve as our collaborators in research. In other words, even with the purest of intentions there is always a danger that the researcher may mislead both him- or herself and the research participants into a false sense of control and security that is ultimately not warranted.

The consequences of a false sense of security can be disastrous. A most extreme instance of a misplaced sense of control and security has been reported by Appell (1978). He notes that Cora DuBois's key informants on Alor were beheaded by the Japanese for claiming that they were under United States protection because of their research relationship to DuBois (Appell 1978:270).[2] Although it is not likely that DuBois explicitly instructed her informants to expect protection of this kind, it still appears that her informants believed that the nature of their relationship with her entailed such privileges, power, and immunity. This raises serious questions about how DuBois understood her own authority, how she explained her presence and role to these people, and what kinds of reciprocal agreements she made with them during the course of her research.

Admittedly, the DuBois case is extreme and, we hope, very unusual. More typical are cases in which researchers assume that they are in a position to protect the subjects of research and explicitly promise such protection without fully understanding that they do not have the ultimate authority to do so. In such cases, the researcher may become an unwitting pawn in a dreadful contest of power and control that will affect the lives of the subjects of research. A dramatic and landmark case was Samuel Popkin's ordeal in the celebrated Pentagon Papers case (cf. Carroll 1973).

Popkin, a professor of political science specializing in Southeast Asia, was subpoenaed in 1972 by a federal grand jury investigating the so-called leak of the infamous Pentagon papers. Because of his academic position, his research interests, his professional contacts, and his extensive knowledge of the politics of the Vietnam War, federal authorities concluded that Popkin had knowledge of who leaked the papers to the press, how this was accomplished, and who had copies of the papers.

Popkin did testify to the grand jury, but he refused to answer seven specific questions designed to elicit the names of his sources of information about the leak. His defense, that answering such questions was a violation of his First Amendment rights, was rejected and Popkin was imprisoned for contempt. With the vigorous support of his colleagues and the professional social science associations, Popkin's case was pursued all the way to the Supreme Court. However, the Supreme Court refused to treat the case seriously, citing as precedent an earlier Court decision that *journalists* had no "special privileges."

Even though the obvious victim in this case appears to be Popkin himself, we must not lose sight of the fact that the system's target was not Popkin, but any information about others that could be gotten out of Popkin, with or without his cooperation. With respect to the potential disposition of Popkin's testimonies, research materials, and data, the implications of this Court decision should be clear. Although we do not know what steps the federal government actually took to gain access to Popkin's materials, it is clear that they had stripped him of legitimacy and rendered him powerless to protect anyone, least of all himself. At the same time, it is also clear that the federal authorities had both the authority and the power to seek out any materials in Popkin's possession and to appropriate them as evidence.

In the aftermath of the Popkin/Pentagon Papers case, the attorney for the American Political Science Association warned that social scientists did not have the constitutional right or the legal authority to guarantee "anonymity" or "confidentiality" to their research subjects (Carroll 1973). As long as the courts can rule that specific claims to anonymity or confidentiality are obstructive to the general public's "right to know," it is neither rational nor ethical for social scientists to make a priori claims to such rights and responsibilities regarding their research subjects (ibid., 272–80).

The Popkin case suggests that it is dangerously naive and patently unfair to elicit information from research subjects on the basis of some authoritatively delivered promise that the researcher alone will determine the ultimate disposition of recorded data. At the very least, both researchers and their research subjects should be wary of falling into the trap of presuming full autonomy with respect to the disposition of research data.

Finally, we must note that there are many research areas and settings that routinely require the researcher to identify carefully and negotiate cautiously conflicting commitments and responsibilities (cf. Everhart 1975; Clinton 1976b; Platt 1976; Punch 1986; ASA 1988). This is frequently the case in contract research, where unanticipated open conflict can emerge among the various definitions and interests of the researcher, the research subjects, and project sponsors/funders at any point during the course of the study.

In some cases, the researcher's perspective, interests, and activities may directly precipitate a conflict from which he or she becomes excluded, losing all further voice or control in the matter. In such extreme cases, the researcher's explicitly professed commitment to "protect" the subjects of research may have no bearing whatsoever on the final outcome of the conflict.

A MISPLACED SENSE OF CONTROL: A CASE STUDY

One of the authors was co-principal investigator in an ethnographic study of patterns of work and use of information resources among staff in a university support organization. The explicit purpose of the study was to provide information that would be of use to administrators in the planning and development of a centralized computing system to support staff work.

There was clear agreement among administrators, staff, and researchers that the value of the ethnographic research was to clarify the nature of work and information use from the perspective of nonadministrative staff. It was openly acknowledged by administrators and staff alike that the administration lacked the detailed comprehension of many aspects of staff work that they needed to understand to develop appropriate technological resources.

In addition to the usual agreements of confidentiality, anonymity, and researcher control over the data, there were agreements that all staff would be provided with copies of our final report and that a general meeting of staff and administrators would be held to discuss the final report. Thus, when we began our research, there were clear and open understandings that our function was to provide a detailed and systematic study that would serve as a resource to focus discussions and begin joint planning by administrative and nonadministrative staff.

When the first draft of the final report was submitted to a select group of administrators for initial comments, most of the administrators were interested and supportive. One administrator, however, directly challenged some of our crucial case-study materials, claiming that we had described work processes that were "in violation of standard procedures" and, therefore, "not representative."[3] When we stood our ground on the "representativeness" of our materials, this administrator challenged us "to prove it" by revealing our sources. We refused, of course, reminding the administrator of previous agreements that had been reached concerning confidentiality, anonymity, and control of the data.

The matter ended in uncomfortable silence and we were never challenged in this way again, but soon we were hearing persistent rumors that this same administrator had been "down on the floor" trying to identify individual staff members and taking measures to prevent future "violations of standard procedures." We responded by attempting to confirm these rumors so that we could discuss the matter openly, but no one among our original informants would admit that they had experienced any pressures at all as a result of our study.

We did discover from our research subjects, however, that the administration had never provided staff with copies of our final report and that there had been no further mention of a general meeting to discuss our findings. When we raised these issues with the administration, we were told that these things were "on the agenda." Six months passed and nothing happened, so we personally delivered copies of the final report to individual staff members, suggesting that they be passed around. We made it clear that we would be delighted to receive any and all responses, but no one ever responded.

Whether or not the troublesome rumors we had initially heard were true (and we had no way of establishing this), we came to understand that there would be little or no chance of our doing anything constructive to mediate a potentially explosive situation we had been instrumental in creating. Our research was finished and we were no longer recognized as players in the game. Both administrators and nonadministrative staff continued to be courteous and friendly to us, but no one seemed interested in involving us in further discussions and no one suggested the need for further research.

*   *   *

In spite of general acceptance of the ethical principle that the individual researcher bears the responsibility for protecting the rights and interests of the subjects of research, it is clear that in many cases it is unreasonable for the researcher to adopt this as a working assumption. On the one hand, it is unreasonable to presuppose that the researcher can be either omniscient or absolutely autonomous. As we have seen, there are too many unforeseen conditions and unpredictable consequences that may, at any time, nullify the researcher's professed commitment to protect.

On the other hand, professional codes of ethics, human subject review committees, and all of the other bureaucratic legitimating mechanisms of contemporary social science research can actually exacerbate the problem by lulling both the researcher and his or her research subjects into a false sense of unbreachable security. This happens quite easily when the researcher, having fulfilled all of the institutional review board requirements and having thoroughly discussed all of the key ethical issues with sponsors and subjects, convinced both him- or herself and the subjects of research that "everyone" is thoroughly protected. As we have attempted to show, there is no essential guarantee that such will be the case.

Ethics by Contract: Can We Protect the Research Relationship?

Cases of conflict like the one outlined above are undoubtedly common in all types of social science research, but they are endemic to applied research. This is because such research is most often undertaken for the express purpose of supporting administrative planning, policymaking, and development and, therefore, typically involves a focused diversity of understandings, interests, and perspectives that provides ample opportunity for debilitating conflict.

The common vehicle for clarifying relevant rights, responsibilities, and interests in such research contexts is the formal contract, which serves to sanction the reciprocal obligations between researcher and sponsor, rather than the informally negotiated agreements between researcher and subjects of research that are the traditional focus of our codes of ethics. Such agreements are usually based on the legal principle that the applied researcher is contracting to perform a professional service that must directly serve rights and interests deemed acceptable to the sponsor. In such an explicitly juridical research model, where rights and responsibilities are contractually specified between researcher and sponsor, the rights of the subjects of research or any other party potentially affected by the research are taken to be either identical to the rights and interests of the sponsor or subordinate to them.

In principle, at least, the contractual model of research offers a specific advantage that noncontracted, independent research normally does not—the explicit focus of ethical decision-making and control is *not* the researcher *alone* but the contract negotiation process itself. In most forms of researcher-initiated, noncontract research, the researcher has to secure permission and solicit cooperation from groups that may have no understanding of or vested interest in the work. In marked contrast to this, the contract researcher is offering a professional service in which the sponsor has a carefully defined vested interest. This, of course, provides the basis for negotiating the specific terms of the contract, for each party is in a strong position to make specific responsibility claims on the other.

Of course, it is still a generally accepted principle that it is unethical for a researcher to accept a research contract that directly threatens the actual subjects of research or any other third party (cf. NAPA 1988). Therefore, the contract researcher is in a much more difficult position than the noncontracted, independent researcher. The crucial ethical dilemma for the contract researcher is to decide *before* contracting to do research whether he or she can justify serving the specific rights and interests of a given sponsor, as well as to decide whether serving those rights and interests will violate the rights of other groups directly involved in the research (cf. NAPA 1988).

However, such teleological omniscience is hardly possible for either the researcher or the sponsor. Central to the problem of "knowing" is that there is no way of predicting what effect the researcher's feedback will have on the sponsor's understanding of his or her own rights and interests, or what the sponsor will actually do with that feedback. Even when researcher and sponsor have honestly negotiated a clear set of initial agreements acceptable to all, both sides may see each other and their respective rights and responsibilities in an entirely new light by the end of the research project. In our collective experience, it is typically unanticipated issues that emerge *during* the course of contractual research that create the greatest difficulties for all parties involved and raise the specter of unethical conduct.

EMERGENT CONFLICTS IN CONTRACT RESEARCH: A CASE STUDY

Our social science research group was a semiautonomous unit within a technology development institute on campus. Although the institute was our administrative home and served as a conduit for much of our funding, much of our research work was conducted independent of the development activities of the institute, and several of our projects did not involve the institute at all. At one point the institute acquired a high level of financial support from a major foundation and a significant amount of equipment from a major computer company to conduct a three-year educational development project in collaboration with campus faculty. One of the funders' requirements for this support was a full assessment of the development project, so the institute contracted with our social science research group to conduct this assessment.

From the beginning, both our research group and the institute's staff agreed that this would be an important development effort in educational computing and that this meant that the course of the development effort would have to be thoroughly documented and analyzed. It was further agreed that our research team's final assessment report was not to be an internal document—it was to be widely advertised and made publicly available upon request.

As time passed, however, this ambitious development project achieved high public visibility and raised equally high expectations for its success, not only on campus but within the software development world and academic computing circles. The project developers increasingly came to feel that the future of the institute depended on the success of this project and anxiety ran high when unforeseen difficulties and delays were encountered. As time went on, the institute administrators came to see this specific project as eclipsing all others in importance and as setting the future course for the institute as a whole.

As the assessment team, however, our research group held no stake in either the success or the failure of this project. Our job was to treat this project as a case study in educational software development and implementation. Documenting and analyzing day-by-day the apparent successes and failures were crucial to our goal of a thorough, detailed case study that would be of value to an audience interested in the benefits and the costs of educational computing.

In short, the emergent character of this specific project was changing the conditions of our previous collaborative efforts and was creating a context within which institute developers and administrators came to understand our assessment work differently from the way we understood it.

The extent to which our perspectives were diverging from common ground became openly acknowledged by both sides when the developers began to encounter difficulties in coordinating efforts with outside suppliers. How to handle these difficulties without jeopardizing these key relationships became a crucial issue for the developers, an issue that they were not eager to have our research team document in detail. From our perspective, however, these coordination difficulties were central to the entire course of the project and had to be carefully documented.

From the emergence of this specific issue to the end of the project, the institute administrators and developers came to believe that our research team was documenting issues that either were relatively unimportant or could be threatening to the future of the institute. From our viewpoint, although the institute was exercising no explicit censorship of our work, institute staff were attempting to guide the course of our research by selectively presenting to us some issues as important and others as unimportant or irrelevant.

The end of the project was marked by disagreements between the institute administrators and our research team over specific issues discussed in early drafts of our final report. And when the final report was finished and became publicly available, we were made to feel that the institute perceived it as a disappointment rather than as a positive contribution. Within a month of the public distribution of our report, the institute administrators had their staff compile a document that listed the many accomplishments of the institute's software developers and that cataloged the wide and positive publicity this project had enjoyed beyond the campus.

Within a few months following the appearance of our final report, our research group and the institute agreed to sever all formal ties and our group moved to a new administrative home within the university.

*　*　*

Cases such as this one (and we believe that this is not at all an unusual one) make it clear that researcher-sponsor joint reliance on the negotiated contract solution to the problem of moral responsibility is no more secure with respect to the actual consequences of research than researcher reliance on the professional code of ethics.

Even in the optimal case of initial consensus, when all parties have clearly defined what is important, necessary, or moral, there can never be a guarantee that all will continue to hold to the same definitions. We take this to be a pointed reminder that the process of social science research, as the process of social life in general, is bounded both by "unacknowledged conditions" and by "unintended consequences" of action that affect the character of the situated understandings of individual agents in a largely unpredictable manner (Giddens 1979).

It is in tacit recognition of this fact that our professional codes of ethics contain a great deal of vagueness and indeterminacy; it is a predictable consequence of this fact that there is now an extensive literature of grounded case studies, which calls for clarification of specific principles within our professional codes of ethics. However, we want to stress that it is apparently not in our power as ordinary social beings to create anticipatory or predictive mechanisms (whether the codes of ethics or the juridical contract) that transcend this essential boundedness of social life.

Let the burden of proof fall on those who believe otherwise, for we have yet to see any theoretical model in the social sciences that can work such analytic magic on daily life; nor have we seen a professional code of ethics that predicts and allows for the resolution of all dilemmas; nor have we seen a contract that could not be hotly disputed. The problems we face in the area of ethics are elemental and essential, but we do not so much need better professional codes and clearer contracts as we need to rethink the epistemological foundations of social science research as these bear directly on issues of moral responsibility.

Toward a Dialogic Conception of Moral Responsibility

We believe that the traditional treatment of ethics as a professional, disciplinary issue has served to reinforce an unacceptable set of assumptions about the character of social science inquiry and the role of the researcher vis-à-vis the world beyond the academic disciplines. Furthermore, we believe that resolving the fundamental dilemmas that have motivated our codes of ethics depends on our willingness and abilities to reconceptualize our relationship to the world beyond the academic disciplines.

It may seem to many that the nature and function of a professional code of ethics is a concern with our own disciplinary practices rather than the practices of those outside the disciplines. On what grounds, it might be objected, could the social sciences sit in judgment on the practices of funders, sponsors, and research subjects? And by what authority could we make such judgments meaningful and efficacious?

In answer to such questions, we would answer that we *already* routinely sit in judgment on all those directly and indirectly involved in our research, just as they sit in judgment on us. From the moment we begin to formulate research questions, methodologies, and practical strategies to the moment we submit reports or manuscripts for publication, we are constantly making ethical judgments and moral choices as an integral feature of the negotiated character of our relationships with "others."

It is no secret that the activities of social science inquiry, from choosing a research topic to disseminating the final results, are all socially negotiated activities that succeed or fail on the basis of reciprocal moral agreements between "us," sponsors, funders, gate-keepers, and subjects of research. At a bare minimum, "we" and "they" must accept, even if only contingently, that each side is willing and able to accept the other's representation of her- or himself. In other words, "we" and "they" must take each other to be moral agents, essentially, and be willing to constitute an ongoing dialogue on that basis and on that basis alone. Such a dialogue must involve a reciprocally constituted and shared notion of moral responsibility.

So far we have attempted to make two major points. First, that our professional codes of ethics entail that we make promises to other people that we are in no privileged position to keep. As we have attempted to show, this is a consequence of having the researcher alone bear the responsibility for ethical decision-making, as if the researcher had the power and authority to control the research process independently of the knowledge, belief, and actions of all others involved in that process. In the preceding sections, we have tried to show why we think this is an unreasonable basis for defining moral responsibility in social science research.

The second point we have tried to make is a more important one, we believe. Simply shifting the focus of ethical decision-making from the researcher alone to the cooperative relationship between researcher and "others" still does not necessarily resolve our ethical dilemmas. In principle, the cooperative focus of the contract agreement does provide a more promising mechanism for defining moral responsibility as a concern shared by all parties to the research agreement, rather than a concern defined and controlled by the researcher alone.

Nevertheless, through examination of a specific case study of contract research gone awry, we have attempted to show that social science research is a social process that often involves shifts and changes in the understandings of participants through time under changing conditions of work. This means that initial consensual agreements may very well come to be contested, perhaps even rejected, by some or by all.

In the past, too many of our discussions of ethical dilemmas in research have involved attempts to assess harm and to assign blame. This follows quite logically from presuming that research, like the social life in which it is embedded, is a deterministic game of control in which one agent's gains result in another's losses. However, if we have successfully made our point that social science research essentially involves a continuous dialogue of a shifting plurality of moral definitions and that, for that reason, the moral consequences of research are essentially unpredictable, then perhaps our discussions of moral responsibility and ethics in research should begin not with assumptions of harm and blame but with honest attempts to understand and to accommodate a plurality of perspectives and definitions in our research, theoretical models, and codes of ethics. Stated bluntly, if our research requires that people outside our disciplines grant legitimacy to our professional interests, perspectives, and definitions, then we must work harder to grant legitimacy to theirs.

Nothing is to be gained, and much lost, by understanding the case studies we have presented in this paper in terms of blame, harm, or control. In our first case study, who is to be blamed for the fact that outside researchers presented an analysis of an organization that a responsible administrator interpreted as evidence that something was wrong in his own organization? In our second case study, who is to be blamed for the fact that the changing conditions of a crucial development project led researchers and administrators to understand the significance of social research in different terms?

What we are calling for is a reconceptualization of social research ethics that is grounded in a more compelling theory of research-as-social-action—one that entails a more dialogic notion of the relations among researchers, sponsors, informants, and the general public, rather than one that rests uncritically on notions of control, harm, and protection.

Habermas's theory of "communicative rationality" points in the right direction because of its insistence on the inherently discursive processes of raising and redeeming "validity claims" that constitute all social interaction (Habermas 1984). From a slightly different perspective, Bakhtin's conception of social life as a "polyphony of voices" is valuable because of its insistence on the importance of accommodating multiple perspectives without reducing the complex "dialogic" fabric of social life to a uniform, "monologic," authoritarian explanation (Bakhtin 1981).

We want to suggest that such discursive and dialogic theories of social process are both valuable and useful because they can provide the basis for conceptualizing ethical decision-making in social research as an ongoing, multivocal process through which researchers, sponsors, and informants search for mutual (if ambiguous) understandings of their respective interests, relationships, and responsibilities in the research context. Such a conception of ethical decision-making could replace prevailing conceptions that either focus too one-sidedly on the responsibilities of the researcher to "others" or seek to employ the contract as a means of control.

ACKNOWLEDGMENTS

The basic perspective and many of the specific ideas in this chapter emerged as unintended consequences of a two-year period of intensive fieldwork and research conducted jointly by the authors. As members of a larger research team during that period, we gratefully acknowledge the generous support provided to our team by the Annenberg/CPB Corporation, the IBM Corporation, and the Pew-Memorial Trust. However, the views presented in this paper are the authors' alone. Consonant with the theoretical position taken in this paper, we recognize that the views of our funders, sponsors, subjects, and research-team colleagues may differ from our own. This would have been a much less coherent chapter without the clear editorial guidance of Carolyn Fluehr-Lobban.

NOTES
   1. We do not intend to enter into a discussion here of the great range of pitfalls and dangers for the researcher today. Suffice it to note that they are many and diverse, ranging from a bewildering array of federal regulations and laws (Wax and Cassell 1979; Chambers 1980) to the "revenges" of articulate "research subjects" (Deloria 1980). See also Bell and Roberts (1984) for an interesting but somewhat depressing collection of articles that testifies to the intensifying political and eco-

nomic pressures social researchers in the United Kingdom face today. Finally, see Punch (1986) for an unusual but enlightening autobiographical account of a researcher fighting bitterly to extricate himself from a complex web of political constraints and legal sanctions that he believes have closed off certain research options and have deprived him of his right to be heard in authoritative fora.

2. Needless to say, we agree completely with Appell in his rejection of recent arguments that subjects of social science research cannot be "harmed" in the same sense as biomedical subjects (cf. contra Reynolds 1972). We think that Cassell (1980) clouds this crucial issue in her critique of the risk/benefit calculus of federal regulations by implying that such "harms" do occur while also claiming that we have no strong evidence of them. Clearly, we must presuppose that harm, in its strongest sense, to research subjects is *always* a potential consequence of social science research. As a fundamental conceptual and methodological issue, we believe it is dangerously naive to assume otherwise. On the other hand, for reasons we discuss in detail below, we find it unreasonable to assume that researchers alone should bear the responsibility for harm.

3. This seems to be a classic instance of what Howard Becker called the "hierarchy of credibility" (1967). Becker argued that it was a basic principle of complex organizations that high-level administrators naturally assumed that the "view from the top" of the organization was the "correct" view; thus, researchers attempting to present any other view would be accused of getting the partial and uninformed view—the "incorrect" view. Although we have seen this principle at work in other studies of complex organizations, in all fairness to the administrative sponsors of our research, we must stress that not all of the administrators connected to our study agreed with the attitude of the particular individual under discussion in this case.

REFERENCES

Appell, G. N.
     1978   *Ethical dilemmas in anthropological inquiry: A case book.* Waltham, Mass.: Crossroads Press.
ASA (Association of Social Anthropologists of the Commonwealth)
     1988   Association of social anthropologists of the commonwealth ethical guidelines for good practice. *Current Anthropology* 29(3):522–27.
Asad, T., ed.
     1973   *Anthropology and the colonial encounter.* London: Ithaca Press.
Bakhtin, M. M.
     1981   *The dialogic imagination.* Austin: University of Texas Press.
Beauchamp, Tom L., and Terry P. Pinkard, eds.
     1983   *Ethics and public policy: An introduction to ethics.* Englewood Cliffs, N.J.: Prentice-Hall.
Becker, H.
     1964   Letter to editor: Against the code of ethics. *American Sociological Review* 29:409–10.
     1967   Whose side are we on? *Social Problems* 14(3):239–47.

Bell, Colin, and Helen Roberts, eds.
1984   *Social researching: Politics, problems and practices*. London: Routledge and Kegan Paul.
Bulmer, Martin, ed.
1982   *Social research ethics*. London: Allen and Unwin.
Carroll, J. D.
1973   Confidentiality of social science research sources and data: The Popkin case. *PS* 6:268–80.
Cassell, Joan
1980   Ethical principles for conducting fieldwork. *American Anthropologist* 82(1):28–41.
Chambers, Erve
1980   Fieldwork and the law: New contexts for ethical decision making. *Social Problems* 27(3):330–41.
Clifford, James
1988   *The predicament of culture*. Cambridge, Mass.: Harvard University Press.
Clinton, C. A.
1976a   The anthropologist as hired hand. *Human Organization* 34:197–204.
1976b   On bargaining with the devil: Contract ethnography and accountability in fieldwork. *Anthropology and Education Quarterly* 8:25–29.
Cushing, Frank H.
1979   *Zuni: Selected writings of Frank Hamilton Cushing*. Lincoln: University of Nebraska Press.
Dawe, Alan
1978   Theories of social action. In *A history of sociological analysis,* ed. T. Bottomore and R. Nisbet, 360–417. New York: Basic Books.
Deloria, V.
1980   Our new research society: Some warnings to social scientists. *Social Problems* 27(3):265–71.
Edsall, J. T.
1975   Scientific freedom and responsibility: Report of the AAAS Committee. *Science* 188:687–93.
Everhart, R. B.
1975   Problems of doing fieldwork in educational evaluation. *Human Organization* 34(2):205–15.
Fabian, Johannes
1983   *Time and the other: How anthropology makes its object*. New York: Columbia University Press.
Fetterman, D. M.
1981a   Guilty knowledge, dirty hands, and other ethical dilemmas: The hazards of contract research. In *Ethnography in educational evaluation,* ed. D. Fetterman. Beverly Hills, Cal.: Sage Publications.
1981b   New perils for the contract ethnographer. *Anthropology and Education Quarterly* 13:71–83.

Friedrichs, R. W.
    1970   Epistemological foundations for a sociological ethic. *American Sociologist* 5:138–40.
Giddens, Anthony
    1979   *Central problems in social theory.* Berkeley: University of California Press.
Haan, N., R. N. Bellah, P. Rabinow, and W. M. Sullivan, eds.
    1983   *Social science as moral inquiry.* New York: Columbia University Press.
Habermas, Jürgen
    1984   *The theory of communicative action.* Boston: Beacon Press.
Karp, I., and M. B. Kendall
    1982   Reflexivity in fieldwork. In *Explaining human behavior,* ed. P. Secord, 249–73.
Kelman, Herbert C.
    1978   Review of behavioral research. In *Encyclopedia of bioethics,* Vol. 5, ed. W. T. Reich, 1470–81.
Malinowski, Bronislaw
    1967   *A diary in the strict sense of the term.* New York: Harcourt, Brace and World.
Marcus, G., and M. Fischer, eds.
    1986   *Anthropology as cultural critique.* Chicago: University of Chicago Press.
NAPA (National Association of Practicing Anthropologists)
    1988   National Association of Practicing Anthropologists' ethical guidelines for practitioners.
Platt, J.
    1976   *The realities of social research.* London: Sussex University Press.
Punch, Maurice
    1986   *The politics and ethics of fieldwork.* London: Sage Publications.
Radin, P.
    1970   *The Winnebago tribe.* Lincoln: University of Nebraska Press.
Reynolds, P. D.
    1972   On the protection of human subjects and social science. *International Social Science Journal* 24:693–719.
Rynkiewich, Michael, and James Spradley, eds.
    1976   *Ethics and anthropology: Dilemmas in fieldwork.* New York: Wiley.
Said, Edward W.
    1978   *Orientalism.* New York: Pantheon.
Toulmin, S.
    1981   *The tyranny of principles.* New York: The Hastings Center Report (December): 31–39.
Warwick, D. P.
    1980   *The teaching of ethics in the social sciences.* New York: The Hastings Center.
Wax, M. L., and J. Cassell, eds.
    1979   *Federal regulations: Ethical issues and social research.* Boulder, Colo.: Westview Press.

Part III

Diverse Voices in the Dialogue for a New Era

Editor's Introduction to Chapter 7

Erve Chambers joins this volume as a past president of the Society for Applied Anthropology (SfAA) and as an outspoken commentator on the post–Vietnam War state of anthropology and the issue of ethics. He brings to this essay an important set of insights stemming from the long-standing history of the involvement of the SfAA with various issues of ethics and professionalism.

It is, perhaps, neither well-known nor appreciated that the first anthropological code of ethics was developed in 1948 from within the SfAA, just seven years after its founding and a full two decades before the American Anthropological Association took any formal action regarding ethics. As pioneers in establishing standards of ethical behavior in the social sciences, Chambers notes that applied anthropologists have always played a key role in shaping ethical positions and commitments for anthropology. In reviewing the SfAA code of 1948 and comparing it with subsequent statements and codes (see Appendixes in this volume), it is clear that the first code of ethics articulated and framed the major issues that were of concern then and are of concern now.

Chambers's chapter focuses on the nature of the discourse that has surrounded the ethics issue and he points to the similarities in language that have come from opposing sides. Indeed, there appears to be a belief in language: that by changing words in a code of ethics, changes in behavior will result. Moreover, Chambers holds that a *real* community of anthropologists, to which the carefully worded code of ethics is aimed, does not exist. "Ethics talk" serves the purpose of facilitating a kind of community solidarity, which has fostered interprofessional competition, creating "good guys" and "bad guys." The "bad guys" of the 1960s and 1970s were applied anthropologists who worked for governments, and some of that stigma carries over into the current period.

Chambers is concerned that narrow interpretation of the PPR can limit employment opportunities that anthropologists seek. He explores the needed balance between ethical responsibility to subjects of research as well as sponsoring clients. He upholds the general consensus regarding confidentiality that is found in the codes of both the AAA and SfAA. Perhaps his most controversial point is his placement of the condemnation and restriction of secret or proprietary research squarely within the politicized context of the Vietnam War.

Chambers sets the record straight on a number of issues involving applied anthropologists. First, he believes they have been the pacesetters in the ethics field within anthropology, and have been wrongfully labeled "bad guys." Second, it is wrong to assume that the current debate over ethics stems *solely* from the employment crisis and the increasing numbers of anthropologists turning to applied anthropology. The ethical dilemmas of today, while in need of a full exploration in light of contemporary world realities, are much the same as those articulated more than four decades ago. Too often polemics cloud the issues that might better be confronted in more reasoned dialogue.

Chapter 7 Acceptable Behaviors
The Evolving Ethos of Ethics Talk

Introduction

IN HIS STORY "Before the Law," Franz Kafka offers the following exchange:

> "I don't agree with that point of view," said K., shaking his head, "for if one accepts it, one must accept as true everything the doorkeeper says. But you yourself have sufficiently proved how impossible it is to do that."
>
> "No," said the priest, "it is not necessary to accept everything as true, one must only accept it as necessary."
>
> "A melancholy conclusion," said K. "It turns lying into a universal principle."

During the 1980s, both the American Anthropological Association (AAA) and the Society for Applied Anthropology (SfAA) have considered revisions to their positions on ethics and professional responsibility. The amount of interest and controversy these attempts have engendered is surprising to some and seems inadequate to others. Among the issues raised have been a number that are generally held to relate most to the requirements of applied anthropology. It has been argued that changes in our ethical positions are needed to accommodate the "recent" professional situation of applied and practicing anthropologists. Such an accommodation has sometimes been viewed as a compromise and weakening of our ethical position. This is an unfortunate approach to the problem. However we might debate the wisdom of specific kinds of revision, it is important to understand that the concerns of applied anthropologists arise not from a willingness to compromise our ethics but from a clear if somewhat different realm of professional and moral experience. Their suggestions are, in other words, meant to strengthen and diversify rather than diminish the ethical position of anthropology. Further, these concerns on the part of some applied anthropologists are not recent but are part of a lengthy engagement in such matters. Applied anthropologists have, through the years, played their parts as both the doorkeepers and outsiders to the keeping of professional ethical standards.

The 1948 Code of Ethics

Shortly before her death, Margaret Mead (1978) summarized her thoughts concerning professional ethics in anthropology. Since Mead was a participant in the creation of the first professional code of ethics for anthropologists developed in the United States (Mead et al. 1949), her contribution to the debate is a valuable resource. First, in discussing the origins of the 1948 code of the Society for Applied Anthropology, Mead alludes to a period in which the involvement of anthropologists in practical matters leaned heavily toward activities which might well be ethically suspect, but not necessarily ethically wrong, if judged by subsequent codes. The large part of the applied work of this time was done as direct involvement in the World War II effort, or on the behalf of American business and industry, or as a part of the United States' supervision of its newly acquired overseas territories.

Mead cites three major challenges to the 1948 code:

It was criticized as being too cold and uncommitted by the advocates of Sol Tax's Action Anthropology. . . . in the 1950s, by those who felt that dynamic equilibrium was a characteristic of closed systems during the expansionist days of early space exploration, when the emphasis was on space as an open system (at the Pittsburgh meeting of the SfAA in 1961), and as lacking political partisanship during the polarizations of the late 1960s and early 1970s. (1978:432)

Mead defends the original code against these criticisms, arguing that they have led to unnecessary division within the field and, mincing few words, that they are the result of professional naiveté:

those who are quickest to denounce their fellow anthropologists for ethnocentrism and imperialism. . . . are also the least likely to be sophisticated about their own cultural biases. So, I regard the uproar that has gone on and continues to go on within the anthropological community primarily as a sign of a lack of sophistication and an inability to establish any real group solidarity. (1978:436)

This is an interesting point to begin further discussion of ways in which the concerns of some applied anthropologists might be included in our most recent deliberations concerning ethical standards. Whether or not we agree with Mead's assessment, it is important to recognize that the issue is not simply one of either incorporating or rejecting the ethical issues that have arisen from a renewed interest in applied anthropology and practice. Rather, applied anthropologists have always played a major role in helping shape our ethical commitments—from having provided the first written code in our country and pioneering among the social sciences to having participated fully in all the subsequent criticisms of that code and its several revisions.

Contemporary readers of the SfAA's 1948 code of ethics should be struck with its essential similarity to all subsequent codes and their revisions. With the exception of a long statement concerning the necessity of viewing societies in "dynamic equilibrium," referred to above by Mead, the "talk" of the 1948 code is very much like the talk of later codes. For the most part, the changes that have occurred are changes in emphasis. The 1948 code and its earliest major revision (SfAA 1963) tend, for example, to give priority to the anthropologist's obligation to Science (the only "constituency" capitalized in the 1963 code). Current codes give first mention to our obligations to the subjects of research. Changes such as these reflect the altered historical sensitivities of our work. It seems codes can be significantly revised in two ways. The most usual is simply to shift priorities. The other way would be to change the nature of the talk itself. Why this talk is so rarely changed is the major subject of the following discussion.

Ethics Talk

With some specific exceptions, anthropologists talk about ethics using pretty much the same words, expressing fairly often the same ideas, and holding some of their colleagues in contempt with just about equal voracity. We tend to agree that anthropologists should do good work which benefits humankind and does no harm. But there is clearly a difference between what is actually said (or meant to be said) when we start discussing ethics and the shared discourse by which we say it. That we can disagree so thoroughly and yet use very similar words to defend our positions is indication that what is being said arises from conditions that may have less to do with the laboriously negotiated and circumspect wording of our ethical statements than they do with the overall phenomena of our professional discourse. In this sense, these conditions are not simply about determining right from wrong behavior. They are a part of virtually unavoidable tensions within a professional dynamic. There are several such conditions which impinge on our discussions.

The first condition is the recognition that our ethics talk, as it is codified, does not always correspond to our ethical behavior. When events give rise to this realization there is renewed concern for professional ethics. The sense that some of our colleagues might have engaged in activities that we feel are unethical often leads to a demand that we change our codes to account for these instances. Similarly, the sense that our codes inappropriately limit or constrain some of our professional activities can lead to a suggestion that our codes be revised in order to permit such activities. On the face of it, these are reasonable expectations and seem healthy in that they *appear* to recognize that our values change over time and in response to new exigencies, and that these changes necessitate revisions in our ethical codes. The talk, however, is rarely about changing values and situational ethics—it is nearly always in reference to what the speakers hold to be absolute values. The intent of most ethics talk, once it passes beyond a stage of gossip, is to turn specific instances of behavior into general principles of behavior. Thus, ethics talk is used to address specific aberrations or omissions in ethical behavior, and this talk results in attempts to revise ethical codes. The revision, curiously, is often little more than a repetition and reemphasis of our already codified general principles. What is going on here?, we might ask.

There are several possible interpretations. In part, our ethics talk moves quickly from specific instances of behavior to general principles meant to govern behavior, because in most instances we have neither the inclination nor the clearly established authority to censure specific behavior. In anthropology, our ethical codes are heavily invested in principles of moral authority (more so perhaps than the codes of most other professions) because many of us tend to believe in a moral universe in which values mold behavior. When we begin to consider revisions in our ethical codes, it is seldom the actual principles that are under attack; rather, it is those specific behaviors that ought not to have occurred but which we seem unable or unwilling to address directly. The function of most ethics talk, then, is largely to reinforce those principles upon which we tend to agree, even though we might disagree as to the interpretation of specific instances of behavior. In other words, troublesome ethical behaviors create professional wounds which are healed by appeals to the moral authority of our ethics codes. However, because we are of a larger society that believes strongly in change and reform, and because we are *a community of professionals who are in competition,* the language of ethics talk is generally expressed as a need to revise rather than celebrate our principles, even though most of our talk does end up celebratory rather than revisionary. This should not surprise us. We have observed and noted similar phenomena in our study of human cultural systems around the world.

In this respect, a second condition to our discussions concerning professional ethics should not be surprising either. A concern for the development of principles of professional ethics assumes that there is a community of anthropologists to which these principles are applicable. It would be more accurate, however, to say that discussions of ethics are about trying to create and enforce the parameters of an imagined community of anthropologists. Thus, differences of opinion regarding our ethics find their language in competing claims for recognition and authority from within our profession. But this striving for recognition and authority is meaningful only so long as we can continue to believe in the community to which it refers—a community that is illusionary in the sense that, rather than creating its parts, it is continually reconstituted by its parts. To maintain the illusion of community, which is necessary if we are to support both competition and meaningful interaction among peers, we cannot afford to permit a specific competing claim to threaten a general principle of behavior that refers to the community as a whole. Thus, we talk the same way, using similar words, in order to maintain the belief that we have something to discuss and yet, within our competing spheres of activity, we often mean different things by the words we use.

These two conditions help explain why it does seem important to discuss revisions in our ethical principles. It is not because the result of those discussions will be a dramatic change in our final talk, which is the code we devise, but because the discussions themselves help maintain and reinforce the community out of which our ethical behaviors emerge. They enable us to interpret ethics talk and adjust ethical behaviors in light of changed circumstances and competition within our little community, even though their language is of a kind that preserves a sense of shared beliefs and absolute values.

One clue to understanding the relationship between interprofessional competition and ethics talk is found in making note of which kinds of ethical issues arise at particular times in the development of our profession. For example, the current tendency, in some sectors of our profession, to be highly critical of applied anthropology on ethical grounds derives in part from a couple of well-known events of the 1960s.[1] This criticism continues not only in relation to still unresolved issues within application, but also in relation to the increased visibility and growth of applied anthropology. On the other hand, it seems curious that no similar outrage emerged during the 1960s (or, for that matter, has yet emerged) in relation to how anthropologists, in their roles as teachers, behave toward their students—despite repeated claims within our lore of professors wrongfully using student research without attribution, knowledge of the sexual harassment of students, and rumors of similar abuses of professorial privilege and power.

Further Conditions of Ethics Talk

In considering the preceding conditions of ethics talk in anthropology, I have observed that such talk helps maintain solidarity while facilitating interprofessional competition. In these two senses, ethics talk is perceived as a closed system that is controlled by professional anthropologists. The idea that professionals are themselves the best judges of the ethics of their behavior has been with us at least since Durkheim (1957). Others have noted that codes of ethical behavior, while presumably intended to protect persons with whom professionals are in contact, are often invested with a tacit dimension in which the primary aim is to protect the profession from outsiders (Appell 1980; Kultgen 1988). The positioning of an inside and outside for ethical decision-making distorts the way we regard ethical problems because it forces us into a style of talk in which the events that give rise to ethical problems are located solely within domains of professional conduct. In reality, all ethical problems are situated in that realm of complex human activity that we sometimes refer to as the "real world"—necessarily, we abstract from this world in order to attempt to resolve our own problems, but in so doing we invariably alter the problem and limit the kinds of solutions that might be achieved (Chambers 1980).

An example can be found in the ways anthropologists have responded to recent government regulations regarding the protection of human research subjects. One response has been to argue that the regulations—pertaining to such matters as informed consent and the requirements for institutional review of research proposals—represent an unnecessary intrusion on the right of anthropologists to oversee their professional behavior. The basis of this argument is that fieldwork is a unique enterprise entailing trust between individuals and that the complex relations involved should not be dictated by bureaucratic fiat (Cassell 1980; Wax 1980). This is not an unreasonable argument. Still, other anthropologists have noted that "outside" regulation of social science research, including fieldwork, may sometimes be necessary simply to permit anthropologists to behave in a way they find ethical, especially as they become involved in more complex relations with research clients and sponsors who are not bound by the ethical standards of anthropology (Chambers and Trend 1981; Akeroyd 1984). Others have stated that federal concern for the protection of human subjects has encouraged them to review more critically their own ethical behaviors (Chrisman 1976).

The determination of ethical standards within a profession requires a distinction between insiders and outsiders. This distinction can also obtain *inter*professionally when, perhaps as a result of increased competition, one faction within a profession attempts to treat another as an outsider rather than as an insider. I have often wondered why so many of our colleagues persist in thinking of applied anthropology and its practice outside academia as something new and recently invented, whereas it clearly is not. One possibility, certainly pertinent to our current discussions of ethics, is that this attitude permits competitors to place application on the "outside" and therefore beyond the province of peer relationships—a phenomenon to be resisted rather than accommodated. In this way, the shortsighted notion that revisions in our current codes of ethics are being considered only in order to accommodate the "new" practical employment situations of applied and practicing anthropologists has become a rallying cry among those who are unsympathetic toward or biased against the idea of applied work—those who, in effect, would like to see applied anthropology outside the realm of accommodation, that is, not a part of the profession.

The definition of the "inside" of a profession is itself fluid, dynamic, and open to contention. Ethics talk is one major way of challenging, negotiating, and sometimes blurring these boundaries. It is a powerful mode of discourse because it evokes considerations of morality and notions of right and wrong behavior. By appealing to feelings of shame and guilt, often by implication rather than on the basis of clear evidence, ethics talk is a superior vehicle for inclusion and exclusion. It is much better, for example, than attempting to draw the line in terms of questions of theoretical orientation or research technique.[2]

Some Instances of Ethics Talk

Many dilemmas in professional ethics arise from interprofessional competition. Although they are often talked out in the terms of disagreements over stated principles of ethical codes, they develop much more often from a perception, if not an ironic appreciation, of the ways in which competing claims of moral authority are used selectively to interpret those principles. This is to say, again, that ethics talk arises out of the perceptions of specific behaviors (and now, it might be suggested, out of specific attitudes toward behaviors) that seem to distort or stand in violation of our general statements of ethics. The discussion so far can be illustrated by considering some of the interpretations that attend the most recent attempts to revise the ethical codes and standards of professional responsibility of two major professional organizations—the American Anthropological Association and the Society for Applied Anthropology.[3]

Both the AAA and the SfAA recognized a need to consider revisions to their ethical positions during the early 1980s. The changing employment situation of anthropologists has often been described as the impetus to this endeavor. As the idea of practicing anthropology outside academia received increased attention within our profession, conflicting sentiments arose. One issue has been whether some general types of employment lead to or encourage unethical behaviors. The counterissue has been whether specific interpretations of the ethics of anthropology unduly limit the employment possibilities of anthropologists. Both of these issues have been argued on the basis of appeals to the general ethics of our profession.

At this juncture, it is fair to note that my bias is on the side of those who are concerned with the ways in which our ethics codes have been used to attempt to exclude or discourage anthropologists from participating in broad areas of specific behaviors, in this case, kinds of nonacademic employment. This does not mean that I am unconcerned with the ethical dilemmas that arise from a broadening of our employment base. Once again, it is worth pointing out that the first ethics code of our profession was developed by applied and practicing anthropologists. At that time, the call for a general statement of ethical principles derived from a concern for the ways in which varied employment situations increase the probability of ethical dilemmas. The need for clear ethical guidelines is considerable in a subfield that relates so routinely to the expectations of others, and that is regularly threatened with the possibility of compromise. Standards of professional ethics not only help guide our behaviors on these occasions but also provide us with something tangible as we try to explain to our clients and employers why we cannot do certain things.

By the same token, some applied anthropologists have suggested that parts of our current ethical codes and principles of professional responsibility seem unduly restrictive, impractical, and, in some cases, unprofessional. I will pursue these arguments by referring to specific sections of the recently revised code of the Society for Applied Anthropology (SfAA 1983) and to the Principles of Professional Responsibility of the American Anthropological Association (AAA 1971), which were revised slightly in 1975 and which have become the major source of contention around which suggestions for further revision revolve.

At the core of this controversy is the weighing of responsibilities toward two major constituencies—the "subjects" of our endeavors and the "clients" or employers for whom we work. In anthropology, our most recently stated ethical guidelines are heavily weighted toward the interests of research subjects. The SfAA code gives research subjects first mention. The AAA principles are even more explicit: "In research, an anthropologist's paramount responsibility is to those he studies. When there is a conflict of interest, these individuals must come first."

Although our current codes recognize that we have ethical obligations not only to research subjects but also to research clients and various employers, these obligations are not well articulated. In the AAA Principles, most of the discussion of relations with clients is specified in terms of situations that should be avoided rather than as professional obligations we might have. It seems especially important to give added recognition to our obligations to clients because sectors of our profession harbor considerable ambivalence toward doing any work outside of an academic base of employment. When they or their students do undertake work outside this base, it has been relatively easy for some of them to justify misleading and even lying to government agencies and corporate clients. This damages the professional reputation of our discipline. We should expect our colleagues to behave in a responsible way toward their clients and employers, just as we expect them to behave responsibly with research subjects. Those of us who have been doing applied work for some time cringe when we see newly graduated colleagues, and occasionally even respected elders, undertake tasks for which they are not qualified, sometimes openly exploiting their employers and doing poor work. By treating what has become a large problem lightly, often by simply wishing it would go away, we only encourage irresponsible conduct and poor performance.

To ask that our profession increase the weight given to considerations of our responsibilities to clients and employers is not necessarily to reduce the weight given to our responsibilities to research subjects. In these matters, we do not have to borrow from one side of the scale in order to expand the reach of our concern to the other side. Even so, the charge that the interests of research subjects should invariably come first is at least open to scrutiny.

Some (certainly not all) applied anthropologists have argued that our profession's insistence upon placing the rights of subjects first pertains in actuality only to certain subjects, and that the position is not strictly one of professional responsibility, but rather a position derived from political ideology. The ethical stance, which is that subjects must be offered the greater part of our protection, becomes a political stance when we assume, as we often do, that anthropologists should have only certain kinds of people as research subjects. These distinctions between obligations to research subjects and research clients lead to issues of confidentiality and to considerations of how confidentiality is or is not maintained by anthropologists. On this matter, the 1983 SfAA code seems clear:

> We shall provide a means throughout our research activities and in subsequent publications to maintain the confidentiality of those we study. The people we study must be made aware of the likely limits of confidentiality and must not be promised a greater degree of confidentiality than can realistically be respected under current legal circumstances in our respective nations. We shall, within the limits of our knowledge, disclose any significant risk to those we study that may result from our activities. (Professional and Ethical Responsibilities, Section 1)

The 1971 AAA Statement of Professional Responsibilities seems equally clear and a shade more forceful: "Informants have a right to remain anonymous. This right should be respected both where it has been promised explicitly and where no clear understanding to the contrary has been reached" (Section 1.c.). The 1975 amendments added a proviso: "Despite every effort being made to preserve anonymity it should be made clear to informants that such anonymity may be compromised unintentionally" (Section 1.c.(1)).

In principle, we extend the promise of confidentiality to everyone, without clear specification of who our "informants" might be. But in reality we are inclined to assure confidentiality only to persons whom we perceive

to be among the world's less privileged or in special need of our protection.
In their reports and ethnographies, anthropologists of all kinds routinely
and often unavoidably violate the confidentiality of people of privilege,
such as government officials and other public figures (Galliher 1980). At
times, this violation is declared to constitute a greater good than our
principles of confidentiality (Nader 1974). In suggesting that our ethical
position should be revised to state clearly that confidentiality cannot be
assured in every case—and to acknowledge that a "compromise" might be
intentional as well as unintentional—one of the things applied anthropologists are doing is asking us to be respectful of the rights of *all* people.
Sometimes a key actor in an ethnographic drama simply cannot be protected. That person deserves to be informed of the possible implications of
taking us into his or her confidence. This consideration is as much deserved
by a corporation executive or a government official as it is deserved by
anyone else.

In these cases, the talk is about confidentiality, but the meaning of the
talk refers to distinctions based on privilege, and these distinctions are
based on theories of sociopolitical order and considerations of morality
about which anthropologists disagree. In a related manner, the principle of
confidentiality is extended to the subjects of research (or, rather, to *some*
kinds of subjects), but is not clearly extended to the clients of research—
and I believe the assumption here is that clients, seen to represent the status
quo and to hold social power, cannot be trusted, whereas the subjects of
research can be trusted. The rationale of this assumption is that "clients"
have the power to do something to "subjects," whereas subjects are without
power. Like most commonly held assumptions, this rationale has merit, but
is oversimplified.

It is also worth noting that neither of the two codes makes a clear
distinction between confidentiality as it pertains to individuals or to groups
and communities. The SfAA code refers to "the people we study," which is
a fairly broad category, whereas the AAA principles refer specifically to
"informants," and thereby, presumably, to individuals. Convention within
anthropology has been to attempt to insure confidentiality by changing the
names of individuals as well as those of communities, although our practice
of the latter has been sporadic and largely ineffective. By the same token,
the practical demands of scientific and collegial communication are generally acknowledged as having precedence over any attempt to assure the
anonymity of larger populations, such as "tribal" groups, even though such

presumably necessary exposure has led to charges of harm visited upon the populations so studied and exposed by anthropologists (Ramos 1987). We can observe then, in these several ways, that the conventions of our ethical behaviors are much more specific and bounded than our codes might suggest. The argument that the interests of a research client might in some cases come before the interests of research subjects is no more unreasonable in principle than the recognition that, in much of our work, the interests of scientific communication have routinely received precedence over a consideration of the full range of interests pertaining to the people we study.

Secret Research

Another issue of general concern, and perhaps the source of the greatest controversy in our current ethics talk, concerns "secret" research.[4] Relative to many other professions, anthropologists have nearly always recognized the extent to which withholding research results from public scrutiny might threaten the interests and well-being of their research subjects. Because most of the knowledge anthropologists have traditionally dealt in has little or no commercial value, client demands for secrecy have largely been based on anthropological research that is politically sensitive or of strategic military significance. As more anthropologists become involved in work that does have commercial value (such as marketing and product research), the problems that arise out of consideration of the dissemination of research results become more complex. The 1983 SfAA code recognizes the principle of public dissemination of research but attempts to balance these interests against the "legitimate proprietary" interests of clients:

> while respecting the needs, responsibilities, and legitimate proprietary interests of our sponsors we should not impede the flow of information about research outcomes and professional practice outcomes.
> We have the obligation to attempt to prevent distortion or suppression of research results or policy recommendations by concerned agencies. [SfAA Code, Section 5]

The 1971 Principles of Professional Responsibility provided by the AAA are much more explicit:

> He [the anthropologist] should not communicate his findings secretly to some and withhold them from others. [Section 2.a.]

He should undertake no secret research or any research whose results cannot be freely derived and publicly reported. [Section 3.a.]

He should enter into no secret agreement with the sponsor regarding the research, results or reports. [Section 5]

Specifically, no secret research, no secret reports or debriefings of any kind should be agreed to or given. [Section 6]

The events that gave rise to the emphasis on secret research in the AAA Principles are well known and are discussed elsewhere in this book. Prior codes and statements have acknowledged the principle of free and open dissemination of research findings, both as an obligation to colleagues and as a protection of research subjects. But the statements concerning secret research in the 1971 Principles are more than a change in emphasis. They constitute one of the few clear changes in ethics talk. As such, they seem unambiguous in their claim to elevate a concern about specific, troublesome behaviors to the status of general principles.

In the aftermath of our nation's ideological, highly emotional, and ultimately correct response to U.S. involvement in the Vietnam War, the prohibition of secret research on the part of anthropologists has gone unchallenged until fairly recently. The three issues that follow are some of the matters that are now emerging and that require further discussion.

First: In practice, anthropologists invariably engage in "secret" research in that they traditionally control the dissemination of their research results. They are free to include and exclude data, to delay publication, or to rush publication, according to their own judgment as to the impact this information might have on others.

Second: The principle of informant confidentiality takes precedence, presumably, over the principle prohibiting secret research. No one has argued that anthropologists do not have the right to maintain "secrets" on the behalf of research subjects. In most cases, this seems to make sense. However, when the principle of confidentiality is extended to ideologically based groups that exercise political influence and power in their own right (Cohen 1976), the toleration of secret activities becomes problematic in that it represents a political decision rather than solely a matter of professional ethics. That the politics and moral issues involved may be ones with which most anthropologists sympathize is beside the point. The issue, unresolved, is whether or not a general principle should favor one group or institution over another. The question is ultimately whether we have the right to presume the wisdom of understanding and distinguishing among the aims and activities of the human social institutions with whom we work and whether, where we lack that wisdom, general principles of ethical conduct should not be applied equally to all groups and institutions.

Third: In effect, *reference to those specific behaviors of the 1960s which gave rise to concerns about secret research is still necessary in order to explain why the 1971 Principles contain this language.* Because the specific behaviors are still required to explain the case, the transition from specific behaviors to general principles does not seem complete. Thus, it can be argued that the actual and unstated general principle is that anthropologists should not work in secrecy with *certain* kinds of sponsors and clients, such as government agencies and private corporations. This lack of completion, or unwillingness to clearly state what is, after all, a contestable world view, leads to a number of ambiguities in the Principles' statements concerning secrecy.

For example, there are a variety of reasons why the dissemination of research findings might reasonably be delayed or withheld altogether. The protection of informants and research communities is one such reason. There are also legitimate client-oriented reasons for delaying preliminary findings regarding research on experimental public programs. The research might, for example, be incomplete, misleading, or even wrong, and premature public exposure could jeopardize the future of a worthwhile program. Further, some research sponsors do seem to have reasonable proprietary interests in the research they support. In some contexts, research techniques and procedures might be "secret" in that they represent a marketable resource. Product research, such as human factors research leading to the design of furniture or marketing research devoted to consumer choice, might also be subject to well-established laws and customs regarding the protection of inventions. These are public rules that seem as legitimate as the copyright protection extended to professional journals and scholarly books.

None of these examples is meant to deny the likelihood that secrecy leads to ethical dilemmas, or that demands for secrecy on the part of research clients (or even of research subjects[5]) might often seem unreasonable and be unacceptable to anthropologists. My point is that the present statements concerning secret research that are included in the 1971 AAA Principles do not stand as general principles that are currently acceptable to a large segment of our profession. They are principles which, because of their ambiguity, are routinely violated. And they are principles that reflect an unstated political and moral bias.

Justice and Morality as a Fourth Condition

In moral philosophy, ethics and justice are not the same thing. Although the balance of ethical positions is not restricted by limited goods, because such goods have no limits, the scales of justice work differently. When the interests of clients and subjects come into actual conflict, something often has to be taken from one to be given to the other. In such cases do we, as the current AAA Principles of Professional Responsibility advise, and as the SfAA code at least implies, always sacrifice the interests of the client or employer to the interests of our research subjects? If we were to agree that our profession should be restricted to a particular ideology and that anthropologists should work only with certain types of research subjects, then perhaps we could take that position. And if we were to agree that anthropologists should never work on the behalf of persons who have power over others, then perhaps we could take that position. But we have no such agreements, and if we did many of us would be guilty of breaches of conduct.

The major change in the ethics talk of anthropology, that having to do with secret research, can be seen as an attempt to move issues of professional ethics out of their more usual realm and into a province of moral authority and ideological preference. From the perspective of some, this will be seen as a desirable state. Others, myself included, see it as a dangerous tendency. This issue relates not only to the larger consideration of how anthropologists perceive their obligations to clients and research subjects, but also to how they honor their obligations to colleagues, some of whom may not share the same beliefs as others.

The measure of justice, while existing in relation to general principles of morality, must still be determined in great part on the basis of particular instances of behavior. What is "just" is best decided free of the defensive constraints and competition of the "inside" that are imposed upon decision-making related to the ethics of professional conduct. The issues related to secret research are among the most important that have to do with our professional conduct, and it is to the credit of anthropology that they have been taken so seriously and have become so much a part of our ethics talk. But, as I have tried to demonstrate, they are not issues that yield easily to general principles. Just as secrecy might, in a love relationship, conceal an adulterous affair or a surprise birthday party, the implications of being secretive in our professional conduct are far more diverse than our present ethical codes imply.

Is Applied Anthropology Unethical?

There is one aspect of our recent discussions of professional ethics that I find especially disturbing. Although I am simplifying, the argument goes something like this. Once upon a time, anthropologists were of a single mind. They came together in harmony, and agreed on most of the essential points of their profession, including how they should behave in public. This era lasted until quite recently, when there were no longer enough jobs in universities to employ all of our students. These students had to do other things. As we now struggle to accommodate the career needs of these students and former students, we are in danger of jeopardizing the harmony we once enjoyed, even to the point of compromising our ethics.

There are three things wrong with this story.

First, I do not believe there was ever a pristine once-upon-a-time for anthropology. (The case of Boas in 1919, described in this volume, offers an early and revealing case for its indelicate handling of ethical issues.) The conditions which gave rise, for example, to the 1971 Principles of Professional Responsibility were particular historical circumstances which represent a brief space in the development of our profession. And although we do not want to forget that moment, neither can we be ruled by it forever or let it blind us to other equally compelling circumstances.

Second, it is not clear that our present crisis, if that is what it is, is the result of anthropologists having to compromise themselves by working outside of academia. I think it is difficult for colleagues who were not students during the late 1960s and early 1970s to realize this. The unrest many of us experienced during that time did not lie simply in the observation that our government could become corrupt. We also learned, or felt we were learning, that our universities and our professors could become equally corrupt. The employment crisis followed a more general, and perhaps an even more profound, erosion of our confidence in academia. Certainly, many young anthropologists do feel they have had to compromise their hopes for an academic position; but as many, if not more, have chosen by preference a career outside academia. Their position does not necessarily represent a compromise. Many of the ethical issues with which we are now struggling would have occurred even if there had been no employment crisis and no such thing as applied anthropology. They are symptoms of a much wider reformation in our way of relating to the rest of the world. Those who feel that these changes should not be taking place are bound to fail in their opposition if they persist in laying the blame upon applied anthropology.

Finally, the notion that the ethical concerns that have been raised by applied anthropologists arose simply out of the need for employment is wrong. To make such a claim is to say that these concerns are only practical matters. It amounts to saying that, if some do not entirely agree with our traditions as they are now held, they do not have an ethical position at all. But, because they are guided by a clear sense and long tradition of ethical concern, applied anthropologists are unlikely to yield to even the most eloquent accounting of the error of their ways. Even the employment issue has in itself an ethical dimension and cannot be regarded solely as a matter of self-interest. The ethical component has to do with the *right* of persons to seek employment and to have their work evaluated without prejudice. We should, for moral as well as practical reasons, use extreme caution in passing judgment upon the career decisions of our colleagues.

Concluding Remarks

I began this chapter with a couple of quotations from Margaret Mead, who was defending the ethical positions of some applied anthropologists. She did this by accusing the critics of these positions of being naive, but her argument is as polemical and naive as most others. Necessity is imposed upon that which is true in many ways. The relativism that has in principle guided anthropologists in their pursuit of the understanding of others can be applied only partially to a re-cognition of their own values. In the face of an ethical dilemma, it is necessary to take a position. But the other aspect of a relativistic ideal, which advises anthropologists to step back and recognize the limits and slippery parameters of the positions they do take, is also often lacking in their ethics talk. This seems unfortunate.

I have had an interest in professional ethics since the beginning of my career. I have seen in myself how quickly an awareness of what I perceive to be a fault or ambiguity in our codes leads to a hardening of my own position—a sense of outrage and a tendency toward polemic that does not yield easily enough to self-understanding. And in this discussion, although I had hoped to avoid it, I see that it has happened again. I find it difficult to separate my sense of what is necessary from a feeling for that which might be true. I feel I am playing a part that needs to be played but that is still clearly only a part. These insights have helped me understand how power-ful a style of discourse our ethics talk can become. With this proviso, I have enjoyed contributing to the dialogue, but I do not expect to be wholly trusted.

ACKNOWLEDGMENTS
Some of these remarks were originally presented in the session "Ethics, Professionalism, and the Future of Anthropology" held at the 1985 Ameri-can Anthropological Association meetings and were subsequently pub-lished in the *Anthropology Newsletter,* volume 27, number 2. I want to thank Setha M. Low for her helpful suggestions.

NOTES
    1. I am referring specifically to the "Thailand controversy," to "Project Cam-elot," and to the American Anthropological Association's publication in 1968 of a job announcement from the Navy Overseas Employment Office for an anthropolo-gist to do research in Vietnam.
    2. The furthest extension of a conflict like this would be a splintering within the profession and a representation of the interests of, in this case, applied anthro-pologists by a separate and independent professional organization. In fact, applied anthropologists have maintained the Society for Applied Anthropology, an organi-zation separate from the American Anthropological Association, for nearly fifty years. It is worth noting, however, that this independence has been maintained largely as a result of distinct organizational goals within the SfAA (such as the interdisciplinary, international, and practicing character of the society). Ethical considerations have contributed little to this separateness. On the other hand, ethics talk has figured prominently in the AAA's recent efforts to be more responsive in its own right to the interests of applied anthropologists. Whether or not this talk might eventually lead to a splintering within the AAA remains to be seen, but seems unlikely. Such an eventuality could be anticipated only if a "clinical" arm of the profession were to develop to such an extent, and with such clarity, as to threaten the existing power base of the discipline on *multiple* grounds. If I am correct in my discussion of the meaning of ethics talk, then it might be predicted that ethics talk, which indirectly serves to support solidarity and maintain *inter*organizational com-petition, would not play a major role in such a splintering. This thesis is supported in part by recognizing that *intra*organizational competition between the SfAA and the AAA has almost never involved conflict on the basis of ethical principles.
    3. These illustrations, drawn from the published "codes" of the American Anthropological Association and the Society for Applied Anthropology, are not intended to set one professional organization against another. I do not argue that one code is better than another, but simply that they have evolved in relation to different perceptions of ethical dilemmas and, in part, in response to the needs of different constituencies within the profession. Still, there is considerable overlap

of membership in the two organizations and it is likely that, except at the extremes of either organization's membership, there is more agreement between members of the two organizations than is apparent from the necessarily partial rendition of the two codes that follows in this chapter.

4. There are any number of possibilities for secrecy in anthropological research. The term might, for example, apply to conditions in which research subjects are not informed of their status or are misled as to the nature of a research inquiry, or it might apply to instances in which the results of research are deliberately withheld by a researcher or research client, perhaps for reasons of proprietary interest, security, or simply to avoid controversy. It is to this latter kind of secrecy that the following discussion refers.

5. As regards research subjects, I have in mind an unpublished case in which anthropologists were conducting a social impact assessment related to the expansion of a reservoir which served as a community's major source of drinking water. Confidentiality was routinely promised to all the interview subjects living near the reservoir. In the course of an interview, one informant who operated a small-scale tanning factory revealed that he regularly dumped animal matter and toxic chemicals into the community's water supply.

REFERENCES
Akeroyd, Anne V.
1984   Ethics in relation to informants, the profession and governments. In *Ethnographic research,* ed. R. F. Ellen. London: Academic Press.
American Anthropological Association (AAA)
1971   Principles of Professional Responsibility. Washington, D.C.: American Anthropological Association. (as amended 1975)
Appell, G. N.
1980   Talking ethics: The uses of moral rhetoric and the function of ethical principles. *Social Problems* 27:350–57.
Cassell, Joan
1980   Ethical principles for conducting fieldwork. *American Anthropologist* 82:28–41.
Chambers, Erve
1980   Fieldwork and the law. *Social Problems* 27:330–41.
Chambers, Erve, and M. G. Trend
1981   Fieldwork ethics in policy-oriented research. *American Anthropologist* 83:626–28.
Chrisman, Noel J.
1976   Secret societies and the ethics of urban fieldwork. In *Ethics and anthropology,* ed. Michael A. Rynkiewich and James P. Spradley. New York: John Wiley & Sons.
Cohen, Fay G.
1976   The American Indian movement and the anthropologist. In *Ethics and anthropology,* ed. Michael A. Rynkiewich and James P. Spradley. New York: John Wiley & Sons.

Durkheim, Emile
1957 *Professional ethics and civic morals.* London: Routledge and Kegan Paul.
Galliher, John F.
1980 Social scientists' ethical responsibilities to superordinates. *Social Problems* 27:298–308.
Kultgen, John
1988 *Ethics and professionalism.* Philadelphia: University of Pennsylvania Press.
Mead, Margaret
1978 The evolving ethics of applied anthropology. In *Applied Anthropology in America,* ed. Elizabeth M. Eddy and William L. Partridge. New York: Columbia University Press.
Mead, Margaret, Eliot D. Chapple, and G. Gordon Brown
1949 Report of the Committee on Ethics. *Human Organization* 9:20–21.
Nader, Laura
1974 Up the anthropologist—perspectives gained from studying up. In *Reinventing Anthropology,* ed. Dell Hymes. New York: Vintage.
Ramos, Alcida R.
1987 Reflecting on the Yanomami. *Cultural Anthropology* 2:284–304.
Society for Applied Anthropology (SfAA)
1963 Statement on ethics of the Society for Applied Anthropology. *Human Organization* 23:237.
1983 Proposed statement on professional and ethical responsibilities. *Human Organization* 42:367.
Wax, Murray L.
1980 Paradoxes of "consent" to the practice of fieldwork. *Social Problems* 27:272–83.

Editor's Introduction to Chapter 8

This chapter brings together the talent and experience of two anthropologists—one academic and one nonacademic. Barbara Frankel, who teaches at Lehigh University, has been active professionally with the Society for Applied Anthropology and chaired its Ethics Committee from 1986 to 1989. M. G. Trend is a full-time applied anthropologist who has served two terms on the Ethics Committee of the SfAA. Their chapter speaks to the anxieties, the uncertainties, and the opportunities that have appeared within a discipline in transition. As they say, "the day of the nonacademically employed anthropologist is here."

After all, it has only been since 1986 that the AAA has reported that more anthropological professionals are working *outside* of academia, yet the authors raise the issue of whether two separate and distinct cultures are forming within anthropology. The split along lines of "pure" research versus applied, client-based "practice" is an obvious fracture, one that parallels the developments that have occurred in other disciplines, such as psychology or sociology. In turn, this raises the question of whether a single code of ethics can be created that is appropriate to all conditions of employment.

Differing with Chambers's conclusions, Frankel and Trend see that economic pressures have been placed on the current generation of anthropologists that have led them to seek employment outside of academia. They believe that the new conditions of employment have placed pressures upon the traditional code of ethics, and that the academic side of the discipline has yet to come to terms with this new reality, intellectually, emotionally, or ethically. This is an important, if not the central, issue in the current need for a "dialogue for a new era."

Frankel and Trend attempt to demythologize the nature of the research that applied anthropologists do, which involves either providing clients with new means of applying existing anthropological data and concepts or creating new knowledge tailored to the client's goals. There is nothing inherently malevolent in any of this; however, there is a tendency for academics to regard it as such.

The authors touch upon some key concerns that anthropologists are likely to have when they work outside of the academy. Applied anthropologists doing proprietary research will often be constrained from publishing their findings, something not usually true of those doing grant-sponsored academic research. Working under pressures of time, applied researchers often lose intellectual control over their material at a much earlier point than do basic researchers. Often, applied anthropologists are junior members of large research teams and, thus, have little say over the design of a project or how the material will be used or disseminated. As a result, applied anthropologists may have their unfinished work released prematurely, or worse, have their best work consigned to the unread "gray literature" of government or corporate reports, rather than published in the best journals in the field.

Such reflections enhance the examination of the issues faced by practicing anthropologists and serve to advance a mutual dialogue between the traditional academic and the newer, applied anthropologist. Frankel and Trend confront difficult issues that should be addressed (and no doubt will be addressed in future developments of this special history of the discipline), such as enforcement mechanisms for ethical codes and licensing of practitioners. They call for the widest possible discussion and debate of these and other issues, thus taking advantage of the opportunity that exists in the discipline at this moment.

Barbara Frankel and M. G. Trend

Chapter 8 Principles, Pressures, and Paychecks
The Anthropologist as Employee

APPLIED ANTHROPOLOGY has arrived. At this moment a significant number of anthropologists—more than half of them, according to one study—are not professors but "practitioners," untenured, probably well-paid by comparison to those of us who work within the academy, and more likely to be living their lives in the fast lane than in the contemplative mode.

Anyone who doubts that the day of the nonacademically employed anthropologist is here need only look at the lists of workshops on the programs of recent meetings of the American Anthropological Association. For example, of the seventeen workshops listed for the 1987 meetings in Chicago, eleven were about how to obtain and/or succeed in business or government jobs. Most of the remaining few were designed to teach skills like computing and proposal-writing, which have become indispensable for people in nonacademic jobs (though they are admittedly useful in academe as well). Only a single workshop was sponsored by an area specialty organization (to teach fieldwork-survival skills in Latin America) and, most striking of all, only one was devoted to helping people find employment in an anthropology department. Surely all this is symptomatic of some sort of culture change.

Another indicator of changing anthropological culture is language. Descriptions of the workshops just enumerated employ an unfamiliar jargon filled with terms such as *impact assessment, resource management, private sector, marketability, packaging,* and *product design.* By contrast, AAA's non-workshop sessions share an idiom that is still comfortably familiar to anyone who was ever an anthropology student. In the scholarly symposia the vocabulary is liberally sprinkled with such terms as *culture areas, symbols, beliefs, native systems, ecology,* and *evolution*—plus an in-group nomenclature peppered with names of obscure and mostly powerless groups of people who inhabit the remoter areas of our world. Such discontinuity in our language of discourse is not entirely new, but it has become more striking than ever before. One can hardly avoid the impression that many of us no longer pretend to share a common tongue at all.

Indeed, it begins to look as though academic anthropologists might be on their way to becoming an anachronistic priesthood in a newly secular world, charged with conducting the traditional rites of intensification connected to certain mysteries of our arcane specialties, and thereby lending sanctity and legitimacy to the discipline. Meanwhile, practitioners act practically, conducting the serious business of profiting from that legitimacy by organizing how-to-do-it workshops that train us for success in the world of affairs, the world of power.

Is anthropology developing two cultures? Perhaps—but the topic of this essay is professional ethics. How do reflections upon the two cultures question bear on that topic? To put the matter quite simply, it seems to us that the bifurcation of any discipline along the axis of "pure" versus "applied" raises questions about legitimacy, perhaps even about licensure and/or sanctioning procedures for ethical violations, that lie somewhat outside the traditional arena of scientific fraud and misconduct that has preoccupied the ethics committees of anthropology's professional organizations in the past.

For an instructive historical parallel that might help us grasp some of the implications of our new situation, we need only examine the experience of the American Psychological Association (APA) in the years since World War II. In the postwar era, the APA[1] had to grapple with thorny ethical problems that came prominently into view when the psychotherapists began to outnumber the scientists in their ranks: How to maintain scientific standards in a world of pragmatic truth? How to insure against quackery that might stain the reputations of academics wearing the mantle of science? Above all, how to prevent abuse of public confidence in a discipline that was bifurcating, with one half subject to traditional constraints of peer review and evaluation, while the other half, in many states, could hang out shingles and practice on people in distress with virtually no surveillance? The APA's solutions to these problems, which include accreditation of programs as well as procedures for credentialing and/or sanctioning individual members (notions generally rejected by anthropological organizations), have been only partly successful, though organization stalwarts have worked diligently on them for more than forty years. The most recent development seems to be a gesture of despair: secession by a substantial segment of the scientific wing of psychology from an organization that has come to be dominated by its therapeutic constituency. The academics have started a group of their own, the American Psychological Society, to which no psychotherapists need apply, although some individuals will maintain membership in both societies (Campbell 1989; Dawes 1989).

This history would lead one to suppose that schismatism between "pure" and "applied" members of any discipline may well be inevitable, while wise and unifying responses to it may, in the very nature of the case, turn out to be elusive. But apart from potential organizational problems, disciplinary bifurcation into "pure" and "applied" communities raises an issue even more central to the present discussion: that is, the question of whether there is, or can be, a single code of ethics appropriate to all anthropological enterprises. Does the increasing nonacademic utilization of anthropological skills and understandings signal a dichotomization of disciplinary ethics to accompany the new divergence in the way we earn our livelihoods? Or is there a right and wrong that flatly applies to the discipline as a whole, and no relativistic nonsense about it?

Let us make no mistake; we are talking about power. Everyone knows the old saw that "knowledge is power." Like many clichés, this one is also a Great Truth—and because knowledge *is* power, once a discipline is recognized as possessing useful knowledge (or the means of getting it) someone will decide it is worth paying for. It is at this juncture that accountability to the purchaser or employer becomes direct.

For a long time the sort of knowledge anthropologists generated did not seem to carry much of a price tag in the corridors of corporate and political power, but lately this has changed considerably. First of all, "qualitative research" of the sort we have traditionally advocated and practiced has attained a new vogue in other disciplines, thus acquiring a certain cachet that has helped people to find employment.[2] Second, many anthropologists have been willing and able to adapt their skills to the needs of a new sort of marketplace, learning to use quantitative methods, meet short deadlines, and become time/cost-effective. In the course of all this, more and more anthropologists have taken on the job of applying what we know to the real world and its problems, not as a sideline but as a full-time career. Some have done so out of a conviction that anthropology should be useful, some because they want to see whether our theories can survive the tests of practice; but most of our students and colleagues who now work in business or government do so in order to survive *as anthropologists* in a shrunken academic market. Once they are there, however, part of the package (especially if they work in government) is concern about power. Another part of it (most central if they work in business) is concern about money. Such concerns are not absent in academe, either, but they take on a new intensity in the world of applied/practicing anthropology.

This may be the place to remark that our title, "Principles, Pressures, and Paychecks," was not idly chosen. It is simply a truism that preoccupation with power and money (regardless of whether they are available in excess or in short supply) creates enormous pressures to succeed at any cost. Is it possible that anthropologists might begin following the example of so many stockbrokers, civil servants, corporate executives, and professionals whose pursuit of money and power nowadays seems to go far beyond what any society can sanely tolerate? The implications of such a phenomenon are serious for any scientific profession, and especially serious for one seeking knowledge about fellow human beings. In a world of increasing temptation to live by an ethic of simple expediency, some compass is urgently needed to guide our ethical course.

The fact that applied (or practicing, or client-centered) research has joined the establishment outside of academe is something that our traditionally academic discipline must learn to deal with at both intellectual and ethical levels. We cannot go on pretending that the problems and predicaments are identical, or that they can be resolved in the same way for everyone, regardless of the world in which they do their daily work. Yet while anthropologists (of all people) must acknowledge the importance of context and local culture in regulating not only practices and principles, but thought itself, it is surely also the case that most of us hold to the somewhat contrary notion that neither goodness nor truth is entirely relative. What can we do with this paradox?

Two Guides to the Perplexed

Two societies have long stood for purity versus application in our discipline: the American Anthropological Association (AAA) and the Society for Applied Anthropology (SfAA). Their memberships overlap substantially, and both societies have possessed official codes of ethics for many years now.[3] Though different in some particulars (including length), the basic structures of the two codes are strikingly similar. Culture-contact and diffusion have undoubtedly played a role in this, but it is likely, too, that the family resemblance is heavily attributable to the dominance of academics in both societies. In decades past, both AAA and SfAA memberships have been made up mostly of people who made their living not by applying anthropology but by teaching it, or even teaching how to apply it[4]—an increasingly popular pursuit.

Both statements of ethical responsibility are, presumably, intended to act as guides to the perplexed. They are similar in other ways as well. The reader is referred to the appendix to this chapter, which contains a preliminary and somewhat crude comparison of the AAA's Principles of Professional Responsibility (1971, 1974), which we have broken into its component parts in the left-hand column, and the SfAA's Professional and Ethical Responsibilities (1983), which is disassembled for comparison on the right. We have arranged the columns so that the provisions of the shorter SfAA document are matched as nearly as possible to those of the AAA code, and in both columns we have indicated those clauses that seem to have no close match on the other side.

Each code lists six constituencies, or publics, made up of individuals or groups with whom one forms an ethical relationship as one goes about his or her anthropological business. By virtue of this relationship, the anthropologist incurs an obligation to consider and protect the interests and/or welfare of each of these several, presumably interested, parties. Differences between the two codes in labeling the six constituencies are slight, though it appears that their areas of maximum vagueness differ: for example, the SfAA's code gives second place in its list of those who must be considered to "the communities affected" by our actions, while the AAA's code mentions only "the public." Conversely, the AAA specifies (albeit in sixth place) obligations to "our own and host governments," whereas the SfAA merely waves a figurative hand toward "society as a whole."

In both documents the constituencies are arranged in what seems to be priority order. First on both lists is "the people we study"—that is, our "informants," who might nowadays be called our "collaborators" (Werner and Schoepfle 1986) or "resource persons" (AAA 1984). Their interests are explicitly described as "paramount" by the AAA, and are to be protected by all means within the anthropologist's power. The SfAA, slightly less emphatic about priorities, merely cautions that if we cannot be sure of protecting people we must at least inform them of any predictable risks.

In both codes, general obligations to all constituencies include honesty and openness. In the case of informants and governments we must be honest regarding our identities and aims; with sponsors or employers, honest about our qualifications; with everyone, including colleagues, students, and the public, we must be honest about our findings. The potential for encountering conflicting claims upon our honesty is obvious—not to mention the clear potential for conflict between requirements of honesty (or openness) and confidentiality (or respect for others' privacy).

In addition, though *confidentiality* must be respected, *secrecy* is forbidden under the codes of both the SfAA and the AAA; and since the line between privacy and secrecy is a fine one, borderline cases become highly debatable (cf. Warren and Laslett 1977). Despite these internal contradictions, however, neither code provides any criteria for deciding which principle or constituency takes precedence in such cases. For example, anthropologists are enjoined to be honest with all constituencies, but clearly if you are honest with certain government bureaucracies seeking information about informants you not only fail to protect their privacy, you may seriously endanger their welfare.[5] Potentially, things can become extremely complicated. For example, an applied anthropologist working for one government agency may promise to protect informants' confidence so as to facilitate research essential to the agency's mission (for example, the treatment of drug addicts) while another agency seeks access to the data in order to carry out the function for which *it* was created (for example, the enforcement of drug statutes).

Neither code provides mechanisms for invoking formal sanctions in cases where ethical precepts are judged to have been violated. In the SfAA case, the Committee on Ethics has traditionally been appointed by the president of the society rather than elected, has no authority to level sanctions, and (last, but hardly least, in these litigious times) it is uninsured. As a result, it has been understandably hesitant to consider the matter of sanctions. In the AAA case, although the committee is elected (and may even carry liability insurance for all we know), it has consistently maintained that it is not its place to judge or punish but, rather, to advise and mediate. Indeed, there is a certain lack of clarity about the ethical codes of all scientific disciplines and, as anyone who thinks about it will realize, this is inevitable. It stems not only from the impossibility of specifying all contingencies, nor even from the imperfection of our definitions, but from recurrent, fundamental conflict between what is required of us as scientists and what is required of us as decent, morally concerned human beings.

To put the matter another way, all anthropologists, academics and practitioners alike, serve at least two masters: science, and their own and others' humanity. The basic demand of science is that we seek and tell the honest truth, insofar as we can know it, without fear or favor. Science is thus widely regarded, in theory at least, as an intrinsically single-valued system—that is to say, in our roles as scientists our only goal should be to *know*.

It is of course true that all disciplines, and the individual scientists within them, are implicitly evaluative in choosing to study certain problems rather than others; indeed, it has been suggested (by Cohen 1980) that our sciences might have looked rather different had their early development taken place in, say, China—or had their practitioners been predominantly female. This, however, is not because the laws of physics or chemistry would then have turned out to be different (or so we must presume). It is because the *extra-scientific* considerations that determine the directions research actually takes (for example, research on female rather than male contraceptive methods) would almost certainly have been different, hence so would have been the problems science chose to address.

Knowledge, then, though surely a high priority, is not quite the whole story when it comes to scientific endeavors. In our roles as human beings— citizens, parents, friends, guests, teachers, employers, and employees— there are clearly other ends to be served. Indeed, ethical sensitivity may sometimes dictate that it is better not to know, or to pretend ignorance, or to suppress knowledge, than to be honest about all that we know; and this is especially so when one's scientific gaze is directed at other human beings. Here, decency may sometimes suggest that clarity of scientific inference should take second place to human and social concerns. The following case gives a plausible scenario for only one sort of potential conflict between scientific and personal conscience. Such a case could be multiplied a thousandfold, and every applied anthropologist will recognize the sort of situation it instantiates.

Imagine that you are working for an organization that has a contract from the federal government to evaluate an experimental program being implemented by a local government agency. The local agency is having trouble navigating the bureaucratic waters at the state level, and there is a real possibility that the project will not be approved. You are the knowledgeable anthropological observer on-site, and you think well of both the project and the local agency's director. Furthermore, the president of the company you work for wants you to make a few suggestions to the director of the agency that might facilitate things at the state level. (After all, if there is no program, there will be nothing to evaluate.)

What do you do? Should you be a nonintervening scientist, tell the president (your boss) that his suggestion is out of order because such behavior would contaminate the data, step back, and let both the contract and a worthy social experiment be canceled? Or should you intervene—not only for the sake of your job, but also for the sake of a good program that will benefit the target population (which happens to be poor/minority/female) and because of your friendship with the agency director?

Here is a stacked situation, no doubt, in which all the human considerations, selfish and unselfish, tend in one direction, whereas all the scientific considerations taught in university methods courses tend in another—but this is not uncommon. Our intuition is that most social scientists would opt to intervene, to act in a helping role. Moreover, we feel rather safe in saying that they will be disappointed if they fail and happy if they succeed. Whether this intervention does, in fact, "contaminate the data" when it comes to evaluation of the project is a complicated question, the complete answer to which would require another essay, but our short answer is that the contamination is not crucial, nor is the fundamental honesty of the scientific evaluation thereby threatened.

It is no great news, really, that the ethical-dilemma potential is tremendous in the human sciences. Indeed, no hard-and-fast rules or recipes can really specify what it *means* in a context of moral decency to be honest with others; what it means to explain your research goals or disclose your sponsorship to an individual, a community, or a government; what it means to protect another's interests (or even to know what they are); or what it means to avoid exploiting others or invading their privacy.

The World of Client-Centered Research

If anthropologists' ethical decisions have always been difficult (and even tragic), if none of us can serve two masters faithfully, then what, if anything, is novel about the plight of the practicing applied anthropologist? For present purposes, we use this term to indicate persons in the employ of (or under contract to) businesses, agencies, or tax-supported institutions, but not connected to universities. These colleagues make their livings as guns for hire: they are paid by clients or employers to use their expertise either (1) to provide the client with means of applying already available anthropological knowledge, or (2) to seek new knowledge specifically tailored to pursuit of the client's own goals.

Such endeavors are not necessarily malevolent, though there is some tendency for academics to regard them as such. It seems to us that the hermeneutic "principle of charity" requires us to assume that anthropological practitioners are not fundamentally different from their university colleagues: they come from the same graduate schools, have studied under the same teachers, and usually think of themselves as serving that most demanding master of all—science itself, with its uncompromising demand for honesty in pursuit of truth. The human pressures on the practitioner are, however, different from those of academe, and their ethical impacts fairly predictable.

We will discuss, briefly, four categories of pressures that may give rise to ethical dilemmas. We call them security pressures, intellectual pressures, self-esteem pressures, and loss-of-control pressures.

SECURITY PRESSURES

The college and university tenure system that we all know and love subjects young scholars to six years of anxiety, then (if they have published, not perished) they win a lifetime of saying and doing pretty much as they please. It is a career line that trades a life of voluntary poverty for the joys of intellectual freedom and job security. By contrast, the employee-anthropologist (or contractor, or consultant) is usually better-paid, but here, too, there is a trade-off. To put the matter baldly: without tenure, one's daily bread depends on pleasing the employer[6] not just in the long run, when one's ground-breaking original work will be appreciated, but in the immediate present. There is, in fact, a saying among researchers who work in contract houses that "you're only as good as your last project." Clearly, this pressure to produce and to please in the short run can entail many compromises, only some of which we can allude to here.

Government contracts, for example, usually contain stipulations under which the contract can be canceled, sometimes merely by giving notice and often without provision for mediating disputes. Experienced contract researchers find themselves well-advised, in fact, to look carefully at clauses pertaining to the settlement of disputes. It is easy to see how compelling a threat to cancel might be if the contract is a big one, and/or the contractor a small one who is dependent on one or two contracts to stay in business at all. Similar considerations apply to employees of corporations, agencies, foundations, and so on—none of which offer tenure, and some of which make it a practice *not* to keep people on for life.

INTELLECTUAL PRESSURES

For employers, especially those that are profit-oriented or politically motivated, knowledge is most often regarded as a commodity rather than a good in itself. At best this instrumental attitude channels inquiry, limiting the choice of research problems to those falling within the client's short-term need to know. These are sometimes, but not necessarily, problems the anthropologist sees as interesting or important. If they are not, too bad.

Rather more threatening to intellectual integrity is the danger that short-run goals and a need to maximize profit, minimize costs, or produce a research product that will satisfy the client create pressures of a sort likely to produce shallow—even erroneous—conclusions. This threat is most acute where a decision has already been made in the halls of economic or political power and is simply intended to be ratified by the research results. (The building of Aswan Dam, and its subsequent justification despite adverse and largely predictable ecological, cultural, and public health impacts, is but one well-known case in point.)

But worst of all from the standpoint of both external ethical codes and the institutionalized internal norms of any science is the employment that requires one to become a party to secrecy, or even to misrepresentation of findings, and to exhibit loyalty not to the truth but to the employer. Everyone is familiar with the notion that science progresses by means of critical challenges to current beliefs. In that case both secrecy and misrepresentation are not just morally shady acts; they are deeply antiscientific and anti-intellectual, for they subvert the progress of knowledge itself. No matter what his or her credentials, then, the individual who falsifies or conceals the truth is no longer a scientist—perhaps a spy, a salesman, or conceivably even a loyal citizen and a public benefactor, but not an anthropologist or any other sort of scientist.

It is surely bad news when it is discovered that erstwhile peers have lost their right to be considered as members of the discipline, having been forced to choose between scientific integrity and a livelihood (or some other important value, perhaps). We should not feel surprised, then, that our colleagues in NAPA ask for a code of ethics that will "shield" them from such pressures as this (cf. Amoss 1986).[7] Which brings us to the next topic.

SELF-ESTEEM PRESSURES
Recognition for one's work is not only a normal desire in most sectors of the modern world, but an especially important ingredient of self-esteem for intellectuals. In a discipline that until lately has been so heavily academic as our own, this recognition has typically been earned in two major ways: through publications, which advertise an individual's contributions among

his or her peers, and through students, who follow in the mentor's footsteps and praise his or her name. These are the standard rewards of meritorious academic achievement. They can also turn nastily into the opposite of rewards, of course. We all know about publish-or-perish pressures on academics, even after tenure, when they seem more closely related to psychological than material security (though perhaps we should not discount the importance of the annual salary increment, either).

The nonacademic anthropologist is unlikely to perish if she or he does not publish and, in fact, the pressures may be in reverse. The employee may be forbidden to publish the results of research on grounds that this would reveal "trade secrets" or otherwise damage the interests of the employer. For example, it seems to be standard practice for such agencies as the World Bank to retain ownership of research data for several years before allowing publication of any portion of it (Kushner 1987). Such suppression or lengthy delay in delivering knowledge to the public clearly violates provisions of both the AAA and the SfAA codes, each of which, in slightly different tones of voice, warns against losing control over the fruits of our professional activities.

In addition, this predicament creates the need for substitute ego-satisfactions for nonpublishers in a discipline where printed works are the prime measure of achievement. In the world of contracts and bureaucracies, recognition often comes in the form of perquisites such as bonuses for securing large contracts, bigger offices, more subordinates, or the keys to the executive washroom. The mechanisms are varied—and not invariably ethically suspect, though they may incur some scorn from threadbare academics. These mechanisms range from ostentatious displays of material symbols that would make Veblen turn in his grave, to inside-dopester satisfactions gleaned in the halls of power, to the worker's pride in exhibiting competence by solving a problem for whomever wants it solved and will pay someone to solve it.

As we have mentioned earlier, and as we all know, the love of money and/or power is the root of much (though surely not all) evil; but the temptation of problem-solving—often enough, without regard to the ethical implications of the problem itself—may be the most insidious ego-trap of all for the academically trained. We are proud of our brains, and we like to use them. Rationalizing that "if I don't do it, someone else will" has undoubtedly led to more than one ethically questionable enterprise being carried out by social scientists eager to solve a puzzle just for the pleasure such activity provides.

LOSS-OF-CONTROL PRESSURES

Even where good scientific work is valued and supported, and even where knowledge may be published, the anthropologist as employee may have a sense of losing control—of alienation from his or her own product. In part this might be due to the employee's lack of power to decide the uses to which knowledge will be put, but even more it may be due to the inability to risk criticizing and/or attempting to influence company or agency policies. The privilege of crankiness, of criticizing one's betters, is a precious one that even the least competent tenured professor possesses. Employees generally lack that privilege.

Loss of control also stems from conditions that are most common within contract research organizations (though some are not entirely unknown in academe). Data may be gathered, then the anthropologist leaves the research team, or a new boss or a new contracting officer arrives and wants things done differently. Or people work in teams in which data are shared, and it sometimes happens that the most entrepreneurial member publishes something from this source without crediting fellow team members. Then there is the ever-pressing necessity, once a project ends, of writing the next grant proposal—which means that a good many pieces of research that could be written up are not. And finally, the contract or agreement under which the researcher should, ideally, retain some autonomy, often contains booby traps—either because the investigator was not wary enough, or because he or she was hungry enough to sign even though it meant substantial loss of control.

Conclusion

Finally, all that has been said sums up to the following general description of the predicament of the anthropologist as employee. First of all, one is likely to learn very early that despite the way the official codes of ethics say it is *supposed* to be, one would be well advised to place the interests of the employer or sponsor before the interests of the people studied, their communities, one's own colleagues, students, host governments, own government, or the general public, all of which are mentioned in the AAA's Principles of Professional Responsibility. In that document the only considerations given to clients' or sponsors' interests are those that insist that anthropologists may not misrepresent their qualifications to their employers, and that permit a sponsor to withdraw from having its name used in connection with publication of the research.

The employee who must, to remain employed, give up control over the release of information stemming from professional activities is, in fact, in direct violation of the ethical code of the AAA, which prohibits clandestine research under any circumstances, and enjoins full and free publication of scientific information. Since 1948, in fact, the AAA's policy has insisted that the only considerations inhibiting publication of research results should be those protecting the welfare of the people and communities we study. The SfAA's code is more lenient on this point, but still obligates the applied anthropologist to "attempt to prevent distortion or suppression of research results or policy recommendations" by employers or other sponsors.

Most serious, in terms of the violation of scientific and ethical norms, is that the anthropologist working outside the academy may be required to refrain from both dissemination of scientific knowledge and public criticism of the uses to which the employer may put such knowledge. If he or she does not accede to this requirement, there is a realistic fear that this will be regarded as disloyalty to the team at best, and whistle-blowing at worst. (We all know what happens to whistle-blowers, who usually receive worse punishments than the malefactors they unmask.)

Remembering that we are using the principle of charity, under which we must assume that similar morals and motives operate among all (or at least most) of us, what sort of an ethic must we espouse? How irreducible is the conflict between scientist and human being which all of us experience in some degree? What hierarchy of values, if any, should we espouse for all anthropologists? How much of a shield can an ethical code offer? Can it help the well-intentioned, who wish to be protected from being asked to do things that they inwardly deplore but feel powerless to refuse on their own? What of the not-so-well-intentioned? Should academics refuse to lend the legitimacy of their scientific status to activities that may be manipulation, or spying, or sales, but are not science—and may be immoral to boot? Should the entire profession support licensing of practitioners, having them take professional oaths?[8] Should we level sanctions and expel people from our organizations when they err? Would it make any difference if we did? Should there be segregation of academic from practicing anthropologists, with each group going its own ethical way?

We end up not with answers, but with questions to which we do not yet begin to know the answers. Indeed, some of these questions may not have answers—but, even so, they need to be placed in some rational order and widely discussed and debated.[9] We may never get to the end of such debates, but the process, we are inclined to think, matters much more than the rules we come up with. We need to stimulate and promote moral awareness and concern, not in some sentimental way, and surely not in an absolutist way, but in a tough-minded way that demands decency even when we cannot define what it is. It's a tall order.

Appendix

Table 8.1 is arranged for the purpose of comparing the two major ethical codes discussed in this chapter, that of the AAA and that of the SfAA, each in the most recent form available when this contribution was written.

Major sections of each code have been given index numbers according to their order in the actual document. Provisions or clauses that are parts of each major section have then been given decimal numbers according to their sequential order within those sections. These subsections or clauses are paraphrased for brevity in many cases; in addition, they have not always been treated as separate provisions in the original documents. To us, however, they appear clearly separable in terms of substantive content, even where not treated as separate provisions of the code in question.

The AAA's Principles of Professional Responsibility (PPR) is disassembled into its component sections and clauses in the left-hand column below, and the SfAA's Professional and Ethical Responsibilities (P&ER) is similarly dissected in the right-hand column. We have preserved the AAA's original order, but the sections and clauses of the SfAA code are rearranged to facilitate comparison to those AAA provisions that seem to parallel them most closely. In both documents, however, there are provisions that lack either equivalents or near approximations in the code of the other organization. We have flagged these clauses by using brackets around their index numbers, and by leaving blank spaces in the adjoining column.

In our chapter we have done only a very partial and selective comparison of the two codes. The reader is here provided with some information that may serve to stimulate some thoughtful conclusions of his or her own. If this is accomplished, then our purpose will have been served.

TABLE 8.1. Comparison of the Ethical Codes of the American Anthropological Association and of the Society for Applied Anthropology

AAA's PPR	*SfAA's PC&ER*
1. RELATIONS WITH THOSE STUDIED	1. TO THE PEOPLE WE STUDY
1.1 their interests are paramount	2.1 show respect for their dignity, integrity, and worth
1.2 we must do all in our power to protect informants':	
1.2.1 physical welfare	
1.2.2 social welfare	
1.2.3 psychological welfare	
1.3 communicate our aims as well as possible	1.3 disclose research goals
1.4 allow informants to remain anonymous:	1.4 maintain confidentiality
1.4.1 whether promised it or not	
1.4.2 regardless of data-gathering techniques used (e.g., tape, film, notes)	
1.4.3 must explain capacities of all recording devices	1.5 warn of limited confidentiality
1.4.4 informants may reject same	
1.4.5 no such device may be used to violate dignity or privacy	
[1.5] we may not exploit informants (thus fair return for services)	
1.6 try to foresee repercussions of research/publication on general population studied	1.6 warn of risks to them
1.7 communicate such anticipated consequences to informants	
[1.8] give informants access to research reports where practicable	
	[1.1] disclose sponsorship
	[1.2] disclose methods
2. TO THE PUBLIC	2. TO THE COMMUNITIES STUDIED
2.1 candor and truth in disseminating results, i.e.:	5.3 accurate reporting of our research and other activities
[2.2] no preferential/secret communication of results	
2.3 no knowing falsification of facts	
2.4 integrity in giving professional opinions/explanations	

TABLE 8.1.   *Continued*

AAA's PPR	SfAA's P&ER
2.5 speak out publicly re: our individual and collective knowledge and/or beliefs	6.1 to give it the benefit of our knowledge and skills
2.5.1 contribute to an adequate definition of reality	6.2 to communicate our understanding of human life
2.5.2 as a basis for public opinion/policy	
3. TO THE DISCIPLINE'S REPUTATION	3. TO SOCIAL SCIENCE COLLEAGUES
3.1 no secret or clandestine research (or appearance of it)	
3.2 no research results kept secret	3.2 share research results
3.3 behavior such that colleagues can follow us into the field	3.1 not to impede their activities
	3.5 not to prejudice communities against colleagues for own gain
	[3.3] share techniques
	[3.4] acknowledge colleagues' contributions to our work
	[3.6] not to prejudice any agency against colleagues for own gain
	[3.7] unmask falsification and distortion by others
4. TO STUDENTS	4. TO TRAINEES AND STUDENTS
[4.1] to be candid in regard to:	
[4.1.1] our academic expectations	
[4.1.2] our evaluations of their performance	
[4.1.3] counsel about career opportunities	
4.1.4 warnings about ethical pressures/enticements	4.3 ethical training
4.2 to be fair in regard to:	
4.2.1 nondiscriminatory selection of them in re: sex, race, class, ethnicity	4.1 nondiscriminatory access to our services
[4.2.3] what we expect of them	
[4.2.4] evaluating performance	
4.3 to be nonexploitive by	
4.3.1 giving appropriate credit for their assistance	4.5 recognition of contributions to our publications/reports
[4.3.2] compensating them justly for time/services	

Table 8.1.   *Continued*

AAA's PPR	SfAA's P&ER
[4.4] to be committed to their welfare and academic progress by:	
[4.4.1] helping them find alternatives to working under pressures to act unethically	
[4.4.2] respond to their interests and desires regarding work and relationships	
4.4.3 supervise and encourage their economic/academic endeavors	4.2 competent and relevant training
[4.4.4] assist in securing support/permission for research	
[4.4.5] assist in securing first professional employment	
4.4.6 strive to improve our own teaching techniques	4.4 continuing education for ourselves
5. TO SPONSORS	5. TO OUR EMPLOYERS AND SPONSORS
5.1 to be honest regarding:	
5.1.1 our qualifications	5.1 accurate reporting of our qualifications
5.1.2 our capabilities	
[5.1.3] our aims	
	[5.2] competent, efficient, timely performance
	[5.4] respect their needs, responsibilities, and legitimate proprietary interests
[5.2] consider sponsor's purposes in terms of their past behavior	
5.3 promise nothing contrary to:	
5.3.1 one's professional ethics	5.6 preventing them from distorting or suppressing our policy recommendations
5.3.2 one's other commitments	
[5.4] require of sponsor full disclosure of their:	
[5.4.1] sources of funds	
[5.4.2] personnel	
[5.4.3] aims as an institution	
[5.4.4] aims for the project	
5.4.5 intended disposition of research results	

TABLE 8.1.   *Continued*

AAA's PPR	SfAA's P&ER
5.5 retain our right to make all ethical decisions regarding:	
5.5.1 research results	5.5 preventing them (or other concerned agencies) from distorting, falsifying, or suppressing research results
5.5.2 research reports	
6. TO OWN AND HOST GOVERNMENTS	6. TO SOCIETY AS A WHOLE
6.1 to be honest/candid in all relationships to both	
6.2 demand that ethical compromise not be a condition of permission to do research	2.2 recommend no action harmful to their interests
[6.3] no agreement to do secret:	
[6.3.1] research	
[6.3.2] reports/debriefings	
[6.4] plan and execute research in cooperation with host society	
[6.5] recognize pluralism of host society in making decisions	

Abbreviations: AAA, American Anthropological Association; PPR, Principles of Professional Responsibility; SfAA, Society for Applied Anthropology; P&ER, Professional and Ethical Responsibilities.

NOTES

    1. There are two other professional organizations that go under these initials: the American Psychiatric Association and the American Philosophical Association. Their histories are not to be confused with that of the psychologists' organization, which is by far the largest of the three.

    2. For example, the history and sociology of science have begun within the last decade to do detailed ethnographic studies of scientific laboratories and the social life of scientists (cf. Latour and Woolgar 1979; Knorr-Cetina 1981; Abir-Am 1989). Even more recently, educational researchers have begun to hail "the ethnographic method" as the new paradigm for their endeavors (cf. Keller 1985; Lincoln 1985; Lincoln and Guba 1985).

    3. The recently formed National Association of Practicing Anthropologists (NAPA) has worked on such a code (cf. Amoss 1986) but at this writing had not yet officially adopted one. In any case, since NAPA is a section of the American

Anthropological Association its membership is, presumably, unable to promulgate a code that would contradict the parent organization's ethical injunctions. We therefore confine our remarks to the documents currently in effect within the two largest independent organizations. These are, respectively, the American Anthropological Association's Principles of Professional Responsibility (approved in 1971 and amended in 1975) and the Society for Applied Anthropology's Professional and Ethical Responsibilities (ratified by the membership in 1983). The history of such codes is lengthy and is taken up in Fluehr-Lobban's chapter, so it need not be reiterated here.

4. The same does not seem to be true of the National Association of Practicing Anthropologists (NAPA), but we have no clear reading. Certainly its directory, while liberally sprinkled with academic addresses, seems predominantly to list people working outside the academy.

5. Many of us still remember the Thailand episode, which brought copious comment for more than a year in the columns of the *Anthropology Newsletter* (1970–71), led to formation of an ad hoc committee to adjudicate the dispute, and was the cause of much acrimonious debate at the AAA's annual meetings in 1971. Such events, and the rifts within the AAA that were engendered then, seem never to have been entirely resolved (cf. Berreman's chapter in this volume).

6. One partial exception to this may be civil service employment, where professionals sometimes have what amounts to tenure; however, they may also have to sign pledges of secrecy and/or loyalty, and/or obtain security clearance in order to be employed at all.

7. This particular kind of structural pressure to ethical compromise is less likely to occur in academe, though we must not forget that other sorts of pressures may and do produce scientific fraud in the university as well. Pressures within the academy seem to have two chief sources (once the scientist has received tenure), one psychological and the other economic: first, an overwhelming desire for fame, and second, competition for research funds along with the freedom and power they bestow. (Cf. Committee on Science and Technology, House of Representatives, 99th Congress, 1987. This volume contains not only testimony but also many citations to the literature on scientific misconduct.)

8. We believe that licensing, if it comes at all, is likeliest to come from pressures generated by practitioners, not by academics. Licensing, historically, is not only a means of trying to insure competent and ethical practice; it is, first and foremost, a way of limiting the supply of persons available for hire, with obvious economic and social benefits to those possessing the necessary credentials (cf. Merton and Gieryn 1982).

9. The SfAA Committee on Ethics has recently submitted proposals to do empirical research on such questions (Frankel and Kaplan 1988). Should such research be funded, we hope that anthropologists will cooperate, not only by responding to our questionnaire, but by supplying us with case materials from which general problems may be abstracted and solutions sought. (Don't sharpen your pencils yet, however; so far no agency seems to see such research as meriting either attention or funding.)

REFERENCES

Abir-Am, Pnina
1989   Toward a historical ethnography of scientific rituals: Interpreting the 50th anniversary of the first X-ray protein photograph. (Forthcoming in *Social Epistemology* 2.)

American Anthropological Association (AAA)
1971   Principles of Professional Responsibility. Washington, D.C.: American Anthropological Association.
1974   Amendment to Principles of Professional Responsibility. Washington, D.C.: American Anthropological Association.
1984   Proposed code of ethics would supersede Principles of Professional Responsibility. *Anthropology Newsletter* 25(7):2.

Amoss, N.
1986   Report from NAPA. *Anthropology Newsletter* 27(5):8.

Campbell, Donald T.
1989   Personal communication.

Cohen, Robert S.
1980   Personal communication.

Committee on Science and Technology, House of Representatives, 99th Congress
1987   Science policy study hearings vol. 22: Research and publications practices. Hearing before the task force on science policy, 14 May 1986 [no. 165]. Washington, D.C.: U.S. Government Printing Office.

Dawes, Robyn
1989   Open letter explaining his reasons for resigning from the American Psychological Association. *APS Observer* 2(1):14–15.

Frankel, Barbara, and Bernice Kaplan
1988   Ethical problems of applied anthropologists. Research proposal submitted to NSF Ethics and Values Studies Unit, with an 8-page draft of a survey instrument included as an appendix. (Available in duplicated form by writing to Frankel, Social Relations, Price 40, Lehigh University, Bethlehem, PA 18015.)

Keller, George
1985   Trees without fruit. *Change* (January-February): 7–10.

Knorr-Cetina, Karin D.
1981   *The manufacture of knowledge*. Oxford: Pergamon.

Kushner, Gilbert
1987   Personal communication.

Latour, Bruno, and Steve Woolgar
1979   *Laboratory life*. Beverly Hills, Cal.: Sage.

Lincoln, Yvonna, ed.
1985   *Organizational theory and inquiry: The paradigm revolution*. Beverly Hills, Cal.: Sage.

Lincoln, Yvonna, and Egon Guba
1985   *Naturalistic inquiry*. Beverly Hills, Cal.: Sage.

Merton, Robert K., and Thomas F. Gieryn
 1982   Institutionalized altruism: The case of the professions. In *Social re-
        search and the practicing professions,* ed. R. K. Merton. Cambridge,
        Mass.: Abt Books.
Society for Applied Anthropology (SfAA)
 1983   Professional and ethical responsibilities. *Human Organization*
        42(4):367; and *Practicing Anthropology* 6(1):15.
Warren, C., and B. Laslett
 1977   Privacy and secrecy. *Journal of Social Issues* 33:43–51.
Werner, Oswald, and G. Mark Schoepfle
 1986   *Systematic fieldwork.* Beverly Hills, Cal.: Sage.

Editor's Introduction to Chapter 9

Among the more recent voices to be heard on the subject of ethics and professionalism are those emanating from the National Association of Practicing Anthropologists (NAPA). Drawing together a new generation of practitioners, NAPA was established in 1983, affiliated with the AAA after its reorganization, and it introduced its own set of ethical guidelines in 1988 to respond more directly to the needs of these professionals. One of the coauthors, Jean Gilbert, chaired the committee charged with drafting these guidelines, while coauthors Nathaniel Tashima and Claudia Fishman were members of the committee.

The motivation for creating a special set of NAPA guidelines stemmed from the view that "practitioners were often faced with issues different in degree or kind from those confronted by anthropologists based in academia," and that the work of practitioners is more policy-related and action-oriented. Indeed, it was concerns about the utility of the AAA code (the Principles of Professional Responsibility), raised by many practitioners that led the AAA to respond by proposing its revision in 1984. This thoughtful essay explains, matter-of-factly, the differences between academic and practicing anthropologists, and addresses the day-to-day ethical and professional concerns of this relatively new breed of anthropologist.

Full-time practitioners of anthropology may well be the most visible group of professionals, a fact that generates a special responsibility for them in representing the discipline to the broader community. They are professionals who are most frequently involved with contract research for clients, thus the importance of clarifying the intent of the employer and the future use of research findings is stressed in their Guidelines. They are also professionals who may be more likely to be involved in multidisciplinary work; thus they promote respect for the methods and approaches of other fields. Likewise, the enhanced public responsibility of the practicing anthropologist to demonstrate the value of anthropological approaches in solving a host of human problems is a service that the full-time practitioner offers to the entire discipline.

M. Jean Gilbert, Nathaniel Tashima, and
Claudia C. Fishman

Chapter 9 Ethics and Practicing Anthropologists' Dialogue with the Larger World

Considerations in the Formulation of Ethical Guidelines for Practicing Anthropologists

Introduction

IN 1986, the Governing Council of the National Association of Practicing Anthropologists (NAPA) requested one of the authors of this chapter (Gilbert) to form a committee to draft guidelines for the ethical conduct of practicing anthropology. In doing so, NAPA recognized that, while practicing anthropologists' ethical concerns coincide to a great extent with those of other anthropologists, practitioners are often faced with issues different in degree or kind from those confronted by anthropologists based in academe. What we lacked as practicing anthropologists was a bridge that took us from the academic to the public domain by defining, in addition to the ethical obligations enjoined on all anthropologists, appropriate behavior in the day-to-day business of anthropology as it is enacted in the larger world. It was felt that stated ethical guidelines could make us more reflective about how we interact with our colleagues and the public and also provide others with a basis for evaluating our behavior. The guidelines needed to take into consideration the fact that, by and large, practitioners are involved in work that is policy-related and action-oriented. That is to say, there is the expectation that the practitioner's research findings not only will be used for theory-building and the advancement of knowledge but also will provide a basis for actions that will impact on the lives of others. The guidelines would also need to show recognition of the fact that practitioner anthropology extends beyond research and frequently involves the anthropologist in widely varied programmatic and advisory capacities. Thus, in phraseology and perspective, the document would need to encompass this broader purview. Finally, issues of accountability are particularly critical for action-oriented researchers. They are frequently hired by one group or constituency to provide information that will inform decision-making and action that will affect the lives of another. To whom is the anthropologist accountable? In what way can the practitioner ethically bridge the gap between groups which may have conflicting stakes in the research or work performed?

The NAPA committee, consisting of Nathaniel Tashima, Claudia Fishman, Barbara Pillsbury, and Jean Gilbert, drafted guidelines, published and presented them for comment, and redrafted them several times prior to their adoption as guidelines for members of NAPA in 1988. The Southern California Applied Anthropological Network (SCAAN) served as a valuable sounding board during the drafting process. This brief discussion will serve as an introduction to the guidelines by reviewing some of the issues that surfaced during the process of their formulation. It should be pointed out, however, that these comments consist of the authors' reflections on these issues and are not to be construed as representative of the views of NAPA, SCAAN, or their members. The guidelines, to which we will refer frequently, are appended to this volume.

Issue 1

Anthropologists, whether they are academic or practicing, share a unique relationship with the people among whom they conduct research. This relationship distinguishes them from most other social scientists and carries particular ethical responsibilities, both scientific and personal. For practicing anthropologists, however, ethical sensitivity is particularly critical since their work generally has a more direct and immediate impact on the lives of people they study or work with.

Anthropologists based in academe and practicing anthropologists share a set of research goals and methods that distinguish them from other behavioral scientists: they seek to produce accurate, detailed descriptions of the actual behaviors of the groups they study and also to convey to the larger world the meanings attributed to those behaviors from the point of view of the actors themselves. They develop these data through systematic fieldwork methods. These methods require that the anthropologist go to the locale and maintain firsthand, lengthy, and intensive contact with the people being studied. Participant observation, in-depth interviews, and the use of key informants, all basic strategies of the ethnographic method, focus attention on the relationship between the individual researcher and the researched in a much more personal manner than is the case with most other types of social science research. The research population *participates* more intensely in the development of data than in other types of research, and for this participation to occur, bonds of trust must be secure between the researcher and the people studied.

Additionally, through its cooperation and participation, the research or resource population acquires a stake in the research results and usually develops quite reasonable expectations and concerns about the data and how it will be used. The data generated by an ethnographer thus differs substantively, for example, from that of a scientist who sends a team of interviewers into a community to implement a survey questionnaire based on the scientist's world view and variables reflecting what the *scientist* deems important. In this latter case, the researcher may never actually be in contact with the "subjects" studied and his or her report back to the larger world is likely to be a highly generalized and compartmentalized review of findings that is no more than an abstract reflection of the group's activities and ideations placed in the context of the researcher's world view.

Unlike the ethnographer, this more distal scientist is responsible for relating neither a precise description of the actual activities of people nor an interpretation of the meaning of those activities from their perspective. In contrast, by dint of actual person-to-person contact and the assumption of the task of interpreting one group's perspectives to others, the ethnographer, whether academic or practitioner, takes on a very personal responsibility. Though much effort can be made to systematize data collection and improve the objectivity and detachment of the ethnographer, in the final analysis the interpretation of the group's reality is often filtered through the researcher alone.

The practicing anthropologist differs significantly from the academic anthropologist in terms of research goals, however. Whereas anthropological work in general seeks to expand theory and provide an understanding of people and their cultures, this information *may or may not* be used by others to formulate actions that affect the lives of the people studied. On the other hand, practitioner's work almost always has the specific goal of generating information upon which decisions can be made or actions taken. Practitioner's work is policy-related and action-oriented. The goal may be, for example, to determine what probable impacts on people's lives or life-styles the building of a specific roadway or dam may have, or, as in social marketing, to find out how to introduce or to implement a particular social change in a culturally acceptable or appropriate way. Therefore, the information developed by a practicing anthropologist is likely to be used to directly affect people's lives. The anthropologist, therefore, has a responsibility to assess whether that impact will be positive or negative and for whom.

The practitioner's sensitive, comprehensive, and in-depth consideration of the ways in which one or several groups of people may be affected by research findings or other factors associated with his or her work is a crucial ethical responsibility. The first statement in NAPA's guidelines calls attention to this overarching principle. Although the researcher must retain scientific objectivity in the collection, analysis, and presentation of the data and in the making of recommendations, he or she is obliged to make clear to those who intend to use the knowledge developed the potential impact, negative and positive, that such use might have on people's welfare. To this it should be added that the anthropologist's assessment of impact cannot ignore the issue of differential power as it accrues to the different groups that will be affected by use of the information or that will use the data as the basis for action. A comprehensive assessment of impact on the welfare of people would include structural constraints operative on the persons or groups party to or affected by the action. The practicing anthropologist should be wary of undertaking work where such a comprehensive assessment is not feasible, an awareness which should be operative *before* a contract is signed or a job accepted (Guideline 3).

Issue 2

Practicing anthropologists encounter numerous situations in which their findings or other aspects of their work impact on the lives of multiple groups of people. Sometimes the interests of the affected groups conflict. How can practitioners deal with this situation in an ethical way?

This issue was introduced frequently and in many different guises as NAPA's members and the committee struggled with the creation of the Ethical Guidelines. As is stated in the introductory paragraph, no code can anticipate unique circumstances, so no hard and fast rules can be laid down. Rather, the practitioner is held responsible for doing some careful thinking throughout any project in which he or she is involved, including determining which groups might potentially be affected and in which ways. Several guidelines are given to help the practitioner deal with conflictive circumstances. Practitioners are advised to make clear to their research population or resource persons the objectives and sponsorship of their activities (NAPA Guidelines, 2; Appendix H). They should make clear their commitment to confidentiality and outline the means they will use to insure confidentiality. By so doing they can give interested parties the opportunity to make their concerns known to the anthropologist and appropriate persons or agencies (NAPA Guidelines, 1). Practitioners should also be prepared to make clear the "assumptions and facts" on which they have based the conduct of their work (introductory paragraph, NAPA Guidelines).

Most important, the guidelines hold the practitioner responsible for carefully reviewing work contracts, clarifying the intent of the employer and the use to be made of projected findings *prior to entering* into a contractual or other relationship with an employer or client (NAPA Guidelines, 1). It is also the ethical responsibility of the practitioner to find out how committed and concerned the employer/client is to (1) issues of confidentiality, and (2) public access to data or information to be developed. At the outset of a project, then, the practitioner has the obligation to determine, as far as possible, whether his or her ethical obligations to respect the rights of others will in turn be respected by the employer. The message is clear: do not sign on the dotted line if you do not know who your work will affect or how the information you develop will be used or to whom it will be made available.

Recognizing that a practitioner who acts with care and in good faith prior to beginning a project may still encounter ethically compromising situations as the project develops, the guidelines point out that such circumstances cannot be ignored but must be dealt with as they occur (NAPA Guidelines, 3).

As can be seen, while the guidelines cannot provide specific ethical "how to's" for solving specific problems, they call attention to general circumstances in which ethical decision-making is critical. They also make it clear that several steps are incumbent upon the practitioner for ensuring ethical practice: (1) acquiring the necessary information for ethical choice-making; (2) considering that information prior to committing to carry out work; (3) remaining sensitive to ethical considerations during the course of work; and (4) publicly articulating the standards undergirding their ethical stance to all interested and affected parties.

Issue 3

Practicing anthropologists, because their daily work involves them with a wide range of agencies, businesses, service providers, policymakers, and communities, are perhaps the most visible of all anthropologists. Moreover, their more directly advisory relationship to the public differs from that of academically based anthropologists. This visibility and relationship carries with them a responsibility to represent the discipline well to the larger world.

There is very often the expectation that the practicing anthropologist will, based on his or her findings or expertise, be able to render expert advice. In this regard, the practicing anthropologist provides a professional service and joins the ranks of other service-providing professionals, such as doctors or lawyers, whose recommendations inform personal and public decisions and actions. This advisory capacity expands our responsibilities into arenas beyond research. The NAPA guidelines recognizes this in its first section by expanding ethical considerations to "decisions, programs or research in which we take part." Just as physicians, clinical psychologists, and lawyers—those in whose counsel the public puts its trust because of perceived professional expertise in a specific arena of human services—are expected to uphold ethical codes, so should specific kinds of ethical conduct be expected from service- and counsel-providing anthropologists.

Academic anthropologists rely primarily on the scholarly community to evaluate the quality and ethical aspects of their research. While the communities among whom they gather data may only vaguely understand their purposes, their "paying customers," such as granting agencies, universities, students, and editors of academic journals, do share some part of the anthropologists' frame of reference.

By contrast, practitioners earn their living in the nonacademic domain, which means that they do research for, communicate insights to, and are paid by persons who may have little understanding of their training or organizing principles. As with other professionals, the larger world knows practicing anthropologists only by how they present themselves, their purposes, and their services in interaction with others. Practitioners are judged by the reasonableness of their methods, which need to be very clearly defined; by their sensitivity to people's needs in specific situations; by their ability to produce data or give counsel that has pragmatic value; and by the ethical standards they expound or demonstrate in everyday interaction.

For example, in our work as practitioners, we occasionally come across persons or even whole communities who questioned the ethics of individuals who had previously done research among them, presenting themselves as anthropologists. We learn to our dismay that their prior experiences with anthropologists (who may or may not have been practitioners) have not been good. It has often happened that anthropologists did research in the community and offered no return for the community's cooperation or participation. Or the anthropologist *did* promise a return of some kind and failed to follow through on the promise. What may have happened in these cases is that an anthropologist or anthropology student studied a community, but gave little real thought as to the expectations of the people studied, why the community allowed the project to proceed, and what further commitments the community thought were necessary to translate theory and findings into action. Certainly, people among whom research is being conducted, along with much of the public, frequently have a different understanding of what research is about from that of the researcher. Most of the time their expectations do revolve around the notion that research will generate findings that will have application in the resolution of a problem or issue rather than simply the advancement of knowledge. When a researcher leaves the site with whatever data has been gathered and is not heard from again (except, perhaps, for publication in journals to which the general public has little access), people's confidence in the ethics undergirding anthropological research is badly shaken, and they are reluctant to have anthropologists in their midst again. The researcher who has left the community for the university or parts unknown does not have to deal with these discontents or with the fact that he or she has created a circumstance that makes it difficult for social scientists (the public does not discriminate between research disciplines as precisely as we do) who come after them.

The practicing anthropologist cannot return to the university environment to build theory on his findings and publish them in scholarly journals; rather, he consistently faces the expectation that his findings will be translated into action or recommendations to others about what actions should be taken. And, frequently, when actions are taken, the practitioner is held at least partly responsible for their impact, pro or con, effective or ineffective, on people's lives. For both practical and ethical reasons, then, the practitioner must attend to and deal forthrightly with expectations that may be raised during the research process and to the way in which the research or program he or she is conducting is interpreted to the public.

Critical to the maintenance of good praxis is the relationship the practitioner has to the client/employer, who is, in a sense, another important "public." Employers come in all sorts, sizes, and levels of organizational complexity, from individuals to corporations to public agencies and governments. Section 3 of the guidelines addresses anthropologist-employer relations. This section adjures the practitioner to be forthright with employers and clients. This recommendation includes communication about many aspects of the practitioner-client relationship: skills and methods, findings and recommendations, and ethical issues.

The guidelines point out that the ethical practitioner has an obligation to be professionally competent. We would expect the anthropologist to interpret this as being current with anthropological theory and skills, being capable of implementing a variety of ethnographic methods, and being able to select methods appropriate for specific tasks. Nothing is gained and much is lost, both ethically and pragmatically, by mystifying or obfuscating the methods through which our work is conducted, thus the guidelines underscore the necessity for clarity in communicating our findings and recommendations, and, by implication, the methods upon which they are based.

Practitioners have the opportunity to demonstrate the efficacy and flexibility of anthropological methods in a wide variety of settings and contexts to many people who might have little prior understanding of the discipline. Clear and nonjargonistic communication not only is the accountable thing to do (people must understand our methods in order to assess them and their results), but also serves to expand public understanding and respect for anthropology as a useful discipline.

Issue 4

Practitioners find themselves in a multidisciplinary world, working with specialists from many disciplines and fields. How do we define the ethics of our relationships to these persons, whether they are trainees or colleagues?

The terminology of academic anthropology, with its emphasis on the university milieu of classes, graduate and undergraduate students, and researchers, fails to encompass adequately the broader world of practicing anthropologists. The work of a practitioner may include program design, project evaluation, service provision, policymaking, training, and group leadership as well as research and teaching. In the language of the NAPA guidelines, we try to allude to this broader world in several ways, for example, by referring to trainees and training situations, as well as students and classes, and "work," which is less specific than "research" with its more academic connotation.

The guidelines (Section 4) point out some of the teaching or training situations that are often part of a practitioner's work. The practitioner may be instructing professionals and nonprofessionals with widely varied backgrounds, rather than undergraduate or graduate anthropology students. It is, for example, not unusual for a practicing anthropologist with a specialization in substance abuse to provide in-service training on cultural issues surrounding use and abuse to highway patrolmen one week and to intern physicians the next. In providing these variable types of instruction, the practitioner must consider the needs of the trainees, making sure to provide bridges that link anthropological data and theoretical interpretations to the needs and understanding of trainees. This not only underscores the anthropologist's respect for trainees, but is "good press" for anthropology, because it makes the relevance of anthropological perspectives, methods, and data concrete for persons outside the discipline.

Oftentimes, too, in the training situations in which practitioners are involved, trainees bring to the encounter important insights derived from their own training and background, frequently culled from much hands-on experience, whether professional or paraprofessional. Thus a model of information-sharing and exchange is usually more appropriate in these situations than a professor-student paradigm (NAPA Guidelines, 4).

Noting that in practicing anthropology, colleagues and collaborators as well as trainees are drawn from a variety of occupations and professions, the guidelines (Point No. 5) point out that both respect for and openness to the methods and perspectives of persons inside *and* outside our discipline are important ethical responsibilities of practitioners. Anthropologists have had a tradition of research typically conducted by the solitary researcher who performs all tasks and orders all phases of a research endeavor. In contrast, the practitioner is likely to be expected to work reciprocally with individuals who do not share anthropological training or perspectives. Frequently, the anthropologist may perform one set of research tasks that feed into or inform a later set performed by a person with another kind of specialized training, as in the case where an ethnographic study is completed prior to and informs the content of an epidemiological survey. The effective coordination of multidisciplinary or team research requires both an understanding of and respect for the methods of the contributing disciplines (Guidelines, 5).

Further, the practitioner is often involved in the development and application of research findings. The charge may be to develop information about an issue or situation, then to design or modify a program, service, or even treatment in accordance with research findings. The practitioner may be responsible also for implementing a program after its design. Alternatively, the anthropologist with a specific area of expertise may be called in in an advisory or evaluative capacity when a program is well under way. In any case, the practitioner, much more than the academic anthropologist, will most likely be involved in teamwork with numerous persons who have skills, information, and ethical standards different from his or hers, but who share power and responsibility.

The need to consider the ethical responsibilities of individuals coming from other occupations and disciplines is also enjoined upon practitioners in section 5. Thus, for example, the anthropologist who is privy to group therapy or counseling sessions of a psychologist as part of an evaluation project must be sensitive and responsive to the issues of client confidentiality and client-therapist rapport in the way the evaluation is conducted and reported.

The multifaceted training and collegial opportunities enjoyed by practicing anthropologists offer a unique opportunity to make clear and public the ethical perspectives of our profession to yet other "publics." It became apparent to the drafters of the guidelines, after reviewing the codified ethical principles of a variety of professions, that anthropological thought engendered a broad, humanistic regard for the welfare of others and a valuation of cultural and group differences that were absent from most ethical codes. Interaction with and training of persons from other walks of life allows for the dissemination and consideration (though not necessarily the adoption!) of this compassionate disciplinary perspective.

Issue 5

As highly visible anthropologists, practitioners have obligations to the discipline to communicate disciplinary perspectives to the wider world and enhance the role of anthropology in public life and policymaking.

There have been an increasing number of calls from within our profession for anthropologists to take a more visible role in public affairs and policymaking. The NAPA guidelines assert that the practitioner does have the responsibility to present the discipline of anthropology to others in a positive way and to emphasize the value of anthropological approaches to resolving human problems (NAPA Guidelines, 6). If the practitioner adheres to the suggestions in the prior sections of the guidelines, the discharge of this responsibility will probably automatically occur. Fortunately, however, there are numerous ways in which the practitioner can actively promote a wider, positive understanding of the discipline.

There are many ways in which individual anthropologists can speak out publicly. We can accept invitations to hold board positions with nonprofit organizations that focus on issues or populations about which our research has given us special knowledge. We can seek and accept positions on county and state commissions and advisory panels. We can provide in-service training to service providers and participate in a variety of teaching and training activities outside of academic settings. We can present some of our papers at multidisciplinary conferences or to conferences attended by service providers, administrators, and policymakers. We can publish accounts of our methods, findings, and, especially, their practical and applied implications, to a wide variety of audiences in clinical and medical journals, social work publications, policy and opinion journals, and even general interest magazines. By "going public" in these and other ways, anthropologists can increase people's awareness of our discipline's perspectives, methods, and ethical views. As more of the public comes to view anthropology as a useful discipline, we will be asked with greater frequency to use our skills and information for the ends that probably attracted most practitioners to the discipline in the first place: to increase human understanding and resolve human problems.

Conclusion

Clearly, the circumstances and situations in which practitioners must make ethical decisions are going to vary, so no "cookbook" prescriptions for ethical behavior can be made. The NAPA guidelines cannot take the place of painstaking and soul-searching deliberation on the part of the individual practitioner. The guidelines, therefore, particularly numbers 1 and 3, advocate a "look before you leap" philosophy based on the overriding principle of respect for the welfare and human rights of all people affected by our work.

Although adopted in its present form by NAPA, the guidelines can be understood as an interim or working document in the sense that it reflects important changes in the discipline but will need to be modified as the field of anthropology continues to evolve in its direction and compass.

Part IV

Components of the Dialogue for a New Era

Editor's Introduction to Chapter 10

This final chapter discusses the major issues and points of view expressed by various authors in this volume, and it takes that dialogue into the 1990s and beyond. The older issues of community and informant confidentiality, responsibility to subjects of research, the relationship to one's own and the host country's government, and the related issue of secret or clandestine research, are examined in light of nearly two decades of review and debate that has occurred within the profession since the introduction of the first general code of ethics in 1971 by the American Anthropological Association.

Newer issues that have been raised in the intervening years since 1971 are identified and discussed, such as the overriding context of the scarcity of academic jobs and the new impetus given to applied and practicing anthropology in the 1970s and 1980s. The practitioner anthropologist working within a context of clients and contract research presents a new challenge to the field of ethics and the profession, since the primary research model that the Principles of Professional Responsibility was based upon was that of the academic researcher in the field. Now the "field" may well be a drug rehabilitation center in a major American city, or a literate, well-informed non-Western cultural group, and newer issues of the proper relationship to those studied and informed consent are raised. The unique history of informed consent as a concept in anthropology is discussed here as well. The core ethical principle of the primary responsibility of the anthropologist being to the people studied is examined in light of the contemporary controversy within the profession over the issue of the return of skeletal remains from museum collections to identifiable Native American communities-descendants. Here the responsibility to science and to the peoples-cultures studied are juxtaposed and difficult choices have been made.

The chapter concludes with an examination of some of the ethical dilemmas posed by the "New Era." The complex set of ethical responsibilities among the various constituents found in contemporary research—the people studied, the client or sponsor, the academic profession—creates a complicated and often confusing situation for the researcher. One solution offered is the development of a consciousness regarding ethics and professional practice such that questions of ethics are raised *before* and *during* research, rather than after the fact or at the time of publication of research results. Newer, more ethically conscious models of research that involve participants are offered as a way to create both better scientists and better science.

Carolyn Fluehr-Lobban

Chapter 10 Ethics and Anthropology in the 1990s and Beyond

THE CRISIS THAT WAS PRECIPITATED by the proposed major revision of the PPR in 1984 was resolved in various ways. The concerns that the National Association of Practicing Anthropologists had with the Principles of Professional Responsibility were met with the drafting and introduction of their own code, Ethical Guidelines for Practitioners, in 1988. The American Anthropological Association, recognizing the need to respond to the transformed nature of the discipline and the new professional, mounted a new effort to revise the PPR with the appointment of a committee to draft a revision of the code. Chaired by Robert Fernea, the committee included both academic and practicing anthropologists. A new draft revision was created in 1989 that bore close resemblance to the original PPR in name and format, although basic change was there in substance and orientation. The new General Principles of Professional Responsibility included nonacademic research on a par with academic research and spoke to the employment of anthropologists in client-based research, government agencies, and private businesses. A fundamental change was effected in the elimination of all references to the AAA condemnation of secret or clandestine research.

An outsider to the field may ask, What has all of the controversy been about? Some insiders may even be puzzled as to why so many battles seem to be waged over issues of ethics. Historically the arena of ethics has been a battleground where differences of morality and professional standards are disputed, but also where more fundamental issues of the profession itself have been sorted out. It may be, as Hakken says in his chapter, that the profession does not have a common culture where philosophy, ideology, and practice are widely shared, so basic questions of ethics and morality, of at least some concern to all practitioners, provide the context within which other professional issues are played out.

A functionalist might argue that a major purpose of professional codes of ethics is to provide the framework for common dialogue within a profession and thus, secondarily, help to bond professionals to each other. This may be so, even if the "bonding" appears to be brought about by conflict wherein professionals argue or disagree with one another but in the end restore equilibrium to the structure. It is not at all clear that this has been the case, for indeed important centrifugal forces have been at work within the AAA during the same period as the crisis over ethics has occurred. At least one part of the recent controversy over ethics has been the underlying tension between academic and practicing anthropologists (to which Halsey, Frankel and Trend, and others refer in their chapters), and the overriding context for the recent exacerbation of that tension has been the scarce economic resource of academic jobs.

New Issues

SCARCITY OF JOBS IN THE 1970S AND 1980S; GROWTH OF APPLIED ANTHROPOLOGY

A number of the contributors to this volume address the issue of the job market, and they disagree about it. Erve Chambers suggests that the ethical issues are much the same as they have always been, and that the academic job market has little to do with the recent controversy. He is fearful, however, that much of the recent "ethics talk" will scare younger professionals away from employment opportunities that may be *perceived* as questionable. Frankel and Trend see the limited academic market for recent Ph.D.'s over the past fifteen years as critical to an understanding of the new economic and intellectual pressures young professionals face, while Berreman, Hakken, and Graves and Shields all allude to the underlying and basic significance of changed employment patterns for anthropologists.

It is important to recall that the demographic shift toward a larger proportion of applied anthropologists than academic anthropologists has only been recorded officially since 1986. There has not been sufficient time to define the new problems of ethics that may have emerged, nor to assess this trend and evaluate its impact on the profession as a whole, together with the issue of ethical standards. A practicing anthropologist might be employed by a Native American rights organization or by the U.S. Bureau of Indian Affairs and, predictably, have different ethical dilemmas and solutions. An academic anthropologist might consult regularly for the U.S. Agency for International Development and, therefore, might conduct both "pure" academic as well as proprietary research.

Chambers, who has argued that polemics often have clouded the real ethical issues, sees an unfortunate stereotyping of applied research as questionable simply because it is client-based. There is, no doubt, a great deal of confusion over the nature of applied research, the degrees of freedom and constraint that can be exercised by the researcher, because the contexts of work are so variable. It is helpful, therefore, that Frankel and Trend offer a definition of applied research about which, at least, professionals can argue. They define applied anthropology as either: (1) providing clients with means of applying existing anthropological data or (2) creating new knowledge tailored to the client's goals. To be sure, the sticking point would be the latter, and the critical nature of the definition of the client's goals vis-à-vis the subjects of research. However, the dialogue has not advanced to this point, where debate and evaluation of different kinds of activities by practicing anthropologists have been considered.

The huge area of development-related anthropological research has only been touched upon in this volume, and, like other important recent trends, it also has not been subject to sufficient critical assessment by the profession. For the large number of anthropologists who have sought development contract work, the challenge of the principal responsibility of the anthropologist "to those they study" (PPR, Section 1) could present real conflicts. The nature of working for massive development agencies, often representing governmental interests, is that the "master" shifts from people studied to the sponsors of research, providing the compromising set of conditions that the client is one's own or another's government. The American Anthropological Association has spoken clearly and on several occasions to the point that anthropologists should exercise caution in pursuing employment or research contracts with their own or host governments (cf. Statement on Problems of Anthropological Research and Ethics 1967; Principles of Professional Responsibility 1971). During the two decades since these statements were made, anthropologists have joined AID and other governmental projects in non-Western countries in record numbers, as part-time or full-time employees. Yet, during the same period, discussions about employment opportunities in these areas of government have outweighed discussion of the ethical implications of this type of work.

With the formation of the National Association of Practicing Anthropologists in the past decade, a new voice and a new constituency within the discipline has emerged. By their own definition, the designation "practicing anthropologist" includes full-time and part-time practitioners who work for clients such as social-service organizations, government agencies, and business and industrial agencies (cf. NAPA Ethical Guidelines, Preamble 1988). The newer dimension to this code is the mention of the business and industrial communities. An applied, "industrial anthropology," like that which exists in sociology, never developed during the first century of anthropology, given the traditional emphases of the field. As the discipline of anthropology and anthropological methods, especially, have come to be understood and appreciated by the business and educational sectors, however, more and more applied anthropological opportunities exist.

The tension that has existed between academic and applied anthropologists surfaced anew as this recent emphasis on the practice of anthropology has emerged. Many traditional academic anthropologists might mistrust or not regard very highly this type of employment. The concerns raised from practicing anthropologists, as early as 1975, that the PPR was "based only on academic considerations" led, ultimately, to the proposed revision of the ethical code in 1984. Those who defend and seek to protect the ethical core of the PPR not only oppose its revision but also might perceive a political or ideological struggle with this new generation of business-oriented, practicing anthropologists. By initiating and backing revision of the PPR, the AAA leaned toward this new constituency, and thereby risked alienating more traditional sectors of its membership.

The greater risk, to which Berreman and also Frankel and Trend refer, is the possibility that the discipline will divide or fracture along academic and practicing lines, and the "holism" that has long been a canon of American anthropology will dissipate. To a large extent that process has already occurred, apart from any controversy over ethics. With long-standing, independent histories of associations like the Society of American Archaeology, the Society for Applied Anthropology, the American Ethnological Society, as well as the appearance of newer organizations now affiliated with the AAA, the process of fission has been more pronounced than that of fusion in the history of anthropology. So, it appears the current debate over ethics is also very much an attempt to confront new realities in the discipline and chart a future course for anthropology in the 1990s and the twenty-first century, according to the way various constituencies might envision it.

Apparently, the 1990s will present a different job-market situation for anthropologists. A recent study, *Prospects for Faculty in the Arts and Sciences: A Study of Factors Affecting Demand and Supply 1987–2012* (*New York Times*, 13 September 1989), projects faculty shortages during the decade of the

1990s that will especially affect disciplines in the humanities and social sciences. Predictably, these shortages reflect the flight from disciplines that offered few opportunities during the preceding two decades. A new job market where academic positions are in demand would relieve many economic pressures, but the impact of the previous period would continue to be felt and, perhaps, result in a broadened and more complex discipline of anthropology—or a divided one.

Old Issues Revived and Reconsidered

CONFIDENTIALITY: COMMUNITY AND INFORMANT ANONYMITY

The dialogue for a new era embraces not only what is new to the field but also a reexamination of ethical principles that have long been a part of the continuing dialogue.

Confidentiality and the protection of community and informant anonymity have been staples in the stock and trade of ethics education in American anthropology. Indeed, the doctrines of privacy, confidentiality, anonymity, and privilege have been cited as centrally relevant to the conduct of research on human subjects (Dalgish 1976). The statements on ethics and the codes reflect this: "Informants have the right to remain anonymous" (PPR 1971, Section 1.c); "We shall provide a means throughout our research activities and in subsequent publications to maintain the confidentiality of those we study" (SfAA Professional and Ethical Responsibilities 1983, Section 1); "These persons [informants] would be informed of our commitment to the principle of confidentiality and of the steps we will take to insure confidentiality" (NAPA 1988, Ethical Guidelines, Section 2). The consensus on this point transcends both time and organization and should, therefore, be unassailable. However, Szklut and Reed in this volume, and others they cite in their work, have questioned the universal applicability of this canon in all research situations. Indeed, anthropological accounts are very often sympathetic, as a result of long-standing familiarity with a community, and anonymity is frequently *not* desired on the part of informants or community leaders, the latter being more likely to have worked closely with the anthropologist.

The same three codes cited above also go to some lengths to caution anthropologists that absolute confidentiality may not always be attainable. "Despite every effort being made to preserve anonymity, it should be made clear to informants that such anonymity may be compromised unintentionally" (PPR, Section 1.c[1]); "The people we study must be made aware of the likely limits of confidentiality" (SfAA Professional and Ethical Responsibilities, Section 1); "[We] should thoroughly investigate and understand all of the limitations on our claims of confidentiality and disclosure" (NAPA Ethical Guidelines, Section 2). According to Szklut and Reed, an ironclad promise of confidentiality is not always sought in field research and need not always be protected in the subsequent publication, as these codes direct. The presumption of desired informant and community confidentiality may not always be so, and this sentiment is reflected in the wording of the 1990 Revised PPR (I.1) where the informant's right to remain anonymous or to receive recognition is respected.

Clearly, one solution would be, as Graves and Shields argue, the discussion and negotiation of the issue *in advance,* without prior assumptions about confidentiality and disclosure. This would be a part of the overall review of the research design and methods with the subjects of research combined with a simple, added discussion about the desirability of confidentiality. The world is a more complex and sophisticated place than it was even a generation ago, and many informants/subjects of research are literate, conscious people for whom questions of confidentiality would be both understood and appreciated.

The matter of confidentiality in the law as it might impact anthropologists and other social scientists is more complicated and technical; simple solutions like those mentioned above do not suffice. Archaeological sites are protected by law in the United States, and the Society of Professional Archaeologists' Code of Ethics directs the archaeologist not to reveal confidential information *unless* required by law (1989, 3.2). The proposed revision of the PPR is the only document to employ such wording when it says, "Where the likelihood exists that others may take legal action to force disclosure of the anonymous identity, resource persons should be advised that the anthropologist may not be able to claim confidentiality" (1984, Section 4). Of course, this may only be noted in passing since this document was never approved and has only historical interest at this point. The recent NAPA Ethical Guidelines do not address the legal issues, perhaps for the reason that the threat of the law and legal suits, even in the abstract, could have an inhibiting, chilling effect on contemplated research contracts.

There is a formal, legal history to the courts' intervention in protection of the researchers' data that is outside of the scope of this volume. Graves and Shields discuss the Popkin case, wherein the U.S. Supreme Court would not offer protection to this political scientist's sources on the ground that "journalists" had no "special privileges." Other courts (such as California's) have ruled that academic researchers are entitled to the same rights to protect confidential sources of information, and that compulsory disclosure would unquestionably stifle research (Culliton 1976).

This dimension of ethics and legal responsibility in anthropological research is sensitive, and is only in the earliest phase of being recognized for its relevance and impact on the discipline. Perhaps this is because there have been no major, national cases of this type in anthropology, and, as was pointed out in the historical survey in chapter 1, the discipline has charted its course in ethical guidelines *in response to* crises precipitated by events, rather than in anticipation of them. The American Sociological Association's code of ethics, also introduced in 1971, recognizes the legal limits of confidentiality placed upon its members, and in straightforward language it says, "Even though research information is not a privileged communication under the law, the sociologist must, as far as possible, protect subjects and informants" (Clapp 1974:734).

RESPONSIBILITY TO SUBJECTS OF RESEARCH

If there is any statement in the Principles of Professional Responsibility that summarizes the core of its philosophy, it is the first statement in the code after the preamble: "In research, anthropologists' paramount responsibility is to those they study. When there is a conflict of interest, these individuals must come first." This guiding, primary responsibility to the subjects of research at once reflects the humanistic essence of the discipline and directs anthropologists' actions toward this special definition of the field. Probably no other single issue was more important in igniting the controversy over ethics in 1984 than the apparent dropping of this core principle. The first principle in the proposed revision says: "Anthropologists must seriously consider their own moral responsibility for their acts when there is a risk that an individual, group, or organization may be hurt, exploited, or jeopardized physically, legally, in reputation, or in self-esteem as a result of these acts." A comparison of the two statements captures some of the tenor of the times in which they were written (in the early 1970s and the early 1980s, respectively) and shows some of the changes that occurred in the discipline in only a decade. The universal moral imperative to those studied that is expressed in the PPR would have been replaced with an individual, highly contextual, personal and legal sense of responsibility. It should be apparent why emotions ran high, and why the organizational response of ANRAP to the proposed revision focused on this shift in paramount responsibility. The strength of this core principle is reflected in the fact that it was left intact in the 1990 Revised Principles of Professional Responsibility.

It might seem to some that the PPR, generated during the heady days of the Vietnam War, had lost some of its relevance, but the basic issue of the relationship to those studied remains alive in the current period. One contemporary interface between anthropologists and indigenous peoples involves the issue of the archaeological remains of burials of native groups in the United States, and the issue has also been raised in Australia, New Zealand, and parts of Africa. In August of 1989, representatives of indigenous groups from these regions met with archaeologists at a conference sponsored by anthropologist Larry Zimmerman of the University of South Dakota; the conference called for a worldwide moratorium on the scientific analysis of anthropological remains until the wishes of the contemporary descendants of these cultures could be determined (Raymond 1989). Halsey (chapter 5) tells us that an informal moratorium on excavation of Native American remains has been in effect in American archaeology for about the past fifteen years. Specifically, the International Indian Treaty Council and the American Indians Against Desecration cited "the anthropologist's primary responsibility to those he studies" as a major substantiation for the correct position regarding ethics and the treatment of anthropological remains. Indeed, the position taken at this forum appears to go beyond the formal ethical principles adopted by the Society of Professional Archaeologists, which states (1989, Section 1.1[c]) that an archaeologist shall "be sensitive to, and respect the legitimate concerns of, groups whose culture histories are the subjects of archeological investigation." The central contemporary issue has been that of the proper treatment of archaeological remains of cultures "whose histories" are the subject of archaeological study. A recent volume on the ethics of archaeological collecting asks the provocative question, Cultural property: whose culture, whose property? (Mauch Messenger 1989).

In 1989, the Smithsonian Institution reached agreement with the U.S. Congress and representatives of national Native American rights groups, such as the National Congress of American Indians, whereby all the archaeological remains of native populations would be returned in cases where tribal descendants could be identified. Robert McC. Adams, secretary of the Smithsonian, was quoted in the press as saying, "It is wonderful and inevitable. We do so with some regret, but everyone would acknowledge that when you face a collision between human rights and scientific study, then scientific values have to take second place" (*Providence Journal-Bulletin,* 13 September 1989, p. A-12).

With the PPR still in effect and a revised version retaining this principle under consideration as of this writing in 1990, the continuing relevance of this point is demonstrated in this case, although the archaeological community in the United States is not unanimous in agreeing to the moratorium or to the return of archaeological remains. Stanford University has recently announced that they will return for reburial the estimated 550 skeletal remains of the ancestors of the Ohlone-Costanoan culture (*Chronicle of Higher Education,* 5 July 1989, p. A-4). Stanford made its decision based on the unanimous recommendation of the anthropology faculty and a provost's advisory committee. An emeritus anthropology professor, Bert Gerow, who collected most of the remains, criticized the decision, saying that "the proper owner of these remains is the scientific community." Other scholars from around the country joined Gerow's protest, for example, Donald Ortner, chair of anthropology at the Smithsonian's National Museum of Natural History, who said that reburial would "forever remove material" that could be analyzed in the future to contribute new information of value to science and to Native Americans.

The NAPA Ethical Guidelines do represent the practicing anthropologist's need to assume responsibility for diverse research and practice settings. As such, the text reads, "Our primary responsibility is to respect and consider the welfare and human rights of all categories of people affected by decisions, programs or research in which we take part" (1988, Section 1). This approach envisions the more complex reality that the anthropologist working for a client faces, as opposed to the relatively simpler research "contract" that exists between the social scientist and the people studied. The principle that paramount responsibility is owed to the subjects of research is a noble, highly moral position that reflects a central humanism in the discipline that many anthropologists note with pride. In this connection, it may be a point that serves a certain function of image-making, and to this degree the PPR, like other codes of ethics, engages in disciplinary public relations. To return to the Vietnam-era temporal context of the PPR, it surely *was* important to get the point across, that first and foremost in anthropological research come the people we study. However, its *continuing* relevance has been demonstrated in the current period over the issue of the return of Native American remains, and the reinforced primacy of human values over scientific inquiry.

Other codes of ethics from related social science disciplines have not taken this position as strongly. The code of ethics of the American Sociological Association states, as its fourth point, the principle that "all research should avoid causing personal harm to subjects used in research" (Clapp 1974:733).

RELATIONSHIP TO ONE'S OWN AND ONE'S HOST GOVERNMENTS
The first anthropological statements and code of ethics are clear in regard to the professional working for the U.S. government. The 1967 Statement on Problems of Anthropological Research and Ethics says (Section III.3), "Anthropologists contemplating or accepting employment in governmental agencies in other than policy-making positions should recognize that they will be committed to agency missions and policies." The PPR pursues this question further (Section 6): "In relation with their own government and with host governments, research anthropologists should be honest and candid. They should demand assurance that they will not be required to compromise their professional responsibilities and ethics as a condition of their permission to pursue research."

While the traditional emphasis has been on the protection of the anthropologist, research sources, and data, some contemporary voices have lamented the lack of an "internal tradition of contributing to policy analysis" for one's own government (Eickelman 1986:34). This was especially apparent during the Iranian crisis, when intelligence analysis failed to assess properly the revolutionary situation and when anthropologists and other social scientists with firsthand knowledge of events in Iran were, generally, not consulted.

Because anthropologists, whether doing academic or applied research, have predominantly carried out their research in non-Western countries or among "third world" people in their own countries, their activities are heavily dependent on access provided through state governments or agencies. The location of research is frequently determined largely by a political context of friendly or normal relations between the national government of the anthropologist and the state wherein the research is to be conducted. Outsiders to the field have observed, "The emphasis in anthropology on the culture and customs of ordinary people may make it the most sensitive discipline of all." This particular comment was made by Kenneth Prewitt, former president of the Social Science Research Council and one of the initiators of U.S.-China exchanges, in discussing the case of Steven Mosher, the Stanford University graduate student dismissed from its program of anthropology for "illegal and seriously unethical conduct" (Coughlin 1987).

After several decades of being generally closed to anthropological research, many believed that future research in China would be jeopardized for American scholars because of Mosher's case.

Possibly the most celebrated instance involving ethics and relations with foreign governments of the 1980s, the Steven Mosher case is complex and, ultimately, resolved in a court of law. But its most significant dimension is that it raises again the delicate issue of the appropriate relationship to one's own and the host government.

Among the first of a new cadre of researchers permitted to work in the Chinese countryside, Mosher had a special responsibility to carry out research in a manner that would not jeopardize future research. Even in countries with which there are established good relations, poor judgment and unethical behavior can harm the opportunities for future research, as Berreman has documented elsewhere for India (1969). Also, for a guest researcher in another country, there is almost always subordination to formal government approval of research and other regulation of one's movements, and there is an informal subordination to local custom that is incumbent on the foreign social scientist. There may be a weakness for certain anthropologists who come from relatively powerful nations in the world community to resist orders and formal restrictions on research activity imposed by relatively less powerful nations. The Mosher case, with all of its complicated scholarly, international, and especially ethical issues, reminds us that the dialogue in which we are engaged is neither abstract nor purely academic.

SECRET-CLANDESTINE RESEARCH;
DISTINGUISHED FROM PROPRIETARY RESEARCH

The matter of intelligence-related research has been a central feature of much of the historical furor over ethics in anthropology. As this volume has shown in the chapters by Berreman, Chamber, Halsey, and me, the issue of secret research has been repeatedly condemned in the discipline, and the apparent dropping of this core feature in the proposed revision of the PPR has ignited other fires of protest.

The PPR, intended for the general membership of the American Anthropological Association, is eminently clear on this point: "Anthropologists should undertake no secret research or any research whose results cannot be freely derived and publicly reported" (3.a). Moreover, "Anthropologists should avoid even the appearance of engaging in clandestine research, by fully and freely disclosing the aims and sponsorship of all research" (3.b). However, the codes designed specifically to assist applied and practicing anthropologists, who are most likely to work in situations that might raise this issue, are not as clear. What is remarkable is that *all* references to secret-clandestine research have been dropped by the revised PPR of 1990. The radical departure that this represents may not be fully appreciated by the present membership unfamiliar with the history of this subject in the discipline.

The SfAA code does not directly mention secret or clandestine research, nor do the new NAPA Ethical Guidelines; however, ethical responsibility and proprietary research are addressed. The SfAA code, after an initial caution that applied anthropologists not engage in actions that impede other researchers' professional activities, says that "while respecting the needs, responsibilities, and legitimate proprietary interests of our sponsors we should not impede the flow of information about research outcomes and professional practice techniques" (Section 3). The former allusion to "actions that impede other's professional activities" is a clear reference for anyone familiar with this particular history in the discipline that secret government research, once disclosed, indeed jeopardizes future research by colleagues. As Berreman shows, secret research is not a matter of simple theoretical interest; its conduct has had serious, damaging ramifications in the history of the field.

The sensitive issue of social scientists working for or collaborating with the Central Intelligence Agency was renewed in the mid-1980s at Harvard with the public disclosure that its director of the Middle East Institute had organized a major conference on Islamic fundamentalism that was sponsored by the CIA, but not acknowledged as such. This type of disclosure and others like it in anthropology, other social sciences, and area studies has fostered a changed CIA policy regarding *its* relationship with scholars. At a 1986 speech at Harvard, Robert Gates, then the CIA's deputy director for intelligence, said that the CIA "will henceforth permit acknowledgement of our funding of research that is later independently published by a scholar unless 1) the scholar requests privacy or 2) we determine that formal, public association of C.I.A. with a specific topic or subject would prove damaging to the United States" (Paul 1986). A great deal of discretion is still permitted the CIA under point 2, but the fact that the agency conceded the point about public disclosure is a measure of the success the academic organizations have achieved regarding covert sponsorship.

In a related vein, an announcement in 1983 that the Defense Intelligence Agency's (DIA) Defense Academic Research Support Program

(DARSP) was inviting requests for proposals from social scientists, including cultural anthropologists, to produce "unclassified, publishable research studies using only source material . . . to obtain a wide range of scholarly and expert . . . viewpoints, appraisals, opinions and assessments to supplement analyses and policy deliberations within the Defense Department" stirred more response among the area studies organizations that had been specifically designated by the DIA invitation. The Board of Directors of the African Studies Association in a 1982 resolution called upon Africanist scholars "to refrain from participation in the Defense Intelligence Agency's program . . . and to oppose participation in that program by their universities and research institutes" (reprinted in *ASA News,* 1990; Delancey 1990). The Ethics Committee of the Middle East Studies Association (MESA), together with representatives from the American Council of Learned Societies and the Social Science Research Council reviewed the request, met with representatives of the DIA in 1984 to explore its proposal. Expressing sentiments that have reverberated throughout the social sciences since Project Camelot, the Ethics Committee urged that scholars and area studies centers "carefully review the complex issues of their responsibilities to the present and future scholarly community before entering into contract research or training agreements with any intelligence agency" (Eickelman and Waldman 1985). Substantially the same position is taken in the Association of American Universities report (Lambert et al. 1984), with the addition that Department of Defense–supported research likewise jeopardizes foreign colleagues with whom American social scientists collaborate.

What is new here is the defense and intelligence establishment's approach to the academic community; it is an approach that incorporates a great deal of the language and concerns of academia regarding research and the majority view that research be open, unclassified, and publishable. What is noteworthy is that, despite the discussion between representatives of the academic community and the DIA, the result, from several professional organizations, was a strong cautionary note to their members regarding their potential response to the DIA's "Requests for Proposals."

Proprietary research, contracted by clients, is significantly different from the above and is protected by the SfAA's mention of the legitimate rights of sponsors; however, once again, the PPR (Section 5) is more cautionary of the anthropologist taking on such employment: "Anthropologists should be especially careful not to promote or imply acceptance of conditions contrary to their professional ethics or competing commitments. This requires that they require of sponsors full disclosure of the sources of funds,

personnel, aims of the institution and the research project, and the disposition of research results." It was, perhaps, a sincere effort to apply this strong
principle in actual research for sponsors that led to some of the questions
that were raised soon after the PPR was introduced. As Graves and Shields
have demonstrated in their chapter, the conditions mentioned above are
difficult to meet and, even if discussed in advance, they may not address
issues that arise during the period of the research; in their case, conditions
changed considerably over the two-year period of research. However, as
they argue, discussion or negotiation of research issues in advance is highly
preferable to the discord that can result from avoidance of ethical matters
involving full disclosure.

The NAPA Ethical Guidelines may be helpful in this regard. They say
in Section 3:

> At the *outset* of a relationship or contract with an employer or client, we have
> an obligation to determine whether or not the work we are requested to
> perform is consistent with our commitment to deal fairly with the rights and
> welfare of persons affected by our work, recognizing that different constituen-
> cies may be affected in different ways. At this time, we should also discuss with
> our employer or client the intended use of the data or materials to be generated
> by our work and clarify the extent to which information developed during our
> activities can be made available to the public.

Presumably, the anthropologist so informed of her or his relationship to
the intent and outcome of research can make a solid ethical judgment as to
acceptance or nonacceptance of a contract. The anthropologist may not be
the sole recipient of predetermined conditions, but she or he can actually
participate in an open negotiation of the conditions and conduct of research. This proactive model is endorsed by Hakken as supporting intervention and clarification of ethical issues before the research is initiated, and
Graves and Shields argue for a plan of monitoring progress on the mutually
agreed upon method of work.

Covert inquiry, more popularly associated with intelligence-gathering
for governments, may involve any ruse, cover, or disguise an anthropologist might use to conceal his or her true identity and purpose. It has been
much debated in the social sciences, with arguments favorable to it stress-
ing the value of information not otherwise obtainable, while others have
opposed its basically dishonest approach. A recent frank and sensitive
discussion of the problem of covert research in an African-American community by a white researcher (Rose 1988) places this issue in a contempo-

rary perspective. Rose, who used covert inquiry, came to reject it, and to question its having any value in ethnographic practice.

Secret-clandestine research still generally remains anathema to anthropological researchers, although no longer specifically censured in the revised code, while covert research is still generally disapproved of; however, proprietary research, with which anthropologists are increasingly involved, is another subject not to be confused with either of the preceding. Client-based research, carefully considered and even negotiated, carries its own particular risks, but they are not of the same magnitude as are the effects of engaging in secret research. Some of these risks are discussed by Frankel and Trend as "pressures": the loss of control one experiences in working for a client, the possible loss of self-esteem suffered by not engaging in traditional academic publishing, the protection of confidentiality and relationship to those studied when one is not the initiator of the study. These risks are real and need to be considered, not simply at the moment before securing employment, but as a part of applied anthropological teaching and training. Such serious attention to the matter of the ethics of working for clients would represent a major advance in the "dialogue for a new era" before the polemics that Chambers and others abhor have their damaging effect.

INFORMED CONSENT: ITS PARTICULAR HISTORY IN ANTHROPOLOGY
Informed consent has become enshrined as a virtual sine qua non for the conduct of medical and biological research where more or less direct cause and effect can be established between participation in research and its outcome. Ideally, this is conceived of as voluntary participation motivated by enlightened self- or group interest. The rights of subjects of research are formally protected in the Department of Health, Education and Welfare's strict guidelines, the "Protection of Human Subjects," which have been generated from the medical-scientific model of research appropriate to the United States and the West in general. Typically, consent forms have been developed which can be administered to subjects of research prior to the initiation of the study. However, anthropological research, utilizing its method of participant observation, traditionally in non-Western countries, does not conform to the model of medical-scientific research.

At the time of post-Camelot, Vietnam War era anthropology, in 1969, Margaret Mead argued for the substitution of voluntary participation for informed consent in anthropological fieldwork, in line with her contention that fieldworker and subject are involved in a joint enterprise. Trust between the anthropologist and informant is critical, and she saw that the stringent rules governing scientific experimentation amounted to a denial of trust. Mead's position stressed the collaborative role of the subject and appropriately summarized the traditional relationship between anthropologist and informant. Although Mead said that the usual research model is for the anthropologist to pay informants for their time and information, she did not raise any ethical questions regarding this "knowledge for hire." To be accurate, the pattern of paying informants is subject to regional variation; while it is normal for researchers to pay Native American informants, this practice is virtually absent in Africa and the Middle East.

Murray Wax (1976) has argued that social science fieldworkers should not be subjected to these rigid controls because the model of the powerful researcher and powerless subject does not apply to social and anthropological fieldwork. Prior written and informed consent, he argues, should be replaced by a detailed accounting of fieldwork that is subject to review by academic and professional peers. This type of monitoring of fieldwork has never been advocated on an organized basis, although many non-Western nations require a formal account of research aims and results before giving the anthropologist permission to commence research or to leave the country.

None of the anthropological codes discussed here, specifically, has used the phrase "informed consent," no doubt because of the legal controls and regulations the phrase conjures in the world of scientific research. Anthropology increasingly is recognized and utilized in other fields because of its major technique of participant observation, which allows the anthropologist-outsider to penetrate a social structure as unobtrusively as possible and observe and record its inner workings. Researchers outside anthropology have recognized the value of this technique for its naturalness, which frequently avoids formal interviews, taping, and questionnaires. It is therefore recognized as a major means of finding out what people actually do, rather than what they say they do. The introduction of informed consent regulations would have a restrictive, even stifling, effect on anthropological research, but the ethical question remains, How do we inform and obtain consent under these conditions of research?

If we examine the codes themselves, they advocate that: (1) the aims of the investigator be communicated as well as possible to the informant (PPR), and (2) the people we study have the right to disclosure of our research goals, methods, and sponsors (SfAA); the NAPA Ethical Guidelines use a similar wording, adding the phrase "full and timely disclosure."

The wording of the PPR reflects some of the concern that traditional anthropological work has often taken place among nonliterate populations wherein the aims of research or even its publication might be incomprehensible. Increasingly, that world is disappearing, and the lives of non-Western peoples have been utterly transformed by colonialism and other forms of Western economic and political influence, mass communications, and an increasingly literate and conscious population which also happens to be the subject of research. Informed consent in this light takes on a new and different meaning, and discussion of sources of funding, research goals, and methods with informants or their legitimate representatives has become more of a necessity in the "new era."

Likewise, if the trend toward more and diversified applied research continues, traditional concepts of informed consent may, indeed, apply to anthropology in the future. Short-term, contract research might not employ the traditional, more time-consuming method of participant observation, and established means of ensuring informed consent may be structured into government or agency-directed projects that employ anthropologists. As such, informed consent, as it is more typically understood and applied in other fields, may increasingly be a factor in research conducted by anthropologists.

Ethical Dilemmas Posed by the "New Era"

There is a clear conflict between the PPR and its primary responsibility to those studied and the codes of the applied and practicing branches of the discipline, wherein the principal responsibility of the anthropologist is shared among a number of constituencies, only one of which is the people studied. In the current dialogue, is this a resolvable conflict? I do not think so, except in the de facto resolution that multiple codes now exist from which the anthropologist may choose, depending upon the research context.

Morally and philosophically, can there be equal responsibility to the people studied and to the client or sponsor, as well as to colleagues and the discipline, or any other interested parties to research? Were the players equal in the planning and conduct of research, there might be some formula that could be generated that might approximate justice and equity. But in the research enterprise, as it is currently constructed in the United States, with its well-established rules for obtaining grants and contracts, the players are *not* equal. Generally speaking, the anthropologist plays a mediating role between funding source and sponsor, and the people to be studied. Funding typically flows from the sponsor, at the top of this particular hierarchy, to the anthropologist, who acts upon the research subjects. There are very few cases where this flow is reversed, although the cases where the researcher is employed by the community are notable and have received a good deal of attention in the past (John 1972).

There are some situations wherein the anthropologist will confront the choice among these unequal players to whom she or he will be *primarily* responsible. These dilemmas will cause confusion to some, especially given the variable emphases of the codes, and painful choices to others. Anthropologists working in large development projects may be torn between honest evaluation in a research project and the powerful national and international aims of the sponsoring agency. Having to choose between continuing work on a project and employment is not attractive to anyone, and might result in a personal choice *not* to think about the ethical implications of one's work.

There is another issue that the codes do not raise, but which is implicit in anthropological debate and practice involving ethics, although this has rarely been discussed as such in the discipline: the issue of relativism and ethics. Cultural relativism, whatever its ultimate scientific merit or contribution, has been a part of the American anthropological world view, teaching, and training since the time of Boas. In a world comprehended by cultural relativism, human behavior is to be observed and recorded, but not judged by any universal standard of ethics or morality. Into this relativistic concept of humanity is injected a universalist principle of research methodology, that in all cases the primary responsibility of the anthropologist is to the people he or she studies. Trained in relativism, many anthropologists will respond that such a principle depends on the context or, perhaps, even on *their* understanding of the aims and intent of research.

G. N. Appell (1974) has raised the matter that the anthropologist is frequently confronted with situations of moral ambiguity, given the variable cultural context of ethical norms, and for this reason, he says, they have not involved themselves with questions of ethics. There is a danger that ethical relativism can flow too easily from cultural relativism. This highly contextual perception and response to ethical dilemmas is easily justified by an individual anthropologist's reference to her or his own conscience, rather than to established principles of a professional organization.

The shift in some of the newer codes to the wording that an individual anthropologist is responsible for her or his own actions in regard to research reflects this tendency, which may be a trend toward individual responsibility and, thus, away from collective, universalist principles.

Anthropologists have been engaged in a dialogue over ethics for seven decades: informally, since Boas's famous letter to the editor in 1919 and formally, since 1949, when the first code of ethics was introduced by the Society for Applied Anthropology. Over the years, many concerned anthropologists have turned their attention to matters of ethics, sometimes placing these issues above their own professional advancement. The often political nature of the crises over ethics that the discipline has experienced makes this an area that some have hesitated to enter or reenter.

Objective review and analysis of the issues have been the only fruitful way to advance this dialogue, and other studies of ethics and anthropology have preceded this one (Beals 1969; Weaver 1973; Rynkiewich and Spradley 1976; Appell 1978; Wax and Cassell 1979; Cassell and Jacobs 1987). These and other significant contributions to the continuing dialogue on ethics have been ably summarized by Murray Wax (1987). The American Association for the Advancement of Science and its Professional Ethics Project and Committee on Scientific Freedom and Responsibility have coordinated efforts among the affiliated professional organizations of the AAAS and have published several helpful reports that place general ethical issues within an interdisciplinary framework (Chalk, Frankel, and Chafer 1980; Frankel 1988).

New Directions Toward a More Consciously Ethical Model of Research

As the discussion and debate over ethics and its proper place in applied or academic research has progressed, parallel and more subtle changes in research methodology have been occurring within both applied and academic branches of the discipline. These developments reflect a changed consciousness regarding the people we study and have grown in a direction that is more egalitarian in regard to the relationship between researcher and subject, and more sensitive to the community aspirations and needs. While it may not be possible to argue a causal connection between the events we have discussed in this volume and the newer paradigms of research to be outlined below, a certain relationship and convergence of ideas can be shown. It may be, after all, that real change occurs in life and not with words put to paper, and this may be one of the more useful aspects of ethical codes and their continual debate and revision.

STUDYING ON A PAR WITH THE "SUBJECTS" RATHER THAN RESEARCH FROM ABOVE

The old, much maligned model of colonial-style research where the anthropologist worked with and for the administrative, occupying government with a subject population has passed with the fading of this older order. Today, anthropologists who work for government agencies like the Bureau of Indian Affairs have adopted a more egalitarian approach to research and practice and have listened to the many voices critical of anthropology raised from native communities, the most notable of whom is Vine Deloria. Archaeologists have listened and responded positively to Native American concerns about excavation of new cemeteries and reburial of ancestral human remains. The new genre of anthropological literature, "reflexive anthropology," in which the field researcher reflects upon her or his experience and its impact on self and on "the other," speaks to this point of the shared humanity of both the researcher and the informant.

The new model of research *involves* the "subject" as a participant in an active way, as an individual or group with a vested interest in the study. Jointly authored and directed projects replace the older model of research from above, planned, executed, and published by the anthropologist alone. Community or individual involvement in the progress of research, thus designed, becomes a condition for its success, not simply a fortuitous by-product of work with informants (cf. Lobban and Coli 1990).

The new model of research may presume a literate, conscious community of informants who may not only participate in research but also read and critique drafts of publishable results.

NEGOTIATION OF CONDITIONS OF RESEARCH, INCLUDING ETHICS

The growing consciousness of the researcher, to which we hope we are contributing with this volume, is such that ethics is increasingly becoming a part of the *plan* of research, rather than an afterthought or an exercise in self-conscious reflection once the study has been completed. Thinking about the ethical issues *in advance,* as several of the authors in this volume have recommended, creates not only better scientists, but better science. The tensions that have been described in this volume—between client and researcher and between researcher and subjects or community—can be greatly alleviated through a process of *prior* negotiation on points of ethics involving the intent and conduct of research and its results. Prior negotiation implies open discussion of the possible ethical dilemmas that might occur during any phase of research from planning to publication, and a clarification of the interests and positions of the various constituencies involved in the study.

Just as the Vietnam War was a watershed period for the growth of consciousness in anthropology and ethics, and for other disciplines in the social sciences and humanities as well, the current period of societal crisis concerning ethics may yield some fresh models and standards for professional behavior. For whatever social forces are at work, at least for the moment "ethics is in," as one journalistic piece has observed (Mulligan 1989), and the opportunity is not one to be lost or taken lightly.

Hopefully, this volume seizes the moment and the opportunity, and not only captures the dialogue of this time but also advances it. By engaging in this process, the anthropologist might withdraw from the project, or the community may not want to participate, or the client may not be able to exercise the kind of freedom required to meet the ethical standards of the former two participants. The inclusion of a discussion of ethics in the planning stage of research is vastly preferable to the potential harm to the profession, to the research enterprise, and to the subjects that might result when such issues are avoided.

We have tried in this volume to examine the long-standing ethical issues in anthropology in a fresh light; to raise some of the newer issues that have emerged during the recent period of change and transition in the field; and, most important, we have tried to establish a framework within anthropology for a dialogue for this new era.

REFERENCES
Appell, G. N.
    1974   Basic issues in the dilemmas and ethical conflicts in anthropological inquiry. *Module* 19:1–28.
    1978   *Ethical dilemmas in anthropological inquiry: A case book*. Waltham, Mass.: Crossroads Press.
Beals, R. L.
    1969   *Politics of social research*. Chicago: Aldine.
Berreman, Gerald
    1969   Academic colonialism: Not so innocent abroad. *The Nation,* 10 November, 505–8.
Cassell, Joan, and Sue-Ellen Jacobs, eds.
    1987   *Handbook on ethical issues in anthropology*. Special publication of the American Anthropological Association, No. 23. Washington, D.C.

234 Carolyn Fluehr-Lobban

Chalk, Rosemary, Mark Frankel, and Sallie Chafer

   1980   *Professional ethics activities in the scientific and engineering societies.* Washington, D.C.: American Association for the Advancement of Science.

Clapp, Jane

   1974   *Professional ethics and insignia.* Metuchen, N.J.: Scarecrow Press.

Coughlin, Ellen K.

   1987   Politics and scholarship mix in China researcher's long battle with Stanford. *Chronicle of Higher Education,* 14 January.

Culliton, B. J.

   1976   Confidentiality: Court declares researcher can protect sources. *Science* 193:465–67.

Dalgish, T. K.

   1976   *Protecting human subjects in social and behavioral research: Ethics, law and the DHEW rules: A critique.* Berkeley: Center for Research in Management Science, University of California.

Delancey, Mark W.

   1990   Open letter to colleagues regarding 1982 DIA resolution. *ASA News,* Quarterly Newsletter for African Studies Association Members, XXIII(2) 1990.

Eickelman, Dale F., and Marilyn Waldman

   1985   A report to the MESA membership from the ethics committee. *Middle East Studies Association Newsletter* 7(1).

Fluehr-Lobban, Carolyn

   1987   *Islamic law and society in the Sudan.* London: Frank Cass and Co., Ltd.

Fluehr-Lobban, Carolyn, and Richard Lobban

   1986   Families, gender and methodology in the Sudan. In *Self, sex and gender in cross-cultural research,* 182–96. Urbana and Chicago: University of Illinois Press.

Frankel, Mark, ed.

   1988   *Science, engineering and ethics, state of the art and future directions.* Report on an AAAS Workshop and Symposium, American Association for the Advancement of Science Office of Freedom and Responsibility (February).

Gert, Bernard

   1988   *Morality, a new justification of the moral rules.* Oxford and New York: Oxford University Press.

Green, Edward C., ed.

   1986   *Practicing developmental anthropology.* Boulder and London: Westview Press.

Greene, Ernestene L., ed.

   1984   *Ethics and values in archaeology.* New York: Free Press.

Hakken, David

   1985   Ethics and professionalism in American anthropology: Commentary. *American Anthropology Newsletter* (May).

John, V. P.

   1972   Learning at Rough Rock. *Human Organization* 31:447–53.

Lambert, Richard D., et al.
  1984   *Beyond growth: The next stages in language and area studies.* Washington, D.C.: Association of American Universities.
Lobban, Richard, and Waltraud Coli
  1990   *Cape Verdeans in Rhode Island.* Providence: Rhode Island Heritage Commission.
Mauch Messenger, P., ed.
  1989   *The ethics of collecting: Whose culture? Cultural property: Whose property?* Albuquerque: University of New Mexico Press.
Mead, Margaret
  1969   Research with human beings: A model derived from anthropological field practice. *Daedalus* 98:361–86.
Mulligan, Hugh
  1989   Ethics is in: From Wall Street to Madison Avenue, ethical standards are now in demand. *Providence Sunday Journal,* 21 May, pp. B-1, B-8.
Orlans, H.
  1973   *Contracting for knowledge.* London: Jossey-Bass.
Paul, Angus
  1986   CIA eases stand on research role: Scholars cautiously welcome shifts. *Chronicle of Higher Education,* 26 February.
Rawls, John
  1972   *Theory of justice.* Cambridge, Mass.: Belknap Press of Harvard University.
Raymond, Chris
  1989a   Some scholars upset by Stanford's decision to return American Indian remains for re-burial by tribe. *Chronicle of Higher Education,* 5 July.
  1989b   American Indians seek moratorium on studies of skeletal remains. *Chronicle of Higher Education,* 16 August.
Rose, Daniel
  1988   *Black Philadelphia street life.* Philadelphia: University of Pennsylvania Press.
Rynkiewich, Michael A., and James P. Spradley, eds.
  1976   *Ethics and anthropology: Dilemmas in fieldwork.* New York: John Wiley & Sons.
Shortage seen for faculty in the 1990s
  1990   *New York Times,* 13 September.
Wax, Murray
  1976   On fieldworkers and those exposed to fieldwork: Federal regulations, moral issues and rights of inquiry. Washington University Occasional Paper, St. Louis.
  1987   Some issues and sources on ethics in anthropology. In *Handbook on ethical issues in anthropology,* ed. J. Cassell and Sue-Ellen Jacobs. Special publication of the American Anthropological Association, No. 23, Washington, D.C.

Wax, Murray, and Joan Cassell, eds.
    1979   *Federal regulation: Ethical issues and social research*. AAAS Symposium No. 36. Boulder, Colo.: Westview Press.
Weaver, Thomas, ed.
    1973   *To see ourselves: Anthropology and modern social issues*. Glenview, Ill.: Scott, Foresman and Co.

Part V

Appendixes

Contents

Printed together for the first time are the following statements of ethical guidelines or codes of ethics that have been adopted by the American Anthropological Association, the Society for Applied Anthropology, the National Association of Practicing Anthropologists, and the Society of Professional Archaeologists, including the first ethical code in anthropology put into effect in 1949 by the Society for Applied Anthropology:

A. Report of the Committee on Ethics, Society for Applied Anthropology, 1949.
B. Statement on Problems of Anthropological Research and Ethics, Adopted by the Council of the American Anthropological Association, March 1967.
C. Statements on Ethics: Principles of Professional Responsibility, Adopted by the Council of the American Anthropological Association, May 1971 (as amended through November 1976).
D. Committee on Ethics: Role and Function of the Committee on Ethics, Adopted by the Council of the American Anthropological Association, May 1971 (as amended through May 1976).
E. The Society of Professional Archaeologists (SOPA), Code of Ethics, Standards of Research Performance and Institutional Standards, 1976.
F. Professional and Ethical Responsibilities, SfAA (revised, 1983).
G. Proposed Code of Ethics Would Supersede Principles of Professional Responsibility, *Anthropology Newsletter,* Vol. 25, No. 7 (October 1984).
H. National Association of Practicing Anthropologists' Ethical Guidelines for Practitioners, 1988.
I. American Anthropological Association, Revised Principles of Professional Responsibility, 1990.

Appendix A

Report of the Committee on Ethics, Society for Applied Anthropology, 1949

CONSIDERATION OF THE DEVELOPMENT of a code of professional ethics for applied anthropologists was inaugurated at a panel discussion at the spring meeting held in New York in May, 1946. It was there moved that a committee be appointed to explore the subject further. This committee made its first report at the business meeting in Chicago in December, 1946. On the basis of the discussion at that meeting, a revised draft was circulated to the entire membership. The responses to this were summarized and were presented at the spring meeting in New Haven in 1947 at a dinner where the speakers had made some comments about legal and medical professional ethics. Later, the report was again revised and circularized with the statement that, after a further revision on the basis of the membership response, it would be acted upon finally at the spring meeting in Philadelphia in 1948. There, the report, once more amended as a result of the mail poll and meeting discussion, was unanimously adopted in substance. At the same time the committee was instructed to rewrite the report, which was still couched in professional jargon, and to publish it in *Applied Anthropology*, now called *Human Organization*. The report as herewith presented is, therefore, the outcome of two and a half years of discussion. For the phrasing of the last paragraph, the committee is heavily indebted to the Committee on Ethics of the International Preparatory Commission for the International Congress on Mental Health, which met in England in 1948.

The following principles are to be regarded as applying specifically to the practice of applied anthropology, as an addition to the anthropologist's own code of ethics which governs his behavior as a private individual, as a citizen, and as a scientist in peace and in war. It is recognized that as different fields of applied anthropology develop, there will be a need to specify behavior appropriate to each field, such as the role of the anthropol-

ogist in hierarchical and bureaucratic structures, the question of the classi-
fication of materials from which a variety of implications might be drawn,
procedures for professionalizing relationships between anthropologists
and collaborators who may be both co-workers and informants, etc. It is
believed that procedures in these special fields can be best developed by
groups of applied anthropologists within each field of industry, government, public relations, communications, etc. However, the general principles outlined in this code are believed to be applicable to the work of all
applied anthropologists. In our present day world, no organization can
bind its members to specific goals or value systems, e.g., on religious,
political or philosophical issues, but it can insist that sound professional
ethics in applied anthropology involves a responsibility for the foreseeable
effects of all applications of professional skills.

The Code

We recognize:
That the applied anthropologist must take responsibility for the effects
of his recommendations, never maintaining that he is merely a technician
unconcerned with the ends toward which his applied scientific skills are
directed.

That the specific means adopted will inevitably determine the ends
attained, hence ends can never be used to justify means and full responsibility must be taken for the ethical and social implications of both means
and ends recommended or employed.

That the specific *area of responsibility* of the applied anthropologist is to
promote a state of dynamic equilibrium within systems of human relationships. This means that the applied anthropologist is concerned either with
maintaining a system of human relationships in a state of dynamic equilibrium or in aiding the resolution of a system into such a new state as to
achieve a greater degree of well-being for the constituent individuals. He is
further concerned with preserving within such a state of equilibrium those
potentialities for change through which greater well-being for the individual can be achieved. The systems of human relationships for which the
applied anthropologist takes responsibility can be defined as the most
inclusive system of interrelationships within which sequential changes in
the actions of persons may be identified.

That within the limits of his skill and conditions of employment he
should take what responsibility he can for the long time effects of his acts,

recognizing that within present anthropological knowledge, predictive skills must be supplemented by continued individual attention to the functioning of such a system.

That an individual is acting as an applied anthropologist whether he is using his scientific skills on behalf of an employer for a fee, or whether he is using them on behalf of an organization or a cause on a voluntary basis, or in any other way in which the application of his anthropological skills will specifically advance some value or goal to which he owes personal allegiance. The applied anthropologist may not in any situation justify a course of action by appealing to a set of values to which he himself owes personal allegiance, unless he is willing to submit this course of action to the same scientific tests he would use in other applied situations.

That no applied anthropologist may undertake a commission on behalf of any interest, or segment, or section of a group, which anthropologically we recognize as an interrelated system of human relationships, without a specific avowal, to those on whose behalf he undertakes the task, of his intention of taking the whole into account.[1] He should recognize also that actions taken on behalf of any such group may create crises in the system or in individual members, and that it is the duty of the applied anthropologist to point out the need for other measures, not previously included in the group's program, to provide for recovery after such crises or disturbances have occurred.

That the applied anthropologist should recognize a special responsibility to use his skill in such a way as to prevent any occurrence which will set in motion a train of events which involves irreversible losses of health or the loss of life to individuals or groups or irreversible damage to the natural productivity of the physical environment.

That the applied anthropologist must take the greatest care to protect his informants, especially in those aspects of confidence which his informants may not be able to stipulate for themselves.[2]

1. It has been emphasized in discussions that the applied anthropologist may properly work for a partisan group within a society (e.g. The National Association of Manufacturers, the Congress of Industrial Organizations, the Anti-Saloon League, the Planned Parenthood League, the National Catholic Rural Life Conference, the National Conference of Christians and Jews, etc.) recognizing that such groups are a significant and important part of our social life and that improvements in the functioning and social understanding of any one such group can be valuable to the whole society. However, the applied anthropologist should also scrutinize all special interest groups as to the possibility of any such group becoming destructive of the larger whole.

2. For example, members of aboriginal groups just entering into complex culture contact situations. The publication of real names of members of pre-literate groups together with records of practices which may at some later time come under public censure or legal interdiction is a case where such care needs exercise.

Finally, applied anthropologists accept as a code of ethics:

To advance those forms of human relationships which contribute to the integrity of the individual human being; to maintain scientific and professional integrity and responsibility without fear or favor to the limit of the foreseeable effects of their actions; to respect both human personality and cultural values; to publish and share new discoveries and methods with colleagues; those are the principles which should be accepted and which should be known to be accepted by all those who work in the disciplines affecting human relationships.

MARGARET MEAD, *Chairman*
ELIOT D. CHAPPLE
G. GORDON BROWN

Appendix B
Statement on Problems of Anthropological Research and Ethics, Adopted by the Council of the American Anthropological Association, March 1967

THE HUMAN CONDITION, past and present, is the concern of anthropologists throughout the world. The study of mankind in varying social, cultural, and ecological situations is essential to our understanding of human nature, of culture, and of society.

Our present knowledge of the range of human behavior is admittedly incomplete. Expansion and refinement of this knowledge depend heavily on international understanding and cooperation in scientific and scholarly inquiry. To maintain the independence and integrity of anthropology as a science, it is necessary that scholars have full opportunity to study peoples and their culture, to publish, disseminate, and openly discuss the results of their research, and to continue their responsibility of protecting the personal privacy of those being studied and assisting in their research.

Constraint, deception, and secrecy have no place in science. Actions which compromise the intellectual integrity and autonomy of research scholars and institutions not only weaken those international understandings essential to our discipline, but in so doing they also threaten any contribution anthropology might make to our own society and to the general interests of human welfare.

The situations which jeopardize research differ from year to year, from country to country, and from discipline to discipline. We are concerned here with problems that affect all the fields of anthropology and which, in varying ways, are shared by the social and behavioral sciences.

I. Freedom of Research

1. The Fellows of the American Anthropological Association reaffirm their resolution of 1948 on freedom of publication and protection of the interests of the persons and groups studied:

Be it resolved: (1) that the American Anthropological Association strongly urge all sponsoring institutions to guarantee their research scientists complete freedom to interpret and publish their findings without censorship or interference; provided that

2. the interests of the persons and communities or other social groups studied are protected; and that

3. in the event that the sponsoring institution does not wish to publish the results nor be identified with the publication, it permit publication of the results, without use of its name as sponsoring agency, through other channels.

—*American Anthropologist* 51:370 (1949)

To extend and strengthen this resolution, the Fellows of the American Anthropological Association endorse the following:

2. Except in the event of a declaration of war by the Congress, academic institutions should not undertake activities or accept contracts in anthropology that are not related to their normal functions of teaching, research, and public service. They should not lend themselves to clandestine activities. We deplore unnecessary restrictive classifications of research reports prepared under contract for the Government, and excessive security regulations imposed on participating academic personnel.

3. The best interests of scientific research are not served by the imposition of external restrictions. The review procedures instituted for foreign area research contracts by the Foreign Affairs Research Council of the Department of State (following a Presidential directive of July, 1965) offer a dangerous potential for censorship of research. Additional demands by some United States agencies for clearance, and for excessively detailed itineraries and field plans from responsible scholars whose research has been approved by their professional peers or academic institutions, are contrary to assurances given by Mr. Thomas L. Hughes, Director of the Bureau of Intelligence and Research, Department of State, to the President of the American Anthropological Association on November 8, 1965, and are incompatible with effective anthropological research.

4. Anthropologists employed or supported by the Government should

be given the greatest possible opportunities to participate in planning research projects, to carry them out, and to publish their findings.

II. Support and Sponsorship

1. The most useful and effective governmental support of anthropology in recent years has come through such agencies as the National Science Foundation, the National Institutes of Health, and the Smithsonian Institution. We welcome support for basic research and training through these and similar institutions.

2. The Fellows take this occasion to express their gratitude to those members of Congress, especially Senator Harris and Representative Fascell, who have so clearly demonstrated their interest in the social sciences, not only through enlarging governmental support for them, but also in establishing channels for social scientists to communicate their opinions to the Government regarding policies that affect the future of the social sciences and their utilization by Government.

3. When queried by individuals representing either host countries or groups being studied, anthropologists should willingly supply evidence of their professional qualifications and associations, their sponsorship and source of funds, and the nature and objectives of the research being undertaken.

4. Anthropologists engaged in research in foreign areas should be especially concerned with the possible effects of their sponsorship and sources of financial support. Although the Department of Defense and other mission-oriented branches of the Government support some basic research in the social sciences, their sponsorship may nevertheless create an extra hazard in the conduct of fieldwork and jeopardize future access to research opportunities in the areas studied.

5. Anthropologists who are considering financial support from independent research organizations should ascertain the full nature of the proposed investigations, including sponsorship and arrangements for publication. It is the responsibility of anthropologists to maintain the highest professional standards and to decline to participate in or to accept support from organizations that permit misrepresentation of technical competence, excessive costs, or concealed sponsorship of activities. Such considerations are especially significant where grants or fellowships are offered by founda-

tions or other organizations which do not publish balance sheets showing their sources of funds.

6. The international reputation of anthropology has been damaged by the activities of unqualified individuals who have falsely claimed to be anthropologists, or who have pretended to be engaged in anthropological research while in fact pursuing other ends. There also is good reason to believe that some anthropologists have used their professional standing and the names of their academic institutions as cloaks for the collection of intelligence information and for intelligence operations. Academic institutions and individual members of the academic community, including students, should scrupulously avoid both involvement in clandestine intelligence activities and the use of the name of anthropology, or the title of anthropologist, as a cover for intelligence activities.

III. Anthropologists in United States Government Service

1. It is desirable that social science advice be made more readily available to the Executive Office of the President.

2. Where the services of anthropologists are needed in agencies of the Government, it is most desirable that professional anthropologists be involved at the project planning stage and in the actual recruitment of necessary personnel. Only in this manner is it possible to provide skilled and effective technical advice.

3. Anthropologists contemplating or accepting employment in governmental agencies in other than policy-making positions should recognize that they will be committed to agency missions and policies. They should seek in advance the clearest possible definition of their expected roles as well as the possibilities for maintaining professional contacts, for continuing to contribute to the profession through publication, and for maintaining professional standards in protecting the privacy of individuals and groups they may study.

Appendix C

Statements on Ethics: Principles of Professional Responsibility, Adopted by the Council of the American Anthropological Association, May 1971 (as amended through November 1976)

Note: *This statement of principles is not intended to supersede previous statements and resolutions of the Association. Its intent is to clarify professional responsibilities in the chief areas of professional concern to anthropologists.*

Preamble:

Anthropologists work in many parts of the world in close personal association with the peoples and situations they study. Their professional situation is, therefore, uniquely varied and complex. They are involved with their discipline, their colleagues, their students, their sponsors, their subjects, their own and host governments, the particular individuals and groups with whom they do their field work, other populations and interest groups in the nations within which they work, and the study of processes and issues affecting general human welfare. In a field of such complex involvements, misunderstandings, conflicts, and the necessity to make choices among conflicting values are bound to arise and to generate ethical dilemmas. It is a prime responsibility of anthropologists to anticipate these and to plan to resolve them in such a way as to do damage neither to those whom they study nor, insofar as possible, to their scholarly community. Where these conditions cannot be met, the anthropologist would be well-advised not to pursue the particular piece of research.

The following principles are deemed fundamental to the anthropologist's responsible, ethical pursuit of the profession.

1. Relations with those studied:

In research, anthropologists' paramount responsibility is to those they study. When there is a conflict of interest, these individuals must come first. Anthropologists must do everything in their power to protect the physical, social, and psychological welfare and to honor the dignity and privacy of those studied.

    a. Where research involves the acquisition of material and information transferred on the assumption of trust between persons, it is axiomatic that the rights, interests, and sensitivities of those studied must be safeguarded.

    b. The aims of the investigation should be communicated as well as possible to the informant.

    c. Informants have a right to remain anonymous. This right should be respected both where it has been promised explicitly and where no clear understanding to the contrary has been reached. These strictures apply to the collection of data by means of cameras, tape recorders, and other data-gathering devices, as well as to data collected in face-to-face interviews or in participant observation. Those being studied should understand the capacities of such devices; they should be free to reject them if they wish; and if they accept them, the results obtained should be consonant with the informant's right to welfare, dignity and privacy.

        (1) Despite every effort being made to preserve anonymity, it should be made clear to informants that such anonymity may be compromised unintentionally.

        (2) When professionals or others have used pseudonyms to maintain anonymity, others should respect this decision and the reasons for it by not revealing indiscriminately the true identity of such committees, persons or other data.

    d. There should be no exploitation of individual informants for personal gain. Fair return should be given them for all services.

    e. There is an obligation to reflect on the foreseeable repercussions of research and publication on the general population being studied.

    f. The anticipated consequences of research should be communicated as fully as possible to the individuals and groups likely to be affected.

    g. In accordance with the Association's general position on clandestine and secret research, no reports should be provided to sponsors that are not also available to the general public and, where practicable, to the population studied.

h. Every effort should be exerted to cooperate with members of the host society in the planning and execution of research projects.

i. All of the above points should be acted upon in full recognition of the social and cultural pluralism of host societies and the consequent plurality of values, interests and demands in those societies. This diversity complicates choice making in research, but ignoring it leads to irresponsible decisions.

2. Responsibility to the public:

Anthropologists are also responsible to the public—all presumed consumers of their professional efforts. To them they owe a commitment to candor and to truth in the dissemination of their research results and in the statement of their opinions as students of humanity.

a. Anthropologists should not communicate findings secretly to some and withhold them from others.

b. Anthropologists should not knowingly falsify or color their findings.

c. In providing professional opinions, anthropologists are responsible not only for their content but also for integrity in explaining both these opinions and their bases.

d. As people who devote their professional lives to understanding people, anthropologists bear a positive responsibility to speak out publicly, both individually and collectively, on what they know and what they believe as a result of their professional expertise gained in the study of human beings. That is, they bear a professional responsibility to contribute to an "adequate definition of reality" upon which public opinion and public policy may be based.

e. In public discourse, anthropologists should be honest about their qualifications and cognizant of the limitations of anthropological expertise.

3. Responsibility to the discipline:

Anthropologists bear responsibility for the good reputation of the discipline and its practitioners.

a. Anthropologists should undertake no secret research or any research whose results cannot be freely derived and publicly reported.

b. Anthropologists should avoid even the appearance of engaging in clandestine research, by fully and freely disclosing the aims and sponsorship of all research.

c. Anthropologists should attempt to maintain such a level of integrity and rapport in the field that, by their behavior and example, they will not jeopardize future research there. The responsibility is not to analyze and report so as to offend no one, but to conduct research in a way consistent with a commitment to honesty, open inquiry, clear communication of sponsorship and research aims, and concern for the welfare and privacy of informants.

d. Anthropologists should not present as their own work, either in speaking or writing, materials directly taken from other sources.

e. When anthropologists participate in actions related to hiring, retention, and advancement, they should ensure that no exclusionary practices be perpetuated against colleagues on the basis of sex, marital status, color, social class, religion, ethnic background, national origin, or other nonacademic attributes. They should, furthermore, refrain from transmitting and resist the use of information irrelevant to professional performance in such personnel actions.

4. Responsibility to students:

In relations with students, anthropologists should be candid, fair, nonexploitative, and committed to the student's welfare and progress.

As Robert Lekachman has suggested, honesty is the essential quality of a good teacher, neutrality is not. Beyond honest teaching, anthropologists as teachers have ethical responsibilities in selection, instruction in ethics, career counseling, academic supervision, evaluation, compensation, and placement.

a. Anthropologists should select students in such a way as to preclude discrimination on the basis of sex, race, ethnic group, social class, and other categories of people indistinguishable by their intellectual potential.

b. Anthropologists should alert students to the ethical problems of research and discourage them from participating in projects employing questionable ethical standards. This should include providing them with information and discussions to protect them from unethical pressures and enticements emanating from possible sponsors, as well as helping them to find acceptable alternatives (see point i below).

c. Anthropologists should be receptive and seriously responsive to students' interest, opinions, and desires in all aspects of their academic work and relationships.

d. Anthropologists should realistically counsel students regarding career opportunities.

e. Anthropologists should conscientiously supervise, encourage and support students in their anthropological and other academic endeavors.

f. Anthropologists should inform students of what is expected of them in their course of study; be fair in the evaluation of their performance; communicate evaluations to the students concerned.

g. Anthropologists should acknowledge in print the student assistance used in their own publications; give appropriate credit (including co-authorship) when student research is used in publication; encourage and assist in publication of worthy student papers; and compensate students justly for the use of their time, energy, and intelligence in research and teaching.

h. Anthropologists should energetically assist students in securing legitimate research support and the necessary permission to pursue research.

i. Anthropologists should energetically assist students in securing professional employment upon completion of their studies.

j. Anthropologists should strive to improve both our techniques of teaching and our techniques for evaluating the effectiveness of our methods of teaching.

5. Responsibility to sponsors:

In relations with sponsors of research, anthropologists should be honest about their qualifications, capabilities, and aims. They thus face the obligation, prior to entering any commitment for research, to reflect sincerely upon the purposes of their sponsors in terms of their past behavior. Anthropologists should be especially careful not to promise or imply acceptance of conditions contrary to their professional ethics or competing commitments. This requires that they require of sponsors full disclosure of the sources of funds, personnel, aims of the institution and the research project, and disposition of research results. Anthropologists must retain the right to make all ethical decisions in their research. They should enter into no secret agreements with sponsors regarding research, results or reports.

6. Responsibilities to one's own government and to host governments:

In relation with their own government and with host governments, research anthropologists should be honest and candid. They should demand assurance that they will not be required to compromise their professional responsibilities and ethics as a condition of their permission to pursue research. Specifically, no secret research, no secret reports or debriefings of any kind should be agreed to or given. If these matters are clearly understood in advance, serious complications and misunderstandings can generally be avoided.

Epilogue:

In the final analysis, anthropological research is a human undertaking, dependent upon choices for which the individual bears ethical as well as scientific responsibility. That responsibility is a human, not superhuman, responsibility. To err is human, to forgive humane. This statement of principles of professional responsibility is not designed to punish, but to provide guidelines which can minimize the occasions upon which there is a need to forgive. When anthropologists, by their actions, jeopardize peoples studied, professional colleagues, students or others, or if they otherwise betray their professional commitments, their colleagues may legitimately inquire into the propriety of those actions, and take such measures as lie within the legitimate powers of their Association as the membership of the Association deems appropriate.

Appendix D

Committee on Ethics: Role and Function of the Committee on Ethics, Adopted by the Council of the American Anthropological Association, May 1971 (as amended through May 1976)

BY ITS VERY EXISTENCE, the Committee on Ethics has been the recipient of appeals from members of the Association for investigation, adjudication, and rectification of ethical issues. Some have appealed on their own behalf, some on behalf of students, colleagues, informants and host populations, some on matters of principle and some on specific transgressions. This response indicates the need which gave rise to the Committee on Ethics and suggests, broadly, the area in which it must function.

Critical response from the membership to proposals for action by the Committee indicates that in defining its functions, great care must be taken to insure that the confidence of the Association is maintained in the performance of the Committee's delicate tasks. One provision for doing so has been to make the Committee an elective such body in the Association aside from the Executive Board. Another provision has been to require that the Committee on Ethics work through (as an adjunct to) the Executive Board, with a member of that Board as a non-voting liaison member. The Committee is not empowered to report directly to the membership nor to act except through the Board.

The following proposals are offered in continuation of this spirit, combining freedom of inquiry with accountability. We draw attention particularly to the fact that we have maintained separation of three functions while being responsive to the obvious need for these functions to be forthrightly, conscientiously, and expeditiously performed: (1) receipt of cases and initial screening thereof (with the judgmental function implicit therein); (2) detailed investigation and recommendations on serious cases;

(3) final judgment and action on all cases. We emphasize that the Committee on Ethics proposes to perform only the first function, and to act only in an advisory capacity to the Executive Board.

Proposals by attending members of the Committee on Ethics concerning its role and functions:

(i) Grievance Procedure:

(1) The Statement of Professional Responsibility prepared by this Committee (when, as and if approved by the membership), together with the 1967 Statement of Problems of Anthropological Research and Ethics, and the body of Resolutions of the Association, shall form the initial basis for defining areas of ethical concern and standards of ethical conduct.

(2) It shall be the responsibility of the Committee on Ethics to review the Statement of Professional Responsibility from time to time as the members see fit or as circumstances dictate or as the membership of the Association requests, revising as appropriate.

(3) The Committee on Ethics will receive correspondence from the membership, the Board or others on issues or instances regarded by their authors as having to do with ethical matters affecting anthropology or the Association, and requiring the attention of the Committee. Communicants will be urged to specify the provisions of the Statements or Resolutions of the Association which they believe to have been violated, jeopardized or called into question, or to specify how they believe them to be inadequate. They will be urged to be as explicit as possible in communicating to the Committee, so that it may be as adequately informed as possible. The procedures will then be:

(a) All communications to the Committee will be circulated at once to all of its members and to no one else. Its members will treat them as entirely confidential.

(1) All parties to the complaint will be notified of it and invited to submit their comments, explanations, evidence, etc.

(b) At periodic meetings, the Committee will review the accumulated correspondence and make initial evaluation of the nature and gravity of each case. This will be a necessary judgmental function, a screening function. The Committee will then transmit all cases, together with the documentation and its recommendations to the Executive Board.

(c) If in the opinion of a majority of the Committee there exists a probable cause for action involving a genuine and serious instance of questionable ethics in terms of the policies and standards of the Association, the Committee would recommend that further action be taken by the Board.

(d) This recommendation would be accepted or rejected by the Executive Board. If accepted, the case would be referred to an ad hoc Committee of Inquiry of three Fellows of the Association, unaffiliated with either the Executive Board or the Committee on Ethics, and appointed for this purpose and this occasion only. This Committee would investigate the case thoroughly and confidentially. Its members would seek legal counsel where appropriate; would speak with individuals, peruse documents, etc. Upon the conclusion of their inquiry, the members of the ad hoc committee would submit a full report and recommendation to the Executive Board, which would then act upon it as its members saw fit.

(e) Any sanctioning mechanisms which might be recommended would have to emerge from the experience of applying this procedure and with the approval of the membership. For example, they might range from simple publication of the ad hoc committee's findings, to a recommendation for expulsion from the Association. Once a mechanism is established, however, it may be applied by the Executive Board upon recommendation of the ad hoc committee. It is now premature to recommend such mechanisms.

(f) All cases not deemed by the Committee on Ethics to merit the further attention of the Executive Board would be referred back to their authors through the Board The Committee on Ethics would in those cases prepare a response which would be turned over to the Executive Board for endorsement and transmittal. This response might be, for example, an indication that the case does not seem to the Committee to entail an ethical issue; that the case is inadequately documented; that the case is trivial, etc. The author might be advised that the matter could more appropriately be pursued at the Departmental or University level, or by some such body as the American Association of University Professors, the American Federation of Teachers, or that legal counsel might best be sought.

(g) Precedents and improvement of procedures will grow out of specific cases and actions. Consequently, the above is a procedure in process, not a static code. We regard this as the core function of the Committee on Ethics.

(ii) Register of Organizations:

To enhance the ability of Fellows and Members to make proper ethical decisions, we suggest that the Association collect and publish the names of organizations and agencies which do not render public accounting of their balance sheets.

(iii) Issuance of Credentials:

To enhance the ability of anthropologists to carry on their work in a research environment increasingly characterized by contradictory political and ethical interests and commitments, we suggest that the Association issue letters of introduction to Fellows and Members who actively solicit its aid. Such letters would detail the professional qualifications of the anthropologist concerned, the nature of his research, and the identity of the sponsor. Application for such letters of introduction would be individual and voluntary. In order to obtain such an instrument, issued under the seal of the Association, an individual would place on file with the Association an application detailing information on the following topics:

> Curriculum vitae of the principal researcher and professional members of his team, including students: names, sexes, ages, academic qualifications, current position and position during the course of the project.
> Project data, including the project name, its purpose, funding agencies and known sources of agency funds, projected time span in the field, location of research, proposed scholarly relations in the host country, (ie, what institutions or scholars will cooperate or be advised of the progress of the research).
> Names of individuals who can be called upon for information about this project and its professional staff.
> Plans for publication; eg, restricted, classified, confidential, etc.
> Plans for other uses of research data; eg, commercial, consultative, etc.

It will be taken for granted that any individual who finds that the information previously furnished to be incomplete or in error will so inform the Association at the earliest possible time. In the event that at a later date it should prove that the information furnished was either incomplete or false, the Association would reserve the right to retract publicly its letter of introduction by any means which it may deem appropriate. If the above conditions are met, issuance of such a letter could not be refused.

Appendix E

The Society of Professional Archaeologists (SOPA), Code of Ethics, Standards of Research Performance and Institutional Standards, 1976

Code of Ethics

ARCHEOLOGY IS A PROFESSION, and the privilege of professional practice requires professional morality and professional responsibility, as well as professional competence, on the part of each practitioner.

I.   The Archeologist's Responsibility to the Public
    1.1 An archeologist shall:
        (a) Recognize a commitment to represent archeology and its research results to the public in a responsible manner;
        (b) Actively support conservation of the archeological research base;
        (c) Be sensitive to, and respect the legitimate concerns of, groups whose culture histories are the subjects of archeological investigation;
        (d) Avoid and discourage exaggerated, misleading, or unwarranted statements about archeological matters that might induce others to engage in unethical or illegal activity;
        (e) Support and comply with the terms of the UNESCO Convention on the means of prohibiting and preventing the illicit import, export, and transfer of ownership of cultural property, as adopted by the General Conference, 14 November 1970, Paris.
    1.2 An archeologist shall not:
        (a) Engage in any illegal or unethical conduct involving archeological matters or knowingly permit the use of his/her name in

support of any illegal or unethical activity involving archeological matters;

(b) Give a professional opinion, make a public report, or give legal testimony involving archeological matters without being as thoroughly informed as might reasonably be expected;

(c) Engage in conduct involving dishonesty, fraud, deceit, or misrepresentation about archeological matters;

(d) Undertake any research that affects the archeological resource base for which she/he is not qualified.

II. The Archeologist's Responsibility to Colleagues

2.1 An archeologist shall:

(a) Give appropriate credit for work done by others;

(b) Stay informed and knowledgeable about developments in his/her field or fields of specialization;

(c) Accurately, and without undue delay, prepare and properly disseminate a description of research done and its results;

(d) Communicate and cooperate with colleagues having common professional interests;

(e) Give due respect to colleagues' interests in, and rights to, information about sites, areas, collections, or data where there is a mutual active or potentially active research concern;

(f) Know and comply with all laws applicable to her/his archeological research, as well as with any relevant procedures promulgated by duly constituted professional organizations;

(g) Report violations of this Code to proper authorities.

2.2 An archeologist shall not:

(a) Falsely or maliciously attempt to injure the reputation of another archeologist;

(b) Commit plagiarism in oral or written communication;

(c) Undertake research that affects the archeological resource base unless reasonably prompt and appropriate analysis and reporting can be expected;

(d) Refuse a reasonable request from a qualified colleague for research data;

(e) Submit a false or misleading application for certification by the Society of Professional Archeologists.

III. The Archeologist's Responsibility to Employers and Clients

3.1 An archeologist shall:

(a) Respect the interests of his/her employer or client, so far as is consistent with the public welfare and this Code and Standards;

(b) Refuse to comply with any request or demand of an employer or client which conflicts with the Code or Standards;

(c) Recommend to employers or clients the employment of other archeologists or other expert consultants upon encountering archeological problems beyond her/his own competence;

(d) Exercise reasonable care to prevent his/her employees, colleagues, associates, and others whose services are utilized by her/him from revealing or using confidential information. Confidential information means information of a non-archeological nature gained in the course of employment which the employer or client has requested be held inviolate, or the disclosure of which would be embarrassing or would be likely to be detrimental to the employer or client. Information ceases to be confidential when the employer or client so indicates or when such information becomes publicly known.

3.2 An archeologist shall <u>not</u>:

(a) Reveal confidential information, unless required to by law;

(b) Use confidential information to the disadvantage of the client or employer;

(c) Use confidential information for the advantage of herself/himself or a third person, unless the employer or client consents after full disclosure;

(d) Accept compensation or anything of value for recommending the employment of another archeologist or other person, unless such compensation or thing of value is fully disclosed to the potential employer or client;

(e) Recommend or participate in any research which does not comply with the requirements of the Standards of Research Performance.

Standards of Research Performance

The research archeologist has a responsibility to attempt to design and conduct projects that will add to our understanding of past cultures and/or that will develop better theories, methods, or techniques for interpreting the archeological record, while causing minimal attrition of the archeological resource base. In the conduct of a research project, the following minimum standards should be followed:

I.   The archeologist has a responsibility to prepare adequately for any research project, whether or not in the field. The archeologist must:

1.1 Assess the adequacy of her/his qualifications for the demands of the project, and minimize inadequacies by acquiring additional expertise, by bringing in associates with the needed qualifications, or by modifying the scope of the project;

1.2 Inform himself/herself of relevant previous research;

1.3 Develop a scientific plan of research which specifies the objectives of the project, takes into account previous relevant research, employs a suitable methodology, and provides for economical use of the resource base (whether such base consists of an excavation site or of specimens) consistent with the objectives of the project;

1.4 Ensure the availability of adequate staff and support facilities to carry the project to completion, and of adequate curatorial facilities for specimens and records;

1.5 Comply with all legal requirements including, without limitation, obtaining all necessary governmental permits and necessary permission from landowners or other persons;

1.6 Determine whether the project is likely to interfere with the program or projects of other scholars and, if there is such likelihood, initiate negotiations to minimize such interference.

II.   In conducting research, the archeologist must follow her/his scientific plan of research, except to the extent that unforeseen circumstances warrant its modification.

III. Procedures for field survey or excavation must meet the following minimal standards:

3.1 If specimens are collected, a system for identifying and recording their provenience must be maintained;

3.2 Uncollected entities, such as environmental or cultural features, depositional strata, and the like, must be fully and accurately recorded by appropriate means, and their location recorded;

3.3 The methods employed in data collection must be fully and accurately described. Significant stratigraphic and/or locational relationships among artifacts, other specimens, and cultural and environmental features must also be fully and accurately recorded;

3.4 All records should be intelligible to other archeologists. If terms lacking commonly held referents are used, they should be clearly defined;

3.5 Insofar as possible, the interests of other researchers should be considered. For example, upper levels of a site should be scientifically excavated and recorded whenever feasible, even if the focus of the project is on underlying levels.

IV. During accessioning, analysis and storage of specimens and records in the laboratory, the archeologist must take precautions to ensure that correlations between the specimens and the field records are maintained, so that prevenience, contextual relationships, and the like are not confused or obscured.

V. Specimens and research records resulting from a project must be deposited at an institution with permanent curatorial facilities.

VI. The archeologist has responsibility for appropriate dissemination of the results of her/his research to the appropriate constituencies with reasonable dispatch:

6.1 Results reviewed as significant contributions to substantive knowledge of the past or to advancements in theory, method or technique should be disseminated to colleagues and other interested persons by appropriate means, such as publications, reports at professional meetings, or letters to colleagues;

6.2 Requests from qualified colleagues for information on research results directly should be honored, if consistent with the researcher's prior rights to publication and with her/his other professional responsibilities;

6.3 Failure to complete a full scholarly report within 10 years after completion of a field project shall be considered as a waiver of an archeologist's right of primacy with respect to analysis and publication of the data. Upon expiration of such 10 year period, or at such earlier time as the archeologist shall determine not to publish the results, such data should be made fully accessible for analysis and publication to other archeologists;

6.4 While contractual obligations in reporting must be respected, archeologists should not enter into a contract which prohibits the archeologist from including her or his own interpretations or conclusions in the contractual reports, or from preserving a continuing right to use the data after completion of the project;

6.5 Archeologists have an obligation to accede to reasonable requests for information from the news media.

Institutional Standards

Archeological research involving collection of original field data and/or acquisition of specimens requires institutional facilities and support services for its successful conduct, and for proper permanent maintenance of the resulting collections and records.

A full-scale archeological field project will require the following facilities and services, normally furnished by or through an institution:

(1) Office space and furniture.

(2) Laboratory space, furniture, and equipment for analysis of specimens and data.

(3) Special facilities such as a darkroom, drafting facilities, conservation laboratory, etc.

(4) Permanent allocation of space, facilities, and equipment for proper maintenance of collections and records equivalent to that specified in the standards of the Association of Systemic Collections.

(5) Field equipment such as vehicles, surveying instruments, etc.

(6) A research library.

(7) Administrative and fiscal control services.

(8) A security system.

(9) Technical specialists such as photographers, curators, conservators, etc.

(10) Publication services.

All the foregoing facilities and services must be adequate to the scope of the project.

Not all archeological research will require all the foregoing facilities and services, but a full-scale field project will. Likewise, all institutions engaging in archeological research will not necessarily require or be able to furnish all such facilities and services from their own resources. Institutions lacking certain facilities or services should arrange for them through cooperative agreements with other institutions.

Appendix F
Professional and Ethical Responsibilities, SfAA (revised 1983)

THIS STATEMENT IS A GUIDE to professional behavior for the members and fellows of the Society for Applied Anthropology. As members or fellows of the Society we shall act in ways that are consistent with the responsibilities stated below irrespective of the specific circumstances of our employment.

1. To the people we study we owe disclosure of our research goals, methods and sponsorship. The participation of people in our research activities shall only be on a voluntary and informed basis. We shall provide a means throughout our research activities and in subsequent publications to maintain the confidentiality of those we study. The people we study must be made aware of the likely limits of confidentiality and must not be promised a greater degree of confidentiality than can be realistically expected under current legal circumstances in our respective nations. We shall, within the limits of our knowledge, disclose any significant risk to those we study that may result from our activities.

2. To the communities ultimately affected by our actions we owe respect for their dignity, integrity and worth. We recognize that human survival is contingent upon the continued existence of a diversity of human communities, and guide our professional activities accordingly. We will avoid taking or recommending action on behalf of a sponsor which is harmful to the interests of a community.

3. To our social science colleagues we have the responsibility to not engage in actions that impede their reasonable professional activities. Among other things this means that, while respecting the needs, responsibilities, and legitimate proprietary interests of our sponsors we should not impede

Editor's Note. The revised statement of Professional and Ethical Responsibilities appearing above was prepared by committee members John van Willigen (Chair), Joan Cassell, Dorothea Theodoratus, M. G. Trend, Murray Wax, and Robert Wulff. The statement was approved in 1983 by vote of the membership of the Society for Applied Anthropology.

the flow of information about research outcomes and professional practice techniques. We shall accurately report the contributions of colleagues to our work. We shall not condone falsification or distortion by others. We should not prejudice communities or agencies against a colleague for reasons of personal gain.

4. To our students, interns or trainees we owe non-discriminatory access to our training services. We shall provide training which is informed, accurate and relevant to the needs of the larger society. We recognize the need for continuing education so as to maintain our skill and knowledge at a high level. Our training should inform students as to their ethical responsibilities. Student contributions to our professional activities, including both research and publication, should be adequately recognized.

5. To our employers and other sponsors we owe accurate reporting of our qualifications and competent, efficient and timely performance of the work we undertake for them. We shall establish a clear understanding with each employer or other sponsor as to the nature of our professional responsibilities. We shall report our research and other activities accurately. We have the obligation to attempt to prevent distortion or suppression of research results or policy recommendations by concerned agencies.

6. To society as a whole we owe the benefit of our special knowledge and skills in interpreting socio-cultural systems. We should communicate our understanding of human life to the society at large.

Appendix G
Proposed Code of Ethics Would Supersede Principles of Professional Responsibility*

THE DRAFT PREAMBLE, Code of Ethics and Role and Function of the Committee on Ethics which follow are presented for discussion. If subsequently approved by Members, these documents would supersede the Principles of Professional Responsibility and Role and Function of Professional Responsibility adopted in 1971, copies of which are available from the Association's offices on request.

Members may address their comments on these drafts to the *Anthropology Newsletter* and to the officers of the Association. The draft documents also will be the subject of discussion at the Open Forum chaired by President-elect June Helm, on Friday evening, November 16, in Denver. In the spring of 1985, the Executive Committee expects to review the comments and suggestions of Members. It may then amend the documents and it will decide at that time whether to ballot the membership in the fall of 1985 or to schedule additional discussion at the 1985 annual meeting before a vote is taken.

By 1975, active concerns had surfaced about aspects of the PPR and the grievance procedures. The growing number of non-academically based anthropologists held that the PPR was based only on academic considerations and it had been demonstrated that the grievance procedures were too slow and did not, as they promise, protect confidentiality. Amendments had extended the PPR well into additional areas covered by law and regulations. Important inconsistencies and ambiguities were found in the various documents relating to ethics, and varying codes of ethics adopted or under consideration by anthropological organizations raised the pros-

*Due to opposition from the membership of the American Anthropological Association, this proposed revision never went into effect.

pect of anthropologists "shopping around" for the most favorable code for their purposes.

The Board asked the Committee on Ethics to consider the problem and propose remedies, which it did. Drafts were circulated to the members of the Committee on Anthropology as a Profession and individual anthropologists for comment. In 1980, an ad hoc committee of five was appointed to prepare revised statements on ethics. Composed of Karl Heider, Chair; Barry Bainton, Alice Brues, Jerald Milanich and John Roberts, the committee submitted its report which was reviewed by the Board, the COE, CAP and individual members who had participated earlier in the process.

By 1982, the Board felt that the draft documents were ready to go to the membership but that they deserved more careful consideration than they might receive while reorganizational issues were being decided. Earlier this year, with reorganization largely in place, both the COE and the Board reviewed the documents again and voted unanimously to open discussion this fall. Because of the time span, the membership of the COE and the Board changed several times; as a consequence, more than 60 members have already participated in the drafts.

Preamble to Code of Ethics

The purpose of this Code of Ethics is to provide a foundation for professional ethical decisions and actions within anthropology and its constituent subdisciplines. The Code is general, because anthropologists' professional situations are varied and complex. However, the Code does not address the many ethical responsibilities which anthropologists, as scholars and scientists, as members of universities, government agencies, business firms and other institutions, confront in their roles as citizen, teacher, employer, employee, and the like. The anthropologist is also bound by the ethical principles which operate in their, and other, occupational and professional contexts.

The work of anthropologists does, however, entail some specific responsibilities which the Code addresses. In the practice of anthropology anthropologists are involved with their discipline, their colleagues, their students, their sponsors, their clients, their subjects, their own and host governments, the particular individuals and groups with whom they do their field work, and other populations and interest groups in the nations within which they work. They study many processes and issues affecting general human welfare. Given such complex involvements, ethical dilemmas may result, and anthropologists may find themselves on opposite sides of issues. One purpose of the Code is to provide a framework within which disclosure of ethical problems and debate on ethical issues can be conducted within anthropology.

Anthropologists have a responsibility to maintain the ethical standards of their profession. The American Anthropological Association, for its part, has an obligation to make its membership aware of the issues involving professional ethics. The following principles are an attempt to address these responsibilities.

Code of Ethics

1. Anthropologists must seriously consider their own moral responsibility for their acts when there is a risk that an individual, group, or organization may be hurt, exploited, or jeopardized physically, legally, in reputation, or in self-esteem as a result of these acts.

2. Anthropologists should communicate as well as possible to their resource persons the aims of their investigations, and should communicate as fully as possible the anticipated consequences of their work to individuals and groups likely to be affected.

3. Where materials and information are acquired on the assumption of trust, then the rights, interests, and sensitivities of the individuals and groups involved should be safeguarded. In addition, such individuals and groups should be advised that, where the likelihood exists that such materials and information will be sought in the course of legal proceedings, the anthropologist may not be able to claim confidentiality.

4. Anthropologists should respect the rights of resource persons, whether individuals, groups or organizations, to remain anonymous if they so desire, or to receive recognition for their contributions. Where the likelihood exists that others may take legal action to force disclosure of the anonymous identity, resource persons should be advised that the anthropologist may not be able to claim confidentiality.

5. Anthropologists should so act in the field or in their professional work that they will not jeopardize ongoing and future research.

6. When engaged in fieldwork or other professional activities, anthropologists should respect the rights of colleagues, including students, already engaged in research there, and should avoid behavior that could interfere with that work.

7. Anthropologists should seek to maintain high standards of integrity and performance in their scholarly, professional and contractual relationships.

8. Anthropologists should in no way attempt to limit freedom of research, communication and publication of their colleagues, including students, except where the professional situation specifically requires that they exercise such a responsibility.

9. Anthropologists should be honest about their qualifications and cognizant of the limitations of their anthropological expertise.

10. Anthropologists should not present as their own work, either in speaking or writing, materials directly taken from other sources.

11. Anthropologists should fully report all sources of financial support in their interpretation of the findings.

12. Anthropologists should make known the disposition and availability of their data, and artifact collections and other materials.

13. Anthropologists should arrange for the proper disposition of their data and materials after their death.

Role and Function of the Committee on Ethics (as amended and adopted by the Board of Directors, 110th Meeting, May 20, 1984)

1. The American Anthropological Association has a responsibility, both to its members and to those outside the profession with whom anthropologists enter into contact in the process of their work, to uphold ethical principles deemed fundamental to the practice of anthropology.

2. The primary mandate of the Committee on Ethics of the American Anthropological Association is to raise awareness of and provide guidance on ethical issues within the membership of the Association and the anthropological community in general. The COE can accomplish this in the following ways:

   a. by periodically reviewing and revising the Association's Code of Ethics;
   b. by encouraging the various sub-disciplines within anthropology to develop codes of ethics relevant to their own particular problems;
   c. by disseminating materials and information on ethics and ethical problems to the anthropological community through special publications and regular columns in the *Anthropology Newsletter;*
   d. by gathering and disseminating information on legal codes that have specific reference to professional anthropological activities;

e. by sponsoring sessions at the annual meetings which can provide a public forum for the discussion of ethical matters;
f. by encouraging undergraduate and graduate programs in anthropology to include information and materials on ethics; and
g. by inviting general queries about ethical problems from the membership.

3. In cases where members have an immediate need for help in solving specific ethical dilemmas or resolving ethical issues involving AAA members the COE may provide guidance on procedures or problem-solving and otherwise provide good offices within a framework of confidentiality.

Appendix H
National Association of Practicing Anthropologists' Ethical Guidelines for Practitioners, 1988

THESE GUIDELINES have been developed by the National Association for the Practice of Anthropology as a guide to the professional and ethical responsibilities that practicing anthropologists should uphold. A practicing anthropologist is a professionally-trained anthropologist who is employed or retained to apply his or her specialized knowledge to problem-solving related to human welfare and human activities. The designation "practicing anthropologist" includes full-time practitioners who work for clients such as social-service organizations, government agencies and business and in-dustrial firms. This term also includes part-time practitioners, usually academically-based anthropologists, who accept occasional assignments with such clients. The substantive work of practicing anthropologists may include applied research, program design and implementation, client advocacy and advisory roles and activities related to the communication of anthropological perspectives. These guidelines are provided with the recognition that practicing anthropologists are involved in many types of policy-related research, frequently affecting individuals and groups with diverse and sometimes conflicting interests. No code or set of guidelines can anticipate unique circumstances or direct practitioner actions in specific situations. The individual practitioner must be willing to make carefully considered ethical choices and be prepared to make clear the assumptions, facts and issues on which those choices are based. These guidelines therefore address *general* contexts, priorities and relationships which should be considered in ethical decision making in anthropological practice.

   1. Our primary responsibility is to respect and consider the welfare and human rights of all categories of people affected by decisions, programs or research in which we take part. However, we recognize that many research and practice settings involve conflicts between benefits accruing to different

parties affected by our research. It is our ethical responsibility, to the extent feasible, to bring to bear on decision making, our own or that of others, information concerning the actual or potential impacts of such activities on all whom they might affect. It is also our responsibility to assure, to the extent possible, that the views of groups so affected are made clear and given full and serious consideration by decision makers and planners, in order to preserve options and choices for affected groups.

2. To our resource persons or research subjects we owe full and timely disclosure of the objectives, methods and sponsorship of our activities. We should recognize the rights of resource persons, whether individuals or groups, to receive recognition for their contributions or to remain anonymous if they so desire or to decline participation altogether. These persons should be informed of our commitment to the principle of confidentiality and of the steps we will take to insure confidentiality. We should be sensitive to issues related to confidentiality throughout the design of research or other activities involving resource persons and should thoroughly investigate and understand all of the limitations on our claims of confidentiality and disclosure.

3. To our employers we owe competent, efficient, fully professional skills and techniques, timely performance of our work and communication of our findings and recommendations in understandable, non-jargonistic language.

As practicing anthropologists, we are frequently involved with employers or clients in legally contracted arrangements. It is our responsibility to carefully review contracts prior to signing and be willing to execute the terms and conditions stipulated in the contract once it has been signed.

At the *outset* of a relationship or contract with an employer or client, we have an obligation to determine whether or not the work we are requested to perform is consistent with our commitment to deal fairly with the rights and welfare of persons affected by our work, recognizing that different constituencies may be affected in different ways. At this time, we should also discuss with our employer or client the intended use of the data or materials to be generated by our work and clarify the extent to which information developed during our activities can be made available to the public. Issues surrounding the protection of subject confidentiality and disclosure of information or findings should be thoroughly reviewed with the potential employer or client. We will not undertake activities which compromise our ethical responsibilities.

We will carry out our work in such a manner that the employer fully understands our ethical priorities, commitments and responsibilities. When, at any time during the course of work performance, the demands of the employer require or appear to require us to violate the ethical standards of our profession, we have the responsibility to clarify the nature of the conflict between the request and our standards and to propose alternatives that are consistent with our standards. If such a conflict cannot be resolved, we should terminate the relationship.

4. In our relations with students and trainees, we will be candid, fair, nonexploitative, nondiscriminatory and committed to the students' or trainees' welfare. We recognize that such mentoring does involve an exchange in which practitioners share their knowledge and experience in return for the significant effort and contribution of the students/trainees. We should be honest and thorough in our presentation of material and should strive to improve our teaching and training techniques and our methods of evaluating the effectiveness of our instruction.

As practicing anthropologists we are frequently called upon to instruct, train or teach individuals, anthropologists and others in non-academic settings (workshop participants, in-service trainees, continuation or certification program trainees and research teams). To such persons, we owe training that is informed, timely and relevant to their needs.

Our instruction should inform both students and trainees of the ethical responsibilities involved in the collection and use of data. To our students and trainees we owe respect for and openness to nonanthropological methods and perspectives. Student and trainee contributions to our work, including publications, should be accurately and completely attributed.

5. To our colleagues, anthropologists and others, we have a responsibility to conduct our work in a manner that facilitates their activities or that does not unjustly compromise their ability to carry out professional work.

The cross-disciplinary nature of the work of practicing anthropologists requires us to be informed and respectful of the disciplinary and professional perspectives, methodologies and ethical requirements of non-anthropological colleagues with whom we work.

We will accurately report the contribution or our colleagues to our research, practice-related activities and publications.

6. To the discipline of anthropology we have a responsibility to act in a manner that presents the discipline to the public and to other professional colleagues in a favorable light. We will point out the value of anthropologi-

cal contributions to the understanding of human problems and human-kind. Where appropriate in the context of our work, we will encourage the use of anthropological approaches and recommend the participation of other anthropologists.

We will contribute to the growth of our discipline through communicating and publishing scientific and practical information about the work in which we are engaged, including, as appropriate, theory, processes, outcomes and professional techniques and methods.

Appendix I
American Anthropological Association, Revised Principles of Professional Responsibility, 1990

Note: This statement enunciates general responsibilities for all anthropologists. Each of the units of the AAA may develop a more detailed statement of ethics specific to their particular professional responsibilities but in all cases consonant with the principles stated herewith.

Preamble

Anthropologists' relations with their discipline, with the individuals and groups among whom they conduct research or to whom they provide services, with their employers and with their own host governments, are varied, complex, sensitive, and sometimes difficult to reconcile. In a field of such complex involvements, misunderstandings, conflicts and the need to make choices among apparently incompatible values are constantly generated. The most fundamental responsibility of anthropologists is to anticipate such difficulties and to resolve them in ways that are compatible with the principles stated here. If such resolution is impossible, anthropological work should not be undertaken or continued.

Anthropologists must respect, protect and promote the rights and the welfare of all of those affected by their work. The following general principles and guidelines are fundamental to ethical anthropological practice.

I. Responsibility to people whose lives and cultures anthropologists study

Anthropologists' first responsibility is to those whose lives and cultures they study. Should conflicts of interest arise, the interests of these people take precedence over other considerations. Anthropologists must do everything in their power to protect the dignity and privacy of the people with whom they work, conduct research or perform other professional activities. Their physical, social and emotional safety and welfare are the professional concerns of the anthropologists who have worked among them.

A. The rights, interests, safety, and sensitivities of those who entrust information to anthropologists must be safeguarded.

1. The right of those providing information to anthropologists either to remain anonymous or to receive recognition is to be respected and defended. It is the responsibility of anthropologists to make every effort to determine the preferences of those providing information and to comply with their wishes.

a. It should be made clear to anyone providing information that despite the anthropologist's best intentions and efforts anonymity may be compromised or recognition fail to materialize.

2. Anthropologists should not reveal the identity of groups or persons whose anonymity is protected through the use of pseudonyms.

3. The aims of all their professional activities should be clearly communicated by anthropologists to those among whom they work.

4. Anthropologists must not exploit individuals or groups for personal gain. They should give fair return for the help and services they receive. They must recognize their debt to the societies in which they work and their obligation to reciprocate in appropriate ways.

5. Anthropologists have an ongoing obligation to assess both the positive and negative consequences of their activities and the publications resulting from those activities. They should inform individuals and groups likely to be affected of any consequences relevant to them that they anticipate. In any case, however, their work must not violate these principles of professional responsibility. *If they anticipate the possibility that such violations might occur they should take steps, including, if necessary, discontinuance of work, to avoid such outcomes.*

6. Whether they are engaged in academic or nonacademic research, anthropologists must be candid about their professional identities. If the results of their activities are not to be made public, this should be made clear to all concerned from the outset.

7. Anthropologists must take into account and, where relevant, make explicit the extent to which their own personal and cultural values affect their professional activities. They must also recognize and deal candidly and judiciously with the effects that the often conflicting demands and values of

employers, sponsors, host governments and research publications may have upon their work.

II. Responsibility to the public

Anthropologists have responsibility to be truthful to the publics that read, hear, or view the products of their work.

A. In expressing professional opinions publicly, anthropologists are not only responsible for the factual content of their statements but also must consider carefully the social and political implications of the information they disseminate. They must do everything in their power to insure that such information is well-understood, properly contextualized and responsibly utilized.

B. Anthropologists bear a positive responsibility to speak out publicly, both individually and collectively, on issues about which they possess professional expertise. That is, they have a professional responsibility to contribute to the formation of informational grounds upon which public policy may be founded. Anthropologists should make clear the bases upon which their positions stand.

C. When engaging in public discourse anthropologists should be candid about their qualifications, and they should recognize and make clear the limits of anthropological expertise.

III. Responsibility to the discipline

Anthropologists bear responsibility for the good reputation of the discipline and its practitioners.

A. The integrity with which anthropologists conduct their affairs, and the rapport that they seek to maintain in the field and in other professional venues must be of an order that justifies trust and confidence. They must not behave in ways that jeopardize either their own or others' future research or professional employment. It is their responsibility to act in ways consistent with commitments to honesty, open inquiry, candor concerning sponsorship and research aims, and concern for the welfare and privacy of all concerned parties. Anthropologists must address such conflicts as do arise among the interests of those parties and attempt to resolve them equitably.

B. Anthropologists must not represent as their own work, either in speaking or writing, materials or ideas directly taken from other sources. Anthropologists must give full credit in speaking or writing to all of their professional colleagues, anthropologists or nonanthropologists, who have contributed to their work.

C. When anthropologists participate in actions relating to hiring, retention and advancement, they should (except in the case of affirmative actions taken to redress historical imbalances) insure that no exclusionary practices should be perpetuated against colleagues on the basis of sex, marital status, color, social class, political convictions, religion, ethnic background, national origin, sexual preference, age, or any other criterion irrelevant to academic performance. Nor should an otherwise qualified individual be excluded on the basis of physical disability. Anthropologists should, furthermore, refrain from transmitting, and resist the use of, information irrelevant to professional performance in personnel actions.

D. The cross-disciplinary nature of the activities of many anthropologists requires that they be informed of, and respect, the requirements of the nonanthropological colleagues with whom they work.

IV. Responsibility to students and trainees

Anthropologists should be candid, fair, and nonexploitative in their dealings with trainees and students, and committed to their welfare and progress. They have continuing responsibility to recognize the changing nature of the discipline, in both its content and its methodology, and further, in novel applications of anthropological knowledge and approaches. They have a further responsibility to convey current understandings to students and trainees.

A. Anthropologists should accept students into their programs in ways precluding and redressing discrimination on the basis of sex, marital status, color, social class, political convictions, religion, ethnic background, national origin, sexual preference, age, or any other criterion irrelevant to academic performance.

B. Anthropologists should strive to improve both their teaching techniques and the methods of evaluating their effectiveness as teachers.

C. Anthropologists should be receptive and genuinely responsive to students' interests, opinions, and needs.

D. Anthropologists should counsel students realistically regarding both academic and nonacademic career opportunities.

E. Anthropologists should be conscientious in supervising, encouraging, and supporting students in their studies, both anthropological and nonanthropological.

F. Anthropologists should inform students of what is expected of them, be fair in the evaluation of their performance, and prompt and reliable in communicating evaluations to them.

G. Anthropologists should impress upon students the ethical problems involved in anthropological work and discourage them from participating in ethically questionable projects.

H. Anthropologists should acknowledge orally and in print student assistance in research and preparation of their work; give appropriate credit for coauthorship or first authorship to students when their research is used in publications or lectures; encourage and assist in publication of worthy student papers; and compensate students justly for the use of their time, energy, and ideas in research, teaching, and other professional activities.

I. Anthropologists should energetically assist students in securing legitimate research support and the necessary permission to pursue research and other professional activities.

J. Anthropologists should vigorously assist students in securing professional placement upon the completion of their studies.

K. Anthropologists should beware of the serious conflicts of interest and exploitation which may result if they engage in sexual relations with students. They must avoid sexual liaisons with students for whose professional training they are in any way responsible.

V. Responsibility to employers, clients, and sponsors

In all dealing with employers, clients, and sponsors anthropologists should be honest about their qualifications, capabilities, and aims. Prior to entering any professional commitment, anthropologists must review the purposes of sponsors, employers, or clients, taking into consideration their past activities and future goals. In working for governmental agencies or private businesses, anthropologists should be especially careful not to promise or imply acceptance of conditions contrary to professional ethics. Anthropologists should be especially careful not to promise or imply acceptance of conditions contrary to professional ethics or competing commitments.

VI. Responsibilities to governments

Anthropologists should be honest and candid in all dealings with their own governments and with host governments. They should ascertain that they will not be required to compromise either their responsibilities or anthropological ethics as a condition of permission to engage in professional activities. Anthropologists are under no professional obligation to provide reports or debriefings of any kind to government officials or employees, unless they have individually and explicitly agreed to do so in the terms of employment.

Epilogue

Anthropological activity requires choices for which anthropologists individually and collectively bear ethical as well as scientific responsibility. This statement is designed to promote discussion and provide general guidelines for ethically responsible decisions. When anthropologists, by their actions, jeopardize peoples studied, professional colleagues, employers, employees, clients, students, or others, or if they otherwise betray their professional commitments, their colleagues may legitimately inquire into the propriety of such actions, and take such measures as lie with legitimate powers of the American Anthropological Association, as the membership of the Association deems appropriate.

About the Contributors

Gerald D. Berreman is Professor of Anthropology at the University of California at Berkeley. He was a member of the AAA Ethics Committee from 1969 to 1971 and participated in the drafting of the Principles of Professional Responsibility; he then served on the Executive Board of the AAA from 1971 to 1974. He has worked primarily in India on questions of social inequality and maintains a continuing interest in ethics and professional responsibility in anthropology.

Erve Chambers is Professor of Anthropology at the University of Maryland, College Park. He is the author of *Applied Anthropology: A Practical Guide,* and has served as President of the Society for Applied Anthropology.

Claudia C. Fishman is a specialist in nutrition-related beliefs and behaviors who has worked in Southeast Asia, Africa, and the Middle East. Currently she works with the Academy for Educational Development and the firm Porter Novelli.

Carolyn Fluehr-Lobban is Professor of Anthropology at Rhode Island College, where she also is Director of International Education. She has researched Islamic subjects in the North African countries of Sudan and Egypt and begins work in Tunisia in 1990. During 1990, she was a Rockefeller Fellow in the Institute for the Study of Applied and Professional Ethics at Dartmouth College.

Barbara Frankel is Professor of Anthropology in the Department of Social Relations at Lehigh University. She is past president of the Philadelphia Anthropological Society, and past Chair of the Ethics Committee of the Society for Applied Anthropology.

M. Jean Gilbert is a medical anthropologist working for Kaiser Permanente's Southern California Regional Offices. Her expertise is in cross-cultural research in substance abuse and the utilization of health care systems.

William Graves III holds a Ph.D. in Anthropology from Indiana University and is currently Assistant Professor of Humanities at Bryant College in Smithfield, Rhode Island.

David Hakken is Associate Professor of Anthropology at SUNY Institute of Technology, where he also teaches Sociology and Computer Science and is Acting Director of the Technology Policy Center. He is reviews editor of the *Anthropology of Work Review.*

John R. Halsey has been state archaeologist in Michigan for the past 14 years. He was instrumental in the development of the state's Archaeological Site File, the official record of archaeological sites in the state designed for their protection.

Robert Roy Reed received his Ph.D. from Indiana University in 1989. He was a Fulbright Fellow in Portugal from 1982 to 1984.

Mark A. Shields holds a Ph.D. in Sociology from Brown University and is currently Assistant Professor of Sociology in the School of Social Sciences at Georgia Institute of Technology.

Jay Szklut received his Ph.D. from Indiana University in 1986. He has conducted fieldwork in rural and small-town America and is currently Research Assistant at the Institute for Economic Development at the University of North Carolina.

Nathaniel Tashima is a co-partner with Cathleen Gretenhart in the anthropological consulting firm LTG Associates, based in Washington, D.C. His extensive work with ethnic groups in the United States has included projects with Asians, Native Americans, Ethiopians, Cubans, Russians, Armenians, and Poles.

M. G. Trend is an applied anthropologist who worked with the Ethics Committee of the Society for Applied Anthropology in the 1983 revision of its code of ethics. He is currently working with the Silver Bullet Research Group in Auburn, Alabama.

General Index

Name Index

Aberle, David, 42–43, 45, 67, 80
Abir-Am, Pnina, 194
Ackerman, Paul W., 126
Adams, Richard N., 42
Adams, Robert McC., 220
Ahmed, Akbar S., 111
Akeroyd, Anne V., 161
Albert, Ethel, 22
Amoss, N., 186, 194
Appell, G. N., 137, 149, 160, 230–31
Arensberg, Conrad M., 99
Asad, Talal, 62, 132, 137

Bainton, Barry, 50, 269
Bakhtin, M. M., 148
Barnes, J. A., 97, 105, 111
Barnett, Stephen A., 68
Barth, Fredrik, 111
Bateson, Gregory, 19, 20
Beals, Ralph L., 18–19, 21, 24, 39, 46, 231
Beauchamp, T. L., 134
Becker, Ernest, 39
Becker, Howard, 133, 149
Beckerman, Stephan, 110
Bell, Colin, 148
Bell, Earl H., 107
Bellah, R. N., 132
Belshaw, Cyril, 67
Benedict, Ruth, 16, 18, 19–20
Bensmen, Joseph, 101, 105
Berreman, Gerald D., 8, 10, 23, 36, 38, 41, 48, 53, 58, 67, 195, 214, 216, 223–24
Berryman, Phillip, 63
Bigelow, Martha M., 120
Black, Deborah Bush, 122
Boas, Franz, 13, 16–18, 25, 28, 32, 39, 62, 67, 170, 230–31
Bodley, John H., 63
Bottomore, T., 155
Bozen, Nicholas L., 127
Brose, David S., 119

Brown, G. Gordon, 156, 245
Brues, Alice, 50, 269
Bulmer, M., 137

Campbell, Donald T., 179
Carr, Kurt W., 120
Carroll, J. D., 138–39
Cass, Lewis, 119
Cassell, Joan, 77, 97, 134–36, 148–49, 161, 231, 266
Chafer, Sallie, 231
Chalk, Rosemary, 231
Chambers, Erve, 10, 130, 134, 148, 153–55, 160–61, 175, 214–15, 223, 227
Chance, Norman A., 43, 68
Chapple, Eliot D., 156, 245
Chrisman, Noel J., 161
Clapp, Jane, 219, 222
Cleland, Charles E., 125
Clifford, J., 136–37
Clinton, C. A., 139
Coburn, Judith, 41
Cohen, Abner, 105
Cohen, Fay G., 111, 167
Cohen, Robert S., 183
Cole, John W., 81, 110
Coli, Waltraud, 232
Cornell, George L., 68, 125
Coughlin, Ellen K., 222
Cox Stevenson, Mathilda, 136
Culliton, B. J., 219
Cushing, F. H., 136

Dalgish, T. K., 217
Davenport, William, 46
Davis, John, 110
Davis, Shelton, 46, 63
Dawe, Alan, 132, 134
Dawes, Robyn, 179
Delancey, Mark W., 240
Deloria, Vine, 134, 137, 148

This book has been set in Linotron Galliard. Galliard was designed for Merganthaler in 1978 by Matthew Carter. Galliard retains many of the features of a sixteenth-century typeface cut by Robert Granjon but has some modifications which give it a more contemporary look.

Printed on acid-free paper.